Understanding Gliding

By the same author

Gliding: A Handbook on Soaring Flight
Beginning Gliding: The Fundamentals of Soaring Flight
Going Solo: A Simple Guide to Soaring
Understanding Flying Weather
Derek Piggott on Gliding

Understanding Gliding

The Principles of Soaring Flight

Derek Piggott

With illustrations by the author

A & C BLACK · LONDON

Published by A & C Black (Publishers) Limited
35 Bedford Row, London WC1R 4JH

First edition 1977, reprinted 1979
Second edition in paperback 1987, revised reprint 1990

ISBN 0 7136 5568 2

A CIP catalogue record for this book is available from
the British Library

Printed and bound in Great Britain by
M & A Thomson Litho Ltd, East Kilbride, Scotland

Contents

Illustrations

Introduction

There are very few mysteries left in flying and yet the majority of glider pilots do not really understand why an aircraft behaves as it does. The fundamental principles are easy to grasp and should not involve complicated mathematical and algebraic formulae. In this book I have tried to write about gliding and soaring in a really practical manner and to explain most of the mysteries.

As I said in *Beginning Gliding*, both 'glider' and 'sailplane' are correct terms to describe soaring aircraft and it is unimportant which we choose to use. In Britain we speak of flying gliders and of gliding, whereas in the USA, and a few other countries, the same aircraft are always known as sailplanes.

Some readers may not be familiar with the use of knots (nautical miles per hour) as a unit of speed in connection with flying. A knot is almost exactly 100 feet per minute and this makes it particularly useful for glider flying where the pilot may want to estimate his gliding angle quickly. For example, a rate of descent of 2 knots at a speed of 60 knots indicates a gliding angle of 1:30 in no wind. The same calculation with the variometer calibrated in feet or metres a second and speeds of miles or kilometres per hour requires a mental calculation involving multiplying by 60 twice, and this is not practical for the average pilot in flight.

It seems probable that, in spite of the move towards metrication, discriminating glider pilots will continue to use knots and nautical miles for measurement, at least in countries where heights are referred to in hundreds and thousands of feet. The nautical mile has the added advantage of being one minute of latitude and this enables a pilot to measure or estimate distances on any map or chart by referring to the distance between lines of latitude, instead of having to find the scale – which may be inaccessible at the time.

Conversion tables are given in Appendix C.

Learning to glide and understanding about gliding are the foundations of soaring flight.

The evolution of the modern sailplane

Before considering how and why a glider flies, it is interesting to trace the evolution of the design and construction of sailplanes up to the present day. The growing enthusiasm for preserving and renovating gliders of historic interest means that many people will actually be able to see examples of early designs both in museums and being flown regularly at gliding sites.

The first successful man-carrying gliders were almost certainly those designed and built by Sir George Cayley, an Englishman, who lived near Scarborough from 1773–1857.

Recent research into his work and the reconstruction and flights of a near replica of one of his man-carriers, have confirmed that Sir George Cayley was the father of the practical aeroplane as we know it today. He understood streamlining and the need for a cambered aerofoil for efficient lifting power. If his discoveries and experiments had been followed up by other enthusiasts, practical flying machines would probably have been in the air almost fifty years earlier.

By 1804 he had evolved the modern conventional layout, with a stabilising tailplane and fin mounted behind the wing, as a result of his experiments with model-size gliders. Although he did not use any lateral control such as wing warping or ailerons, many of his machines used dihedral and had the wings mounted high above the centre of gravity in order to provide extra lateral stability. Encouraged by the success of his smaller models he built very large machines and tested them with ballast before attempting flights, first with animals and finally with human passengers. History recounts how his coachman resigned after being flown across the valley at Brompton Dale in 1853. At the time Sir George was 80, and therefore unable to fly himself.

After Cayley's death there was little progress in the design of heavier than air machines until 1891 when Otto Lilienthal built and flew a number of hang gliders in Germany. Similar types of glider were flown by Percy Pilcher and other pioneers, but since the only means of controlling them was by the pilot shifting his weight, their success was rather limited and there were several fatal accidents.

At about the same time, Orville and Wilbur Wright started their experiments with gliders in the USA, but, unlike their predecessors, they relied upon proper controls rather than built-in stability. This involved them in the problems of learning to fly but gave them enough control to correct the effects of gusts of wind and to make turns. They made many soaring flights using the upcurrent created by the wind blowing over a ridge of hills, including one very notable flight of nine and three-quarter minutes. However, gliding was for

1 All motorless aircraft are gliders. Sailplanes are gliders designed for soaring flight.

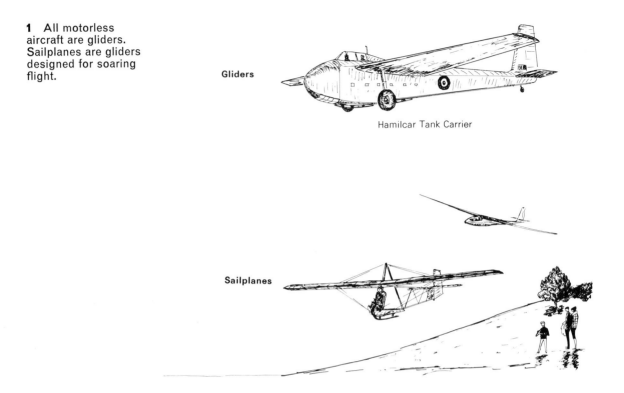

Gliders

Hamilcar Tank Carrier

Sailplanes

them a means of teaching themselves how to fly and as soon as they had developed a suitable engine, they concentrated on the problem of producing a practical powered machine.

The possibility of making long, soaring flights with gliders was more or less forgotten until after the First World War. Then many German pilots and flying enthusiasts realised that gliding was a way of flying which they could afford and which had not been specifically denied to them by the terms of the Versailles treaty. As a result, within a few years glider flights were being measured in hours instead of minutes and the sport of soaring was established in many countries.

Whereas the First World War had resulted in rapid advances in aircraft design, it was the spirit of friendly competition and, in particular, the enthusiasm inspired by the international gliding competitions held in Germany in the 1920s and 1930s which were responsible for the development of the high performance sailplane.

The effect of the wind blowing over a ridge of hills was well understood by this time and with an adequate wind strength in the right direction, hill soaring was possible with comparatively low-performance gliders. The strength of the hill lift depends mainly on the wind speed and the average angle of the slope, and even a moderate wind of 20 knots blowing up a slope of 1:3 will produce an upcurrent of about 600 feet per minute.

It is not difficult, therefore, to produce a satisfactory hill soaring machine for use in strong wind conditions. Since the rate of sink is proportional to both the gliding angle and the flying speed, an acceptably low sink rate may be obtained just by making the glider fly slowly, even if the gliding angle is relatively poor. A low flying speed is largely a matter of building a very light machine with a large wing area; i.e. having a low wing loading. The weight of the wing structure can be kept very low if it is wire or strut braced. This would have a serious drag penalty at high speed but for normal hill soaring at low speed the extra drag is not sufficient to affect the soaring performance significantly.

The modern Rogallo type of sailwing hang glider is an extreme example of a large wing area and low weight. The gliding angle is only about 5:1 but, with its low flying speed of about 20 knots, it can be soared quite successfully in strong winds if the slope of the hill is steep. However, unless you happen to live in an area with good hills and strong winds, flying this kind of machine will not be very rewarding.

The pioneers of the 1920s found this out for themselves and soon realised the need to obtain much lower rates of sink in order to be able to soar in light winds. It was still important to keep the wing loading and flying speed low, but an improvement in the gliding angle was even more valuable. This could only come from an increase in efficiency – that is by improving the lift and reducing the drag.

Up to this stage of development most of the gliders relied on two mainspars in the wing to take both the bending loads and the twisting forces which act on a wing in flight. Struts or wires were used to stop the twisting tendency and they also greatly reduced the strength and weight of the spars necessary for a strong, stiff wing. Gliders were becoming much more streamlined and soon the drag of the struts represented a significant amount of the total drag of the whole machine and could no longer be tolerated. Doing away with the struts and using a cantilever wing required a much stronger and heavier main spar and it also presented new problems in keeping the wing sufficiently stiff. Torsional stiffness is of vital importance because there is a very distinctive tendency for a wing to twist at high speeds and when the ailerons are used. If this happens the ailerons become ineffective, or produce the opposite effect, and the twisting may even result in structural failure.

The solution to this problem was to adopt the D, or torsion box leading edge to the wing. With this design the main spar takes the bending and shear loads and the torsion box prevents the wing from twisting. In addition, the thin plywood skin used for the torsion box greatly improves the shape and surface of the leading edge and enhances the performance. Not only the rate of sink at low speeds but also the gliding angle at a higher speed were much improved, so that the glider could make more headway against stronger winds. This meant that it could make better progress from one hill to another and so fly across country.

It was at about this stage of development that glider pilots began to notice

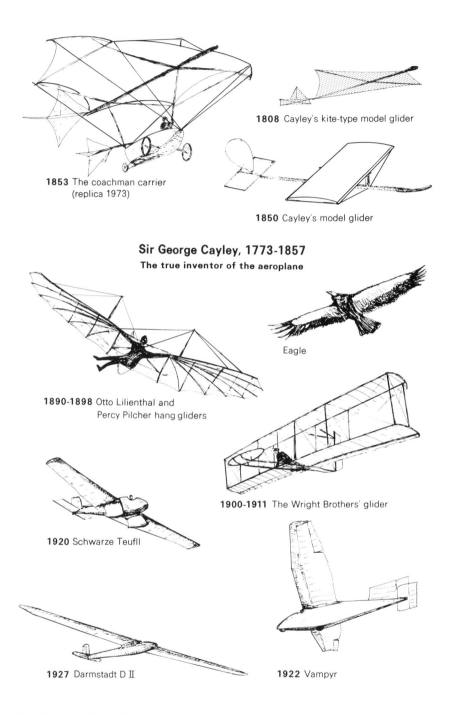

1808 Cayley's kite-type model glider

1853 The coachman carrier
(replica 1973)

1850 Cayley's model glider

Sir George Cayley, 1773-1857
The true inventor of the aeroplane

Eagle

1890-1898 Otto Lilienthal and
Percy Pilcher hang gliders

1900-1911 The Wright Brothers' glider

1920 Schwarze Teufll

1927 Darmstadt D II

1922 Vampyr

2 The evolution of the modern sailplane 1800–1927.

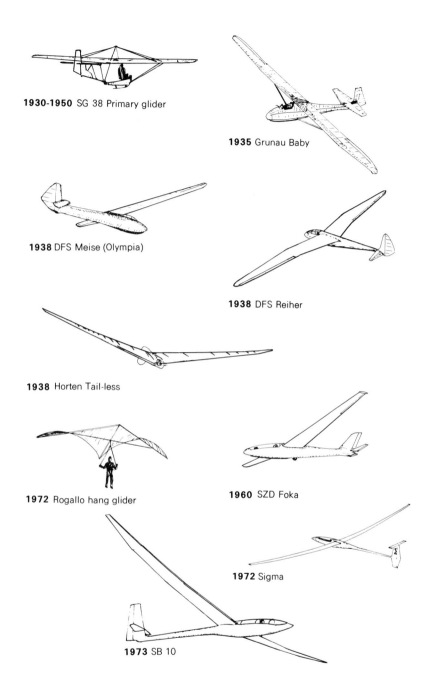

1930-1950 SG 38 Primary glider

1935 Grunau Baby

1938 DFS Meise (Olympia)

1938 DFS Reiher

1938 Horten Tail-less

1972 Rogallo hang glider

1960 SZD Foka

1972 Sigma

1973 SB 10

3   Sailplane development from 1935–1973.

that whenever shower clouds drifted over their hill sites the lift improved and they were able to climb to much greater heights. Soon the pilots were deliberately leaving their hill lift to explore the area under the clouds for this new kind of lift. The glider pilot had at last become free of his dependence on the hills and the wind. Cross-country flying, as we know it today, had begun.

It did not take long to discover that the most efficient way to climb under and inside these cumulus clouds was to circle like the birds. A simple type of variometer was soon developed to help the pilot find the best areas of lift and within a short time flights of over a hundred miles were not uncommon.

It soon became clear that the so-called cloud lift was really the result of thermals leaving the ground and that these often occurred in spite of there being no actual cloud formation. Whereas with hill soaring the primary aim had been to keep a very low rate of descent, with thermalling it became more important to have a flat gliding angle so that more air could be covered in the search for the next thermal. It also became very important to be able to turn quickly and manoeuvre as accurately as possible in the turbulent air of the thermals.

While the hill lift was limited to a few times the height of the hill, thermals usually went to three or four thousand feet and often gave rates of climb of several hundred feet per minute. The penalty of a slight increase in the rate of sink of the glider became insignificant compared with the bonus of being able to glide a little further in search of a new thermal. It became an advantage to reduce the drag even at the expense of extra weight. The very thick, bulbous aerofoils which had been developed for hill soaring machines were replaced by thinner, more streamlined ones. These perhaps did not produce quite so much lift at low speeds but they had far less drag when the glider was flown with extra speed against the wind or through sinking air between thermals.

As the gliding angles improved, so the problems of landing in a restricted area became much worse and the technique of sideslipping down was inadequate as a means of approaching steeply over tall trees or other obstructions. Spoilers and airbrakes were introduced in order to give the pilot an easy way to control the approach and to make a spot landing.

By the outbreak of the Second World War, glider designs were very refined and the best machines had glide ratios of about 1:30. An international competition for the design of a 15 metre span glider suitable for use in the Olympic games had inspired many fine designs and although these games never took place because of the outbreak of war, the winning design by Hans Jacob, known in Germany as the Meise and elsewhere as the Olympia, was produced all over the world in large numbers. The design set new standards in control and handling, had powerful airbrakes, a good all-round soaring performance, and yet was suitable for even a beginner to fly.

At about the same time, the German Horten brothers were developing their flying wing designs to challenge the conventional machines such as the Weihe (pronounced as in *Via*duct) and the Darmstadt D30. In spite of the

Horten's very clean design and the elimination of a normal stabiliser and fuselage, the conventional Weihe remained supreme in championship flying.

During the war years, the quest for faster fighters and bombers led to research and the development of the so-called laminar flow aerofoils. Wind tunnel tests in the USA had shown that the NACA 6000 series of aerofoils offered a possible bonus for gliders as well as powered machines. However, the problem of constructing a lightweight glider wing with a good enough surface to obtain this bonus still had to be solved. It was easy with a thick metal skin on a powered machine but quite another problem with the plywood skin of a glider, which is often only one-sixteenth of an inch thick.

In order to maintain the necessary smoothness, the ply skin of the torsion box had to be extended back over most of the wing. The spacing of the supporting ribs had also to be closed up to prevent the plywood sagging. Most importantly, the contours of the whole wing had to be built to hitherto unthought of tolerances while keeping the weight as low as possible.

The new low-drag sections were an almost instant success. There was a noticeable improvement in both the best gliding angle and the gliding angles at higher speeds. In addition there was an unexpected advantage in the form of better aileron control. It soon became clear that the reason for having to use large, wide chord ailerons on the earlier designs was that the wings had been twisting under load. The thicker skins needed for the laminar flow wings resulted in a much stiffer wing and allowed the designer to reduce the size of the ailerons considerably.

Soon all but the basic training machines were using laminar flow aerofoils and in the quest for still better performance designers began to look again at the fuselage shape and wing root joints for ways of reducing the drag further.

Up to this time pilots had been sitting more or less normally in an upright position but by redesigning the control runs so that they were either side of the cockpit instead of under the seat, and by making the pilot's position less upright, designers found the frontal area could be reduced. The conventional front skid and main wheel were other sources of drag which had to be eliminated and this was achieved by moving the wheel forward to ahead of the centre of gravity and by making it retract.

Pilots soon learned to accept the less upright seating position as comfortable and necessary in the interest of lower drag. Before this, good forward visibility had been considered essential and a bulbous canopy shape had been usual. A few designs apeared with the pilot laid out flat in the slimmest possible fuselage, but this extreme soon gave way to the present day compromise of the pilot sitting at an angle of about 45°.

Later, the same principles of maintaining laminar flow over the wing were applied in three dimensional flow over the nose of the fuselage. This involved calculating the pressure gradient over the nose and reshaping it very accurately. Since any joint or step in the surface would result in turbulent flow, the forward portion of the canopy became fixed so that the joint did not occur until the airflow was past the transition point. Designers also began to pay much more attention to sealing the canopy in order to eliminate any leakage of air which might cause further turbulence. The risk of leakage was also reduced by venting at the tail to reduce the pressure slightly inside the fuselage and cockpit.

Once the airflow in the boundary layer has become turbulent there is less tendency for it to separate and leave the surface than when it is laminar. Many gliders took advantage of this by reducing the cross-section of the fuselage behind the wing and adopting a pod and boom type of fuselage. The drag reduction is the result of a reduction in surface area and there is therefore less skin friction. As with a wing aerofoil, laminar flow cannot be maintained at all speeds and angles of attack on the fuselage nose. The use of variable camber wing flaps helped to extend the range of speeds for maintaining extensive laminar flow over both the wing and the nose of the fuselage by reducing the change in angle of attack required for varying the speed. It is possible to make quite a large change in flying speed by raising and lowering the flaps with little or no change in fuselage attitude.

In the USA Doctor Raspet pioneered the development of the modern glider with his work in reducing drag by eliminating surface wavyness and by improving the design of the wing roots and other drag producing areas.

But perhaps the most outstanding contribution to the advancement of glider design has come from Professor Wortman and Doctor Eppler, two German scientists who developed special aerofoils for gliders. These have now superseded the earlier NACA 6000 series and are used on almost all recent designs (1976).

The problem of improving the performance of a modern glider still further can be understood when it is realised that the total drag of a machine weighing 900 lb flying at about 50 knots is in the order of 20–30 lb. The performance is therefore drastically reduced by dust and dirt on the wing, or by the failure to seal any joints in the wing root with adhesive tape.

The requirements for the ultimate soaring machine are conflicting ones. In order to use thermals efficiently the glider must have easy handling and good control response so that it can be manoeuvred quickly into the centre of the lift. It must also have a low rate of sink at low speeds in order to use small weak thermals. A low speed gives a small radius of turn and is frequently the key factor which determines whether a particular type of glider can stay up in difficult soaring conditions. However, in cruising flight between areas of lift it needs a flat gliding angle at high speed, and, of course, at the end of the flight it must be easy to land in a confined space.

Good low-speed performance for thermalling is best obtained by having a low wing loading, since the wing loading determines the minimum flying speed, and the radius of turn is proportional to the speed. However, good performance at high speed is easiest to obtain with a high wing loading since this increases the speed for the best gliding angle.

If the lift is strong, the glider with a high wing loading will average a much higher speed, in spite of climbing less efficiently. However, if the lift is very weak it might be unable to climb at all and the extra wing loading is a definite disadvantage. The need for adjustment according to the conditions is to some extent met by carrying jettisonable water ballast in the wings. On a promising looking day when the lift is strong, the wing loading can then be increased by filling up the ballast tanks before take off. If the lift becomes weak and there is a risk that the glider will be unable to stay up, the water can be jettisoned so that the wing loading is reduced again to give the lowest possible sinking speed. Unfortunately, if the weather improves a few minutes later the pilot cannot reverse the process and must make do with his light weight and slower machine for the rest of the flight. The use of water ballast is not new but has become worthwhile owing to the intense competition to achieve the highest possible performance.

The alternative to carrying water ballast is to change the effective wing loading, either by changing the wing area in flight or by altering the aerofoil in order to change the lift coefficient. The wing area may be increased by extending wing flaps for circling flight in the thermals, and reduced again by retracting them for efficient high-speed flight between thermals. However, this is not easy to do without incurring drag losses which more than offset the advantages gained. It is very difficult to design a wing with an extending flap which does not have joints and slots which leak air and create extra drag. In most cases these losses cancel out the advantages, and a simple, clean wing without the complication and weight of flaps is just as efficient. Once the structural problem of making the flaps without the resultant excessive drag losses has been solved, variable geometry like this offers a significant improvement in performance because it allows a much higher wing loading to be used for better performance at high speeds while retaining satisfactory low-speed performance for circling flight and climbing. Unlike water ballast, the two configurations can be used again and again during the same flight.

The use of trailing edge flaps, which vary the camber of the aerofoil, give much the same effect but on a smaller scale. They are easier to construct without large weight or drag penalties. In many machines the ailerons are arranged to raise and droop as the flaps are moved up and down, which has the effect of changing the camber of the wing along the complete span. Unfortunately, when the flaps and ailerons are lowered for low-speed flight, the aileron drag is increased. This spoils the handling of the machine at low speeds and necessitates the use of much more rudder, just at the time when it is important to control the aircraft easily and accurately in order to centre into the strongest lift.

It is difficult to predict what improvements are still possible apart from the development of even better aerofoils. Many of the more recent designs have had some rather poor features which have tended to make them unnecessarily difficult to land, or prone to damage on the ground. Apart from these points it is in the structural design that most improvement may be hoped for.

Since the adoption of the laminar flow wing sections, designers have shown great ingenuity in trying out new forms of wing structures in order to produce accurate, smooth surfaces. Some tried stabilising thin plywood skins with numbers of spanwise stringers to eliminate the need for a heavy main spar (SHK and Foka). Others tried using very thick top and bottom plywood skins to form a large box spar and then building fairing shapes onto the leading and trailing edge (Finnish Vasama).

Metal structures are also used in some gliders and have various advantages. However, unless the skins are reasonably thick the surface is scarcely smooth enough to make the best use of the modern aerofoils. A thin skin tends to buckle under load and it is a skilled business to rivet thin skins and smooth out any joints with filler. Stabilising the skin with foam materials and honeycombs has also been tried with varying degrees of success (HP10 and prototype BG100).

Perhaps the most striking advance in structural design has been the introduction of glass fibre for primary structure. This was almost entirely due to the wonderful work of the students at various universities and technical institutes in Germany who pioneered the design of glass fibre machines and carried out the testing of the new materials and structures. Almost overnight the supremacy of the wooden gliders was challenged by this material. It had only previously been used for fairing shapes such as the fuselage nose cone and other minor non-load-carrying parts. One of the greatest advantages of the new material was the exceptional smoothness and surface finish which could be obtained with it and its resistance to warping in hot or wet climates. It also lent itself to moulding into complex three dimensional curves which would be impossible or very expensive to duplicate in metal or wood.

A further development, which at the time of writing is still being explored, is the use of carbon fibres to supplement the glass. This results in a much lighter and stiffer structure than normal glass fibre. However, it is very expensive at present and has only just begun being used extensively in a production machine.

Contrary to many predictions, the introduction of glass fibre construction has not radically reduced the cost of producing gliders although it has resulted in an improvement in finish and performance. Although the glider is produced from moulds, it still requires a large number of man hours to complete, and the laying-up of the glass matting and rovings is a skilled job needing careful supervision. Much of the structure cannot be adequately inspected after it has been made, and if a workman misses out one layer of glass matting the strength of that part may be seriously affected, no one being any the wiser until a structural failure has occurred. Glass fibre is not a miracle material as it is heavy, expensive and rather springy. In many parts of a glider an unnecessary extra amount of material has to be used in order to produce a reasonably stiff structure and prevent flutter. This makes it rather heavy compared with a good metal structure.

The most needed breakthrough now is probably in simplifying glider design to reduce the cost of production. There has been a tendency for designers to use all metal, all wood, or all glass fibre, which is not necessarily the best or the cheapest thing to do. Future designs will probably include a mixture of materials, using each one in the way in which it is most efficient and economical.

Apart from the gliders which are specifically designed for competitive or cross-country soaring, there will always be a need for basic trainers and for gliders designed for the inexperienced pilot to fly solo and gain experience. Again, one of the prime considerations is low cost, but ease of maintenance and repair is also important.

With any kind of training machine, whether it is a motor car or aircraft, there are various possible philosophies. A very simple, foolproof machine will make the initial training easier and will perhaps reduce the number and seriousness of any accidents. However, unless the student is given experience on a less forgiving machine he is liable to have problems at a later stage when he converts to a machine which has different characteristics.

A training machine with difficult flying characteristics would necessitate more comprehensive and perhaps longer training before going solo, but might lead to a higher standard of flying in the long term. However, it might also result in a much larger percentage of trainees being unable to reach a safe solo standard.

It seems best, on balance, to have docile and forgiving machines for all the early training and solo flying. This does not mean having a poor performance but rather a low stalling speed and good airbrakes. The low stalling speed reduces the shocks and risk of damage in the event of a bad landing and the effective airbrakes help to eliminate the risk of the beginner being unable to get down in a confined area.

Most of the modern high-performance machines are docile and easy to handle in flight but from every point of view the beginner is well-advised to gain some cross-country and field landing experience before buying a contest machine. By flying a slightly inferior machine, a pilot learns to work harder to get the best out of it against his competitors and competition of this sort is the best stimulus for improving flying and soaring skill. More important still, it enables a pilot to gain confidence in his ability to select fields and land in them, before flying machines which require a much higher degree of skill and accuracy to spot-land.

2 How and why a glider flies

Most people take flying very much for granted when they are passengers in an airliner, and do not worry themselves about why and how the aeroplane flies. However, when you start learning to fly, you will soon find yourself wondering what can go wrong. You will want to know a little more about it in order to believe that flying is really as safe as it appears from the ground.

It is not necessary to have any detailed knowledge of aerodynamics or of meteorology to become a good soaring pilot. However, the pilot who does have some extra knowledge will be at a definite advantage, as in all walks of life. In practice though, as you gain experience, it is likely that you will get a sudden thirst for knowledge in order to understand how to improve your flying.

The explanations which follow will form a basis for understanding the principles of flight. Further simple explanations about the theory of flight will be found in my other books. However, you will not find any mathematical formulae in them as piloting is all a very practical business.

Propulsion With a powered aircraft the thrust of the jet engines or propellers drives the machine through the air so that the wings can develop the lift to support its weight.

In gliding flight, the aircraft must descend and use the force of gravity to maintain a steady speed. This is exactly the same principle as the cyclist freewheeling down a hill. If the hill is too gentle, the cycle moves too slowly to keep control and balance. Similarly, if the glider pilot attempts to fly in too shallow a glide, or on the level, the speed becomes too slow for good control and the wings are unable to produce enough lift to support the weight in steady flight.

With a bicycle the angle of slope required for a certain speed will depend upon the friction or 'drag' of the cycle. Extra friction caused by applying

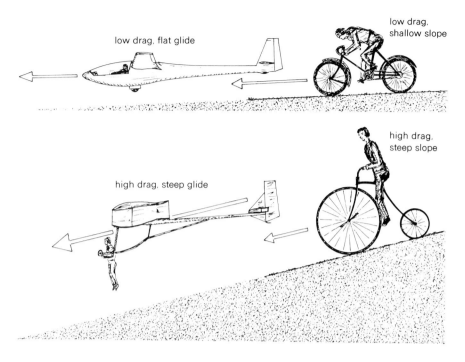

4 The gliding angle compared with a freewheeling bicycle. With high drag a steeper slope is needed to maintain speed.

low drag, flat glide

low drag, shallow slope

high drag, steep slope

high drag, steep glide

the wheel brakes continuously would make a much steeper slope necessary for freewheeling at a given speed.

In the same way with gliders, a crude machine with struts and wires will have much higher drag and will, therefore, need a steeper descent to maintain speed. A very flat angle of glide is only possible with a highly streamlined aircraft fitted with a very efficient wing (Fig. 4).

Speed can only be maintained with either the bicycle or the glider when they are moving down their respective slopes. They are both being propelled by gravity and are converting their height (potential energy) into speed and distance (kinetic energy).

Any attempt to make the bicycle freewheel uphill is doomed to failure, although, if it has excess speed, it will be possible to ride level or go up a short slope while the excess speed is used up. Similarly with the glider, extra speed may be turned into height by 'zooming' upwards for a few moments. But any attempt to keep climbing or to fly level for more than a few seconds would result in the speed becoming too low for controlled flight and the glider would soon stall and start to lose height again.

The glider must, therefore, start any flight by being launched or released at height. It may be carried to the top of a hill and thrown off, be pulled up by a winch or car, like a kite on a string, or it may be towed to height by another aircraft and then released. It begins to glide down and, in the absence of any rising air and apart from any momentary zooms, the whole flight will be a gradual descent to the ground.

The majority of gliders fly most efficiently at about 50 miles per hour and lose height at 150–200 feet per minute. Whereas the cyclist has very limited freedom to turn and zig-zag down any hill, the glider pilot's hill slopes away in any direction that he cares to point the glider. He can also vary the angle of the slope, making it steeper if he wishes, but he must not attempt to climb, or to glide down a slope which is too shallow to maintain the minimum speed for support and control.

Soaring flight We must now consider how the glider can make use of rising air to gain height without losing flying speed. A simple explanation is shown in Fig. 5.

Imagine that you are walking down a stationary escalator at the rate of 200 steps every minute. This is equivalent to gliding normally in still air and losing 200 feet per minute.

Now the stairs start to move slowly upwards so that, although you continue walking at the same pace, it now takes you much longer to reach the bottom of the stairway. This situation is similar to the glider flying into weakly rising air, thus slightly reducing the rate of descent (known usually as 'reduced sink').

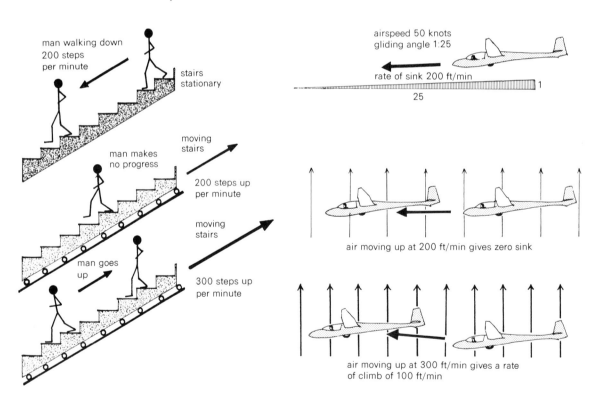

5 How a glider gains height in rising air. Like the man on the escalator, the glider gains height although it is moving down continuously through the surrounding air.

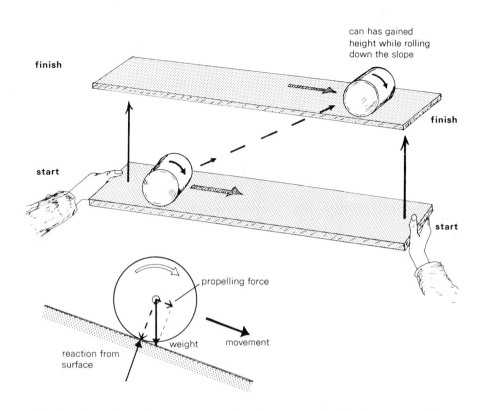

can has gained height while rolling down the slope

finish

finish

start

start

propelling force

weight   movement

reaction from surface

6 The force of gravity propels an object down an inclined surface, even when the surface is lifted bodily upward. In the same way a glider is propelled by gravity as it gains height in rising air.

If the speed of the escalator is increased to give a movement upwards of 200 steps per minute you will get nowhere, although you continue walking steadily down the stairs ('zero sink' in the glider).

Any further increase in the rate of ascent of the stairs results in your being gradually taken to the top of the escalator, in spite of walking downwards continuously. This is what happens when the glider is soaring and has flown into air which is rising more rapidly than the glider sinks. It does not matter whether this air is rising vertically or at an angle, as when blowing over a hill. The effect of gravity is not changed by the glider flying in rising air so that in relation to the ground it is actually gaining height. Fig. 6 shows a little experiment you can do at home to confirm this last statement.

Take a tin can and roll it down a sloping board set at a slight angle. This represents the glider in a steady glide. Then, start it off again at the top, but at the same time lift the board upwards. The can continues to roll steadily even when the movement is quick enough for it to reach the bottom of the board when it is higher than the starting point.

The major difference between all these examples and the aeroplane or glider is that the cyclist or object is supported by a solid surface, whereas aircraft have to get their support by flying fast enough to develop the necessary amount of lift. In this respect, the wing of an aircraft is similar to water skis, which only support their rider when the speed and angle of the ski is sufficient to develop enough lift to do so.

The wing

The wing of an aircraft is designed to create the lift which supports the weight of the whole machine. It does this by acting as a deflector, pushing the air downwards behind it as it moves through the air. When the air is pushed downwards by the wing the reaction tends to raise the wing upwards with the force that we call lift. Since the wing is doing work in forcing the air downwards, a certain amount of resistance is inevitable. In aerodynamics, resistance to motion is always known as drag.

For efficient flight, the wing must be designed to give a large amount of lift in relation to the amount of drag that it produces at the same time.

The crudest form of wing is just a flat plate set at an angle to the direction of movement as in Fig. 7. Air is deflected downwards by the lower surface and the reaction to this is lift and drag (unfortunately not much lift and rather a lot of drag in this case). If the angle is increased, more lift is created but at the expense of even more drag because the airflow over the top surface of the flat plate breaks away at the sharp 'leading edge' and forms turbulent eddies which cause excessive drag. Practical flying machines might have been delayed for many years had it not been for the realisation that a cambered wing section as also shown in Fig. 7 offered both greatly increased lift and a greatly reduced amount of drag. With a cambered aerofoil, even at quite large angles the air flows smoothly over the cambered leading edge and down over the top surface of the wing. But, in addition, the cambered shape is efficient at reducing the air pressure slightly over the wing and this effect accounts for up to two-thirds of the total lift created. In simple terms, the cambered wing is better at deflecting the airflow downwards, and is a much more streamlined shape which creates far less drag. This is fortunate, as the designer needs a fairly deep wing section in order to have room to put the spars for strengthening the wing. A flat section would be structurally difficult – if not impossible.

Bernoulli's theorem

Bernoulli's theorem concerns the properties of fluids in motion and is a very useful way of explaining the greater lifting properties of a cambered aerofoil. For all practical purposes air behaves in a similar manner to a fluid, provided that the speed of an object through it is well below that of sound (760 m.p.h. at sea level).

Bernoulli's theorem states that in the streamlined flow of a perfect fluid (one with no viscosity) the sum of the energies remains constant. In other words, if there is a change in potential energy or height, there will be a corresponding change in pressure or speed of the flow. Similarly, if there is

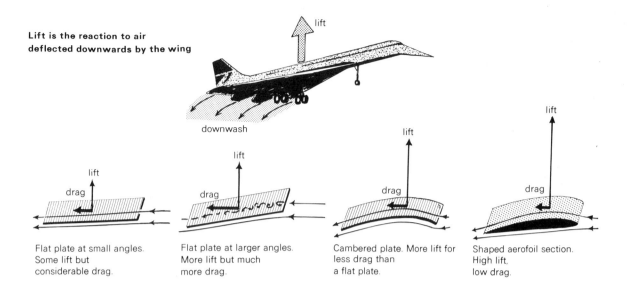

Lift is the reaction to air deflected downwards by the wing

lift

downwash

lift

lift

lift

lift

drag

drag

drag

drag

Flat plate at small angles.
Some lift but
considerable drag.

Flat plate at larger angles.
More lift but much
more drag.

Cambered plate. More lift for
less drag than
a flat plate.

Shaped aerofoil section.
High lift,
low drag.

7 The wing as a simple deflector. From flat plates to aerofoils. The cambered aerofoil is more efficient and also provides the necessary depth for proper wing spars.

no change in height, an increase in the speed of flow, for example, will result in a corresponding decrease in pressure (Fig. 8**a** and **b**).

At first sight it may seem questionable that if a fluid or gas, like air, flowing through a smooth restriction is *accelerated*, the pressure in the narrow part is reduced. This is because the flow has to speed up in order to allow the same volume of fluid or air to flow through the narrow restriction as is flowing along the larger diameter tube. Because the speed of flow is increased (more kinetic energy) the pressure drops.

This will happen with any *smooth* restriction and is known as a 'venturi effect'. A venturi is a tube with a smooth restriction in it designed to produce a suction. The same principle is used to draw fuel through the jets of a carburettor and also in many paint spray guns.

The relation between a venturi tube and the top surface of an aerofoil is easiest to explain diagrammatically. Fig. 8**d** shows two curved plates mounted in a wind tunnel with the airflow blowing through them. The speed of the air is increased as it passes through the narrow gap and this results in a drop in the pressure. An increase in the speed gives a marked further drop in the pressure, an important fact to remember when considering the variations in lift with speed. If the angles of the plates are changed to give a narrower restriction as in Fig. 8**f**, the result is again a further reduction in the pressure.

This venturi effect still occurs if the top plate is replaced by a flat one, or even if the top plate is removed altogether. In this case, the layers of air above the single curved plate act as the top of the restriction. The similarity

8 Bernoulli's theorem explains the cambered aerofoil and the operation of flaps and control surfaces.

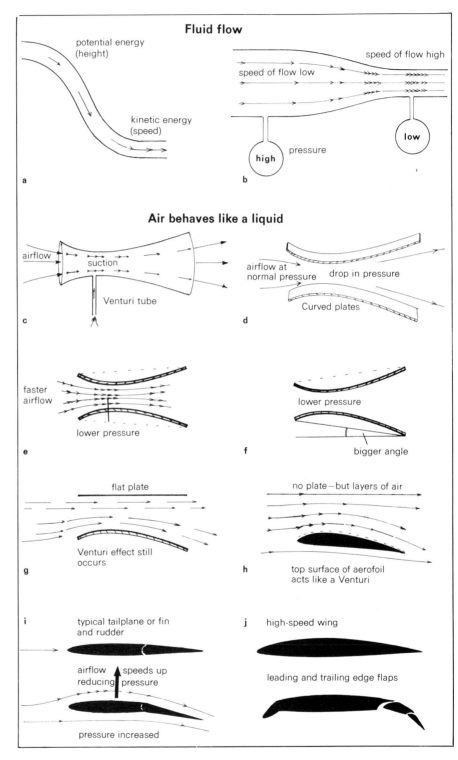

Fluid flow

potential energy (height)

kinetic energy (speed)

a

speed of flow high

speed of flow low

high   pressure   low

b

Air behaves like a liquid

airflow   suction

Venturi tube

c

airflow at normal pressure   drop in pressure

Curved plates

d

faster airflow

lower pressure

e

lower pressure

bigger angle

f

flat plate

Venturi effect still occurs

g

no plate—but layers of air

top surface of aerofoil acts like a Venturi

h

typical tailplane or fin and rudder

airflow speeds up reducing pressure

pressure increased

i

high-speed wing

leading and trailing edge flaps

j

between this example and the top surface of a cambered aerofoil can be seen clearly (Fig. 8**h**).

As a wing moves through the air the airflow over the cambered top surface is speeded up, reducing the pressure. At the same time the airflow below the wing is being deflected downwards and slowed down slightly so that the pressure in this region is increased. These changes in pressure give the upward reaction we call lift. In fact the majority of the lift comes from the drop in pressure above the wing and only about one-third from the increase in pressure below.

If the angle of attack of the wing is increased more the venturi effect above the cambered top surface is greater and the pressure is decreased further, giving even more lift. However, there is a limit to the angle at which the airflow will remain streamlined and steady and beyond this the wing will become stalled. The turbulent flow prevents the speeding up of the air and so a large amount of the lift is lost.

The action of all the conventional controls on an aircraft can be explained by these facts. For example, when the elevator is depressed by moving the stick forward, the streamlined symmetrical aerofoil of the stabiliser is modified into a cambered shape (Fig. 8**i**). The airflow above the tail is speeded up, reducing pressure, and the airflow below the tail is slowed down, increasing pressure. These changes result in an upward reaction which lifts the tail. Similarly, the use of the rudder modifies the aerofoil of the fin and rudder into a cambered shape and produces a side force. The ailerons increase and decrease the camber of the wingtips so that the lift is changed and the aircraft is banked over.

The variations in pressure above and below the wing are really quite small. For example, on a glider weighing 600 lb with a wing area of 150 square feet, each square foot of wing supports an average of 4 lb. However, since atmospheric pressure is about 14.7 lb per square *inch*, the average pressure above the wing would only be reduced to 14.68 lb per square inch. It is therefore completely wrong to describe any wing as having a vacuum above it, although it is reasonable to say that the aircraft is kept up by suction!

For a wing of a given area, a large wing span is much more efficient (making more lift for less drag) because along its increased length it affects more air in a given time. This factor, known as the 'aspect ratio', is discussed in more detail on page 110. However, it is both more expensive and much more difficult to make wings with a large span and a small chord without their becoming either heavy or too flexible. Wings for gliders are always a compromise between weight, strength, efficiency and cost.

Although the lift and drag of a wing depend upon a number of factors (density of the air, speed of the airflow, area of the wing, aspect ratio and angle of attack, to mention the main ones) for practical purposes the lift developed in flight depends on only two of these factors – the airspeed and the angle at which the wing meets the airflow, known as the 'angle of attack'. Air density is also important, but only when operating in the tropics or at high altitudes where the air is less dense than at sea level.

The way in which a wing develops lift can be demonstrated very easily with a model wing, or even just a strip of card. If you want to try a few experiments, find a strip of thin cardboard about 15 inches long and 3 or 4 inches wide. This will act as a crude wing with a 'flat plate' section. You could give it a little camber to make it more like a real wing and give it a more efficient lifting surface.

Speed   First, hold the strip by one end at a slight angle of attack and move it horizontally through the air. You will feel it tending to react upwards as it pushes air down and creates lift. Try moving it much more quickly, but at the same angle. Notice the big increase in the lift with the higher speed. It may also be possible to feel the extra resistance or drag as well at the higher speed.

Actually the lift (and, unfortunately, drag, as we never get something for nothing) increases with the square of the speed, i.e., double the speed and the lift increases 4 times; treble the speed – 9 times the lift (and 9 times the drag!). This square law is most easily explained if we consider what is happening to the air as it meets the wing. At twice the speed, the air meets the wing twice as hard, but also, in a given time, twice as much air passes over the wing. Looked at in this way, it is not surprising that both lift and drag increase so rapidly with more speed.

In practice this means that quite a small increase in speed is needed to produce the extra lift required for carrying a large load, a fact that has many important implications even in gliders. Twice the lift, for example, requires only 1.4 times the speed ($\sqrt{2} = 1.4$). It also results in the gliding angle deteriorating badly at higher speeds because of the large increase in drag.

Angle of attack   The angle of attack, as explained, is the angle at which the wing meets the air in flight. This sounds very simple, but unfortunately it is not always easy to know exactly in which direction the aircraft is moving. Fig. 9 clarifies a few special situations when the angle is not obvious. In order to avoid complicating the issue even further it is easiest to ignore the wind and imagine that it is always a dead calm day. As the reader will see in a later chapter, this is quite an acceptable assumption since a steady wind has no effect on an aircraft, apart from changing its ground speed.

Notice that the angle of attack of the wing can be quite unrelated to the attitude of the aircraft. It is often easiest to imagine that the aircraft is stationary and the air is moving towards it – this is similar to the situation in a wind tunnel where the aircraft is held fixed while the air is blown at it. The airflow meeting the aircraft in flight is known as the *relative* airflow. In no wind, this is the exact opposite to the direction of movement of the aircraft (see Fig. 10).

The relative airflow depends only upon the direction of flight and this can be quite different from the direction in which the nose and fuselage are

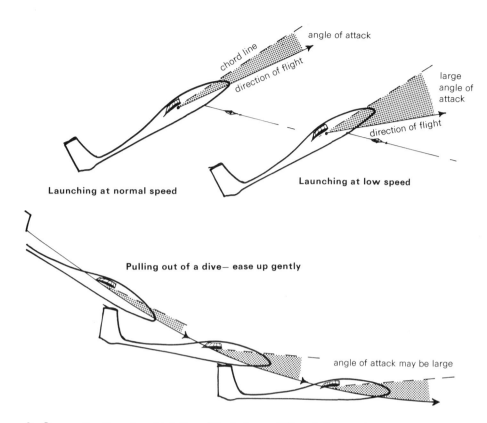

9 Some situations in which the attitude bears little relation to the angle of attack. On a winch launch a steep angle is only safe while the speed is normal. At low speed the same angle of climb results in a large angle of attack and a risk of stalling. Sharp pull-outs can result in the wing being pulled to a large angle so that it stalls in spite of the nose down attitude and relatively high speed.

pointing. Notice that we try to avoid using the term 'wind' for anything other than the actual wind. Once in the air, we do not feel wind in an open glider. It is just airflow – the relative airflow.

Angle of incidence (sometimes known as the Rigger's angle of incidence)

Normally the wings of an aircraft are set at a fixed angle of incidence to the fuselage (Fig. 10) so that a variation in the angle of attack involves a change in the angle of the whole aircraft in relation to the relative airflow. A heavy and complex mechanism would be required to change the wing angle on the fuselage in flight and there are few advantages in doing so in normal aircraft. However, for the ultimate in performance in gliders the designer may try to keep the line of the fuselage accurately along the line of flight to minimise the drag. The wing is set at the best angle for cruising flight and then, for faster or slower speeds, instead of lowering or raising the nose and spoiling the fuselage angle, the wing flaps are raised or lowered. This has an effect similar to changing the wing incidence but it also improves the wing efficiency

10 The angle of incidence and the angle of attack. The angle of incidence is fixed whereas the angle of attack varies according to the direction of flight.

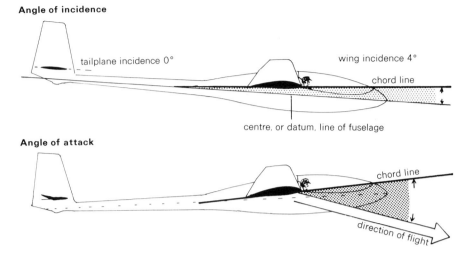

Angle of incidence

tailplane incidence 0°   wing incidence 4°

chord line

centre, or datum, line of fuselage

Angle of attack

chord line

direction of flight

too. Modern low-drag wing sections are most efficient over quite a small range of angles. Instead of having to increase the angle of attack to maintain the lift at low speeds, the flap is lowered so that the all-important front section of the wing still meets the air at much the same angle and remains efficient. Similarly, when the flap is raised, the glider can fly at a much higher speed without upsetting the flow over the main portion of the wing. On some machines, such as the ASW 12, the pilot is provided with a spirit level so that he can keep the fuselage at, or near, the correct attitude. In this case, he adjusts his speed with a combination of movements of the flap and attitude in order to keep the fuselage in line and the drag to a minimum. Fortunately, most gliders do not have the complication of flaps so the pilot does not normally have to be so clever!

Lift and drag   Going back to the strip of card, the effect of some changes in the angle of attack are obvious. As the angle is increased, more lift is developed and more effort is needed to move the strip through the air. Both the lift and the drag have increased. At even larger angles it becomes obvious that the main increase is an increase in drag.

A cambered aerofoil is much more efficient than a flat plate and, even by bending our crude cardboard wing into a cambered shape, the improvement in the lift at small angles can be detected.

A wind tunnel is required to find out more about the relationship between lift and drag and the speed and angle of attack of a wing. Most wing sections produce some lift at small negative angles of attack because of the reduction in pressure over the cambered top surface. If the speed of the airflow is kept constant, the lift increases steadily with an increase in the angle of attack until it reaches a certain angle, usually about 15°–20°, depending mainly on the exact shape of the aerofoil. Any further increase in angle results in a *drop* in the amount of lift. At this point, the airflow above the wing has broken away into turbulent flow so that, instead of the wing deflecting the air smoothly and efficiently downwards, it leaves a trail of eddies and swirls behind it. The amount of lift is reduced drastically and the amount of drag greatly increased by all the turbulent airflow in the wake of the wing. The wing is then said to be stalled (Fig. 11).

If the wing angle is reduced even slightly below the angle at which the airflow broke up, smooth flow will be re-established immediately. This angle is known as the 'stalling angle' (or sometimes as the critical angle) and experiments show that the angle remains, for all practical purposes, the same, regardless of the speed of the airflow. For example, if a certain design of aerofoil stalls at 16° at 30 knots, it will also stall at about 16° at any speed up to about 400 knots. (At very high speeds the effects of compressibility of the air begin to have a significant effect.)

This also has important implications in flight. It means that whenever the wing angle gets too large, lift will be lost suddenly and the aircraft will stall and lose height. This will happen at any speed and *not* only at very low speeds, although it will probably be much more difficult for the pilot to pull

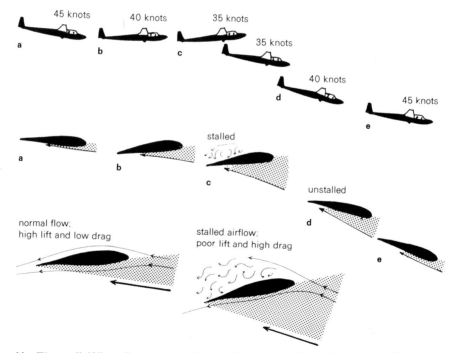

11 The stall. When the wing reaches too large an angle of attack, the airflow above the wing becomes turbulent, reducing the lift and increasing the drag. The glider sinks rapidly, dropping its nose for a few seconds, until normal flight is resumed as the pilot relaxes the backward movement of the stick.

the wing accidentally to such a large angle in normal flight. However, the lift will be regained immediately the wing angle is reduced to less than the critical angle.

Steady flight is only possible while the wing remains below the stalling angle. Stalling occurs whenever the angle of attack of the wing exceeds the stalling angle and is in fact nothing to do with the speed of the airflow. A more comprehensive explanation of the effects of the wing stalling follows on page 41.

The balancing act When an aeroplane or glider is in steady straight flight the forces acting on it are exactly balanced and in equilibrium. Fig. 12 shows the forces acting on a powered aircraft and a glider. It may seem strange that the lift from the wings is exactly equal to the weight in straight and level flight in the powered machine. Any more lift would result in an acceleration upwards, in the same way as any extra thrust from the engine and propeller would result in a gain in speed until such time as the drag became equal to the thrust.

The pilot does not need to think about this balance of forces when he flies the aircraft. If the balance is not perfect the aircraft automatically tries to sort the problem out for itself, so that it can fly steadily again. Like other bodies, aircraft always tend to settle in a steady state of motion.

When gliding, the aircraft has only three forces acting on it – lift, drag and weight. In steady flight the weight is balanced by the combination of the lift

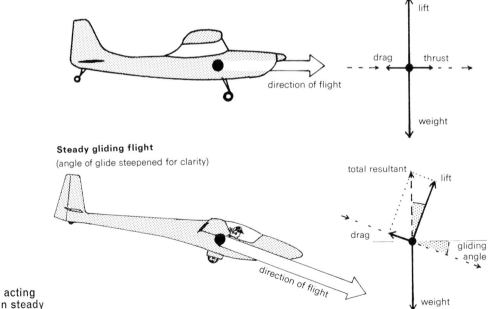

Straight and level flight

lift

drag · · · · thrust

direction of flight

weight

Steady gliding flight
(angle of glide steepened for clarity)

total resultant

lift

drag

gliding angle

direction of flight

weight

12 The forces acting on the aircraft in steady flight are balanced.

and drag. The moves by which the glider rebalances these forces automatically after being disturbed in steady flight are interesting, if somewhat complex, and are happening almost continuously on a bumpy day.

Suppose that for some reason, perhaps a sudden change in the wind speed, the airspeed of the glider decreases by a few knots. Less speed will result in less lift and, since the glider was in steady flight before this loss, the reduction in lift will upset the balance of the forces. For a few moments the weight force will win and there will be an increase in the rate of sink and a steeper glide path. However, the steeper glide will result in the airflow coming up to meet the wing at a larger angle of attack than before. This will increase the lift, which will help to check the higher rate of sink. At the same time the steeper angle of descent causes a gradual increase in speed towards the original figure. This also gives extra lift, which will help to reduce the rate of sink. Less sink will reduce the angle of glide again and after a further series of minor adjustments between the speed and angle of attack and glide-path, the glider will find itself once again in steady straight flight at the original speed! To the pilot this is mainly of academic interest except to demonstrate that the aircraft is always trying to settle down.

Steady flight can be established in a glider at any speed, from its maximum permissible speed down to the stalling speed. Since the lift from the wing depends on the angle of attack and the airspeed, knowing that the forces have to be in balance for a steady glide we can understand how this balance is achieved at various speeds.

If, for a moment, we make the approximation that with a glider the lift must always be equal to the weight (this is true during the hold off for a landing when the aircraft is flying level, but is only approximate for descents when it is the combination of lift and drag which must equal the weight) then it will be seen that sufficient lift will be produced at a small angle of attack to fly steadily at high speed. At a lower flying speed the angle of attack will have to be larger to maintain the lift and balance the weight. In fact, as the speed is changed the flight path adjusts itself after a few seconds until the angle of attack gives just the correct amount of lift to balance out the weight.

The actual gliding angle settles down after a short while and will depend only upon the proportions of the lift and drag of the aircraft at that speed and attitude. If the drag is rather high in proportion to the lift, the angle of glide will be steep. Fig. 13 shows a number of situations, and it can be seen by comparing them that the gliding angle is, in fact, the angle making up the triangle formed by the vectors representing the lift and drag forces. (Appendix B explains vector diagrams in a simple way.) Nothing else affects the gliding angle in a steady glide. A flat gliding angle can, therefore, only be achieved by a very clean and streamlined glider with an efficient wing. This alone can give the large lift required with small drag.

If the aircraft is reasonably stable it can be made to settle down at its normal cruising speed and fly 'hands off'. It is then said to be trimmed for

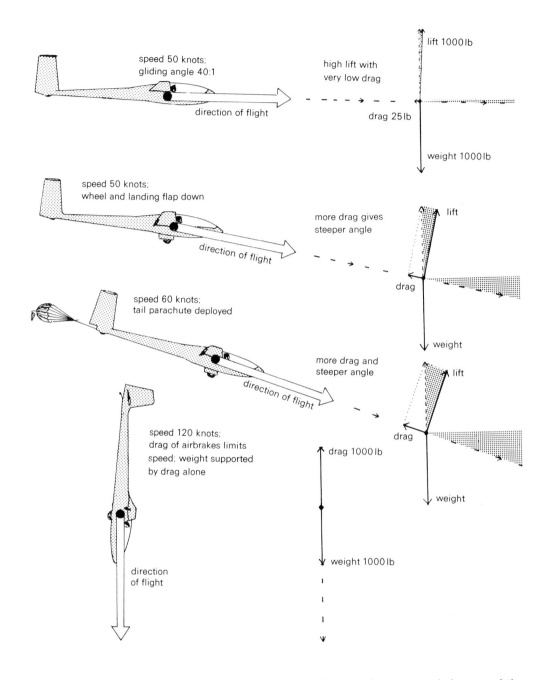

speed 50 knots;
gliding angle 40:1

high lift with
very low drag

direction of flight

lift 1000 lb

drag 25 lb

weight 1000 lb

speed 50 knots;
wheel and landing flap down

direction of flight

more drag gives
steeper angle

lift

drag

weight

speed 60 knots;
tail parachute deployed

direction of flight

more drag and
steeper angle

lift

drag

weight

speed 120 knots;
drag of airbrakes limits
speed; weight supported
by drag alone

direction
of flight

drag 1000 lb

weight 1000 lb

13 The gliding angle and the lift/drag ratio. In steady flight the forces must balance and the gliding angle is dependent *only* on the lift/drag ratio.

that speed. This speed will correspond with a certain definite angle of attack, so that the combination of lift and drag exactly balance the weight.

The function of the elevator

Because of the stability the controls have to be used to change the angle of attack. For example, to hold an increased angle of attack and so fly more slowly, a constant backward pressure and movement on the stick will be required. If this is relaxed, the aircraft will resume the trimmed speed and attitude.

The function of the elevator is, therefore, only to change the angle at which the wing meets the airflow. This alters the amount of lift being produced and it is the change in the lift which makes the aircraft change direction; nose up if the lift exceeds the amount required for steady flight at that speed, or nose down if the lift is reduced so that the weight exceeds the lift.

If the wing has been pulled up to a slightly larger angle rather quickly

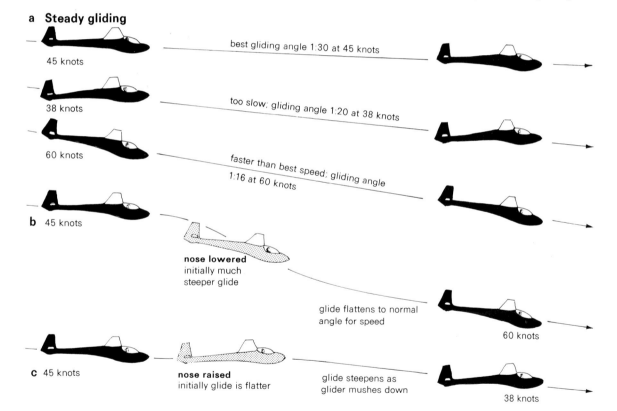

a Steady gliding

45 knots

best gliding angle 1:30 at 45 knots

38 knots

too slow: gliding angle 1:20 at 38 knots

60 knots

faster than best speed: gliding angle 1:16 at 60 knots

b 45 knots

nose lowered initially much steeper glide

glide flattens to normal angle for speed

60 knots

c 45 knots

nose raised initially glide is flatter

glide steepens as glider mushes down

38 knots

14 a The relationship between the attitude and the gliding angle in a steady glide. **b** The effect of lowering the nose quickly. Initially the glide is much steeper until the speed and glide settle down. **c** The effect of raising the nose quickly. Initially the glider flies level, or even gains a few feet; then it begins to sink more rapidly and the gliding angle becomes much steeper than at the best gliding speed.

the glider loses some speed after a few seconds as it levels out for a moment. This loss of speed causes a reduction in the lift which results in the glider starting to sink again. The final result is that although the attitude of the glider has become slightly more nose high, the glidepath is steeper (Fig. 14). The airflow is moving upwards towards the wing at a larger angle because of the sinking movement of the aircraft, and this change in the angle of attack increases the lift again and restores the balance of forces. The final gliding angle has become steeper because, at the lower speed, the wing is meeting the airflow at a less efficient angle. In proportion to the lift being developed, the drag is much greater than at the normal gliding speed and it is ultimately this spoiling of the lift/drag ratio which causes the spoiling of the gliding angle.

Conversely, when the stick is moved forward a little in cruising flight the initial effect is to lower the nose and reduce the angle of attack of the wing slightly. This reduces the lift and drag momentarily so that the glider sinks into a steeper descent for a few seconds. However, the increasing rate of descent results in an immediate change in the direction of the relative airflow, so that after a few moments of steeper descent, the glidepath settles to an angle which is a little less steep. As the cruising speed is increased, the angle of attack of the wing is automatically reduced to maintain the balance of lift and weight until steady flight is achieved.

In steady flight the position of the stick determines the angle of attack of the wing and the airspeed. Backward movements result in larger angles and lower speeds, forward movements give smaller angles and higher speeds. Since the wing only stalls at large angles of attack, the pilot should be conscious of the approximate stick position and avoid holding it back continuously. In effect, the position of the stick in steady flight is an angle of attack indicator and gives warning of potential trouble from stalling (Fig. 15).

It is vital to understand that in spite of being called an elevator, pulling the nose up can only result in a momentary gain of height. After a few seconds, as the speed decreases and in spite of the backward position of the stick, the aircraft will sink again, or will stall and drop its nose.

The elevator trimmer is usually an adjustable tab on the elevator, or a spring tensioning device which applies a small force to the stick one way or the other as required. Whereas the trimmer affects whether the aircraft will fly 'hands off' at a certain speed it does not have much, if any, effect on the position of the stick. The stick position controls the angle of attack of the wing and – as we have seen – can provide the pilot with an indication of the situation in steady flight. When the stick is being held well back the angle of attack is large and the aircraft must be close to the stall, regardless of the apparent position of the nose in relation to the horizon. This is important. In a tight turn, the nose may even be a little lower than the normal cruising position but if the stick is being held well back near the end of its range, the angle of attack *is* large and the aircraft *is* close to the stall.

Landing is the perfect example of varying the speed and angle of attack

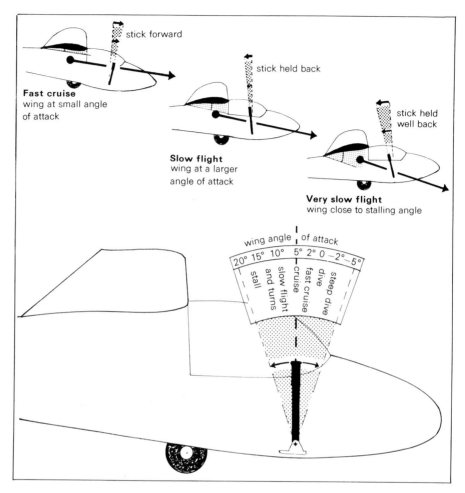

15 The stick position and the angle of attack. A large backward position in gentle turns or straight flight is a warning sign that the glider is close to the stall.

to keep the lift exactly constant and balance the weight. Watch a glider or powered aircraft as it completes the round out and flies level just above the ground. Fig. 16 shows what happens. At point **a** the glider in the drawing has just levelled out at about 50 knots. In order to fly level the weight must now be exactly balanced by the lift, or the aircraft will either sink or balloon upwards. Because of the relatively high speed (giving plenty of lift) the angle of attack of the wing will be quite small. At this moment the glider will be flying in a rather nose down attitude which might cause damage to the front skid (or propeller in the motor glider or powered aircraft) on landing. The landing would also be at a much higher speed than necessary with a greater risk of damage on rough ground.

However, as soon as the glider has started to round out and fly level it begins to lose speed, because, like a bicycle, it loses speed when it is no longer freewheeling downhill. As speed is lost the lift from the wings decreases and, if this is allowed to happen, the glider will start to sink because the weight is not being balanced correctly. In order to prevent the sinking the pilot must bring the wing to a slightly larger angle of attack so that, although the speed has decreased, the same amount of lift is being generated to balance out the weight (point **b**). The speed will continue to fall and the pilot must gradually increase the wing angle still further to keep the total lift constant. In practice, all he does is to try and fly the machine level a few feet above the ground. He stops any tendency for the aircraft to sink by moving back on the stick to raise the nose a little, so increasing the angle of attack. Eventually, as the wing gets too close to the stalling angle, the controls cannot prevent the aircraft from sinking gently onto the ground (**c**). Providing, that is, that the ground is close at hand!

If the backward movement on the stick is made too quickly, the wing angle will be too great for the speed, and instead of just balancing the weight the lift will be more than is needed for a few seconds. The aircraft will then 'balloon' up instead of just flying level. However, if the controls are held still, the speed will drop a little further after a few seconds so that once again there is not quite enough lift to maintain level flight. So, with no help from

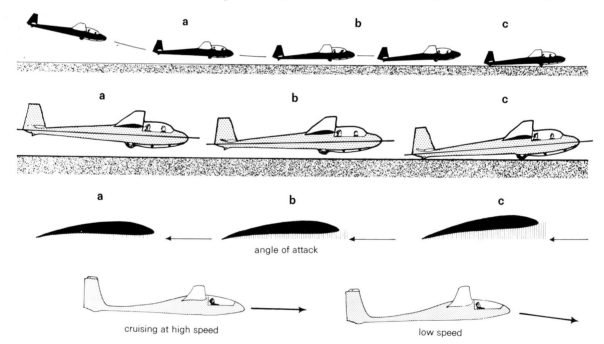

16 Landing. As the glider loses speed during the hold off the lift is maintained by gradually raising the nose to increase the angle of attack of the wing. At high speed the glider flies at a small angle of attack in a nose down attitude while at low speed the angle of attack is much larger and the glider flies in a nose high attitude.

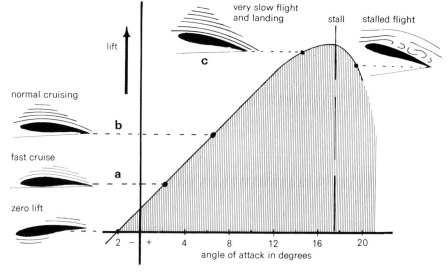

17 Variations in lift with the angle of attack. Maximum lift occurs just before the stalling angle, in this case 17°.

the pilot, the glider will begin to sink again. Then the lowered speed will require a further increase in angle of attack to develop more lift to level the glider out once more.

In steady straight flight the relationship between airspeed and angle of attack is a similar one. At high speeds the angle of attack will be very small whereas at low speed the angle will be large and not far from the critical angle and the stall. Thus the control of flight at low speed has to be much more precise and care must be taken to avoid stalling (Fig. 17).

Stalling If the wing is pulled beyond the stalling angle, the aircraft will have insufficient lift for a few moments to fly properly and support its weight. It will lose height rapidly until the wing is allowed to return to a smaller angle so that it can unstall and make lift normally (Fig. 11).

Fortunately, with most aircraft there is a distinctive nose down pitching movement as the wing stalls. Of course, even when the airflow breaks up over the top surface of the wing, some lift is still being produced. However, this remaining lift acts further back along the wing than usual causing a nose down pitching movement as the aircraft sinks. This movement helps to reduce the angle of attack of the wing so that, if anything, the wing is trying to unstall itself. In fact almost all gliders will unstall themselves if they are allowed to do so, i.e. as long as the pilot does not attempt to stop the nose from dropping.

(Not all modern jet aircraft are like this. Most Delta wings, and highly swept-back winged types with high tailplanes, tend to pitch nose up at the stall. This is inclined to prevent the recovery from being made quickly, if at all. On these types, special stall warning and anti-stall devices are fitted to try to ensure that an accidental stall cannot happen.)

Mention has already been made of the difficulties of telling whether the angle of attack is large or small in flight. The attitude of the aircraft, that is the position of the nose in relation to the horizon, is not always an accurate guide. For example, even in a normal gliding attitude the speed might be very low if there were excessive drag. This might happen if the airbrakes came open accidentally without the knowledge of the pilot. In steady flight at low speed the glider is bound to be sinking rather steeply so that the wing meets the air at a large angle of attack. Otherwise there would not be sufficient lift to support the weight at the low speed and provide a balance of forces.

Manoeuvring and its effect on the stalling speed

The aeroplane would be a useless means of transport if it were unable to manoeuvre in all three dimensions. In the case of the glider, and of all conventional aeroplanes, almost all the power to manoeuvre is obtained by varying the lift from the wings, and not, as might at first be thought, by means of the tail surfaces.

For example, if a glider or aeroplane needs to be pulled out of a dive quickly, a large additional upward force is needed to make it change direction. The pilot eases back on the stick and raises the elevators producing an extra download on the tailplane. This force acting at the rear of the fuselage brings the whole aircraft, including the wing, to a slightly greater nose up angle so that the wing develops extra lift. It is this extra lift which provides the force to make the aircraft change direction and pull out of the dive.

Similarly, when going into a dive the movement of the elevator lowers the nose a little and reduces the wing lift, but in this case, unless it is a very violent movement, the change in direction occurs because the force of gravity is stronger at that moment than the reduced lift from the wings and it begins to pull the aircraft downwards.

Whenever some additional force is required to change direction in a nose up or nose down sense, it can only come from variations in the lift from the wings. When more lift is required it must be obtained by more speed or a larger angle of attack, or a combination of these two factors. If extra lift is required for a manoeuvre more speed will be necessary unless the angle of attack is changed. This means that if the angle of attack is very close to the stalling angle, a higher speed is needed, i.e. the stalling speed has been raised by the manoeuvre.

Increased lift is required for any increase in the load that the wings have to support, whether it is simply additional weight (heavier pilots or water ballast) or is due to manoeuvring. The greater the wing loading, the more lift required and, therefore, the higher the speed needed to produce that lift, and the higher the stalling speed. (Fig. 18.)

The wing loading of an aircraft is the total weight divided by the wing area. For example, with a modern glider the total weight of 900 lb supported by a wing area of 150 square feet gives a wing loading of 6 lb/sq. ft.

When the loading on the aircraft is increased or decreased by manoeuvring,

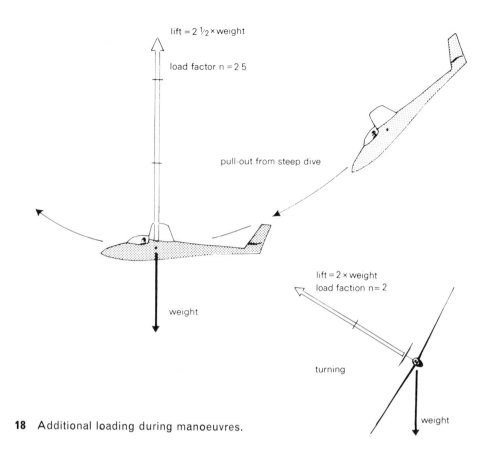

lift = 2 ½ × weight

load factor n = 2.5

pull-out from steep dive

weight

lift = 2 × weight
load faction n = 2

turning

weight

18 Additional loading during manoeuvres.

it is normal to refer to an increase or decrease in the load factor (n). As with an increase in the actual weight, increasing the load factor means that the wings must develop more lift. This means an increase in the stalling speed during the manoeuvre.

Extra loading is produced whenever the pilot pulls back on the stick sharply. The inertia of the aircraft tends to make it continue along its original flight path and resist the attempt to change its direction of movement. The wing has to be pulled to a larger angle of attack to provide the large amount of extra lift required and this makes the aircraft appear to mush through the air in a slightly nose high attitude as it changes direction.

In most light aircraft and gliders any really harsh backward movement on the stick at speeds of less than about twice the normal stalling speed, will pull the wing beyond its stalling angle so that a high speed stall occurs. (The term 'high speed stall' is used for any stall occurring above the normal level flight stalling speed during manoeuvring and is nothing to do with high speed flight.) This would be dangerously near the limit of the strength of the structure of many light aircraft as at speeds of over twice the normal stalling speed the load on the wings could be four times greater than normal (4g). The pilot must, therefore, learn to use his controls gently and avoid harsh backward movements at speeds above twice the stalling speed. At lower speeds, any attempt to make a sharp pull up will just stall the wing, reducing the lift and preventing high loads which might damage the structure.

Heavier and faster types of aircraft are usually much easier to stall in steep turns and violent manoeuvres because of their extra inertia and more powerful controls. The result of a high speed stall on these machines is generally more spectacular since any uneven stalling of the wings will cause a rapid wing drop, and a prompt forward movement on the stick may be necessary to stop the aircraft rolling past the vertical!

Only some of the normal low speed stalling characteristics will be seen and felt during a high speed stall in a glider. Close to, or at, the stall, the buffet will begin and it will be impossible to continue raising the nose, or if turning, to tighten the turn any further. Either the nose or one wing will drop and, until the wing is allowed to unstall by relaxing the backward pressure, the buffet will continue and height will be lost rapidly.

Turning Turning is a little more complex than a pure pitching manoeuvre since it

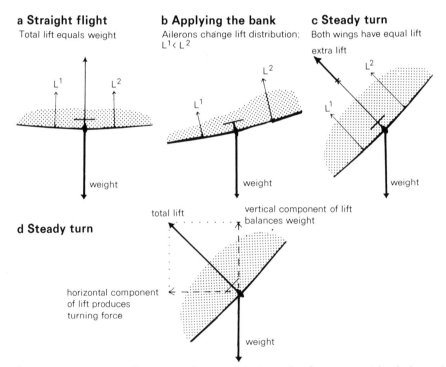

a Straight flight
Total lift equals weight

b Applying the bank
Ailerons change lift distribution;
$L^1 < L^2$

c Steady turn
Both wings have equal lift

d Steady turn

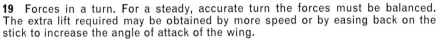

19 Forces in a turn. For a steady, accurate turn the forces must be balanced. The extra lift required may be obtained by more speed or by easing back on the stick to increase the angle of attack of the wing.

combines pitching, rolling and yawing movements.

Early aircraft, such as the Wright Brothers' machine and the Bleriot, used wing warping, and literally twisted the wings to different angles of incidence to vary the lift on opposite wings in order to apply bank. Then the French, and an American named Curtiss, introduced movable flaps out on the wingtips and called them 'ailerons'.

Once again this is an example of changing the lift in order to manoeuvre the aircraft. Extra lift on one wing and reduced lift on the other result in the aircraft rolling over when the ailerons are used to apply or to take off the bank (Fig. 19).

Fundamentally, turns are a matter of applying the bank and then of increasing the total lift by easing back on the stick to increase the angle of attack of the wing. The rudder plays only a minor part and is best described as the control which keeps the aircraft pointing into the airflow during normal flight. Particularly with gliders, movements of the rudder are essential to keep the aircraft from swinging sideways as it is rolled into and out of turns and a small amount of rudder is usually required throughout the turn on a glider. On faster, powered aircraft, the directional stability is much stronger, so that the required amount of yaw in the direction of the turn occurs automatically when the bank is applied and the aircraft slips slightly towards the lower wing.

The actual turning force is produced by the wing lift as the wings are banked over. At small angles of bank this force is fairly weak, so that the use of opposite rudder is enough to stop the turn and convert it into a sideslip. Any further bank results in a slipping turn which is only a useful manoeuvre if you need to lose height very quickly and do not mind turning at the same time.

The glide is a much steeper descent in a slipping turn because of the very high drag of the fuselage as it slides sideways through the air. This has much the same effect as the extra drag caused by using the airbrakes. The effectiveness of the rudder in being able to oppose the results of the bank depends upon the design of the aircraft. If the directional stability is strong, the rudder will be unable to prevent the aircraft weathercocking round into the airflow in even a gently banked sideslip. With less directional stability the rudder will be able to yaw the aircraft to a much larger angle. The designer of a high-performance glider will usually try to use the smallest fin and rudder that will give adequate directional stability and a good spin recovery. As a result most of them can be sideslipped effectively.

Aileron drag
(Fig. 20.)

The rudder power should also be sufficient to stop any adverse yaw created by the ailerons as the bank is applied (see page 181 for more detail about this). A larger fin usually gives the result of less adverse yaw from the aileron drag because the fin tends to keep the aircraft straight. It also makes the need for precise co-ordination less essential and so makes the machine a little easier to fly accurately, but it costs valuable weight and drag because of the

20 Adverse yaw caused by aileron drag. Whenever the aileron creates extra lift the drag is also increased.

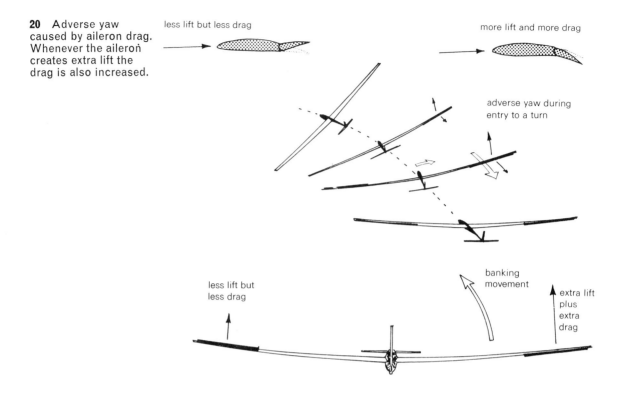

less lift but less drag

more lift and more drag

adverse yaw during entry to a turn

less lift but less drag

banking movement

extra lift plus extra drag

larger surfaces. On powered machines, where the drag and weight are less critical, the directional stability is usually much stronger and, since the aileron drag has less leverage on the shorter wings, little or no rudder is needed for turns. As soon as the aircraft is banked over and begins to sideslip slightly towards the lower wing, the powerful directional stability weather-cocks the machine round into line with the airflow and provides the small amount of yawing needed for the turn (Fig. 21).

When flying a glider the rudder must be used to eliminate the adverse yaw caused by the ailerons. The large wing span gives any extra drag caused

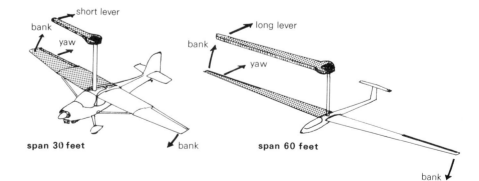

21 The adverse yaw caused by aileron drag depends mainly on the length of wing span.

short lever

bank

yaw

bank

span 30 feet

long lever

bank

yaw

bank

span 60 feet

bank

by the ailerons a very big leverage so that, in spite of careful design of the ailerons, a distinct swing does occur with most gliders unless the stick and rudder are moved together.

The effect of extra rudder in a turn

Although the rudder is able to prevent a turn provided that the angle of bank is shallow, extra rudder applied in the direction of the turn has scarcely any effect in increasing the rate of turn. Initially, as the rudder is applied, the nose swings rapidly across the horizon so that there is an impression of changing direction. Then after the initial yaw the turn continues at very nearly the same rate as it would without the extra rudder. However, too much rudder has roughly the same effect as applying full airbrake and the sideways skidding through the air creates vast amounts of extra drag so that more height is lost, or alternatively the airspeed will decrease rapidly with a risk of stalling. With a large angle of yaw like this, the inner wingtip is bound to stall first and a full spin can develop very rapidly (Fig. 32, page 61).

Unfortunately, at times when the aircraft is skidding or slipping badly, the pilot is usually only able to guess at the flying speed. The normal noise

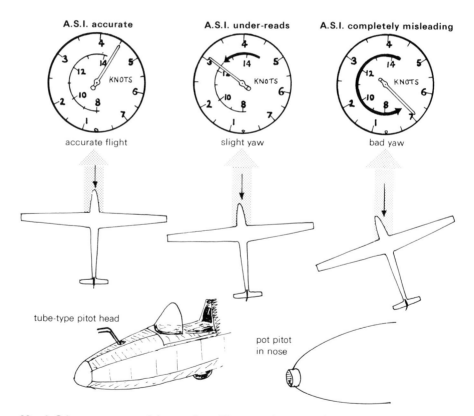

22 A.S.I. errors caused by yawing. The pot pitots used to avoid icing in cloud suffer serious errors in yawed flight, particularly during spinning and sideslipping.

of the airflow is badly disturbed by the air meeting the fuselage at a large angle and the airspeed indicator becomes useless, or at best unreliable. At large angles of yaw the needle of the A.S.I. usually moves back towards, or even beyond, the zero position and it can appear to show quite a high speed when the aircraft is, in fact, nearly stalled (Fig. 22).

This is caused by the rather crude nose pitot often used on gliders in order to avoid ice blocking the system in cloud. The A.S.I. is really only an air pressure gauge connected to a forward facing tube or chamber in the nose. As speed is gained the pressure builds up in the chamber and the instrument records the increase in pressure as an increase in speed. However, if the airflow is striking the nose at an angle, completely false readings can occur. This happens during spinning and whenever the aircraft is slipping or skidding badly.

It will be seen from the explanation of lateral stability and dihedral in Fig. 110 on page 177 that any yaw will result in an increase in the bank. If an excessive amount of rudder is held on and an attempt is made to stop the overbanking by using the aileron to 'hold off' the bank, the aileron drag will increase the yawing still further. There is a grave possibility that the downward movement of the aileron which, in effect, increases the angle of attack of that wingtip, may precipitate the stall (Fig. 23). With such a large amount of pro-spin rudder, a full spin of at least one or two turns is inevitable.

23 Using large aileron movements to stop the wing dropping near the stall can in fact result in the wingtip becoming stalled and dropping further.

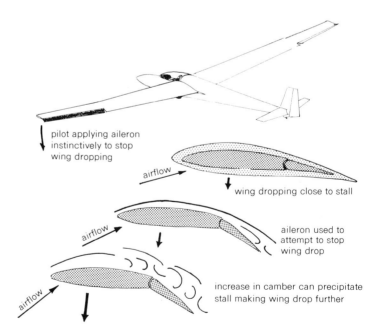

pilot applying aileron instinctively to stop wing dropping

airflow

wing dropping close to stall

airflow

aileron used to attempt to stop wing drop

airflow

increase in camber can precipitate stall making wing drop further

This kind of situation can happen very easily in a glider. If an unexpected amount of height is lost, with the result that the glider is left in a position where a low turn is inevitable, the natural tendency will be to start a gently-banked turn to avoid turning steeply near the ground. There will then be a temptation to apply more and more rudder in an attempt to get round the turn and into the landing area without using any more bank. The drag will immediately increase considerably, so that even more height will be lost. Since by this time there is little or no height left, the pilot is bound to try and stop the loss of height by pulling back on the stick. At the same time he will have stopped the overbanking tendency caused by the extra rudder by applying opposite aileron. From then on the die is cast: if there is sufficient height the glider will almost certainly stall and spin. Alternatively, it will collide with the ground in its skidding turn and cartwheel (Fig. 24).

Fortunately, most gliders give the pilot definite warning signs that too much rudder is being used and that there is a danger of an imminent stall and spin. If, at any time, it is necessary to use a very large amount of opposite aileron to prevent the tendency for the bank to increase during the turn

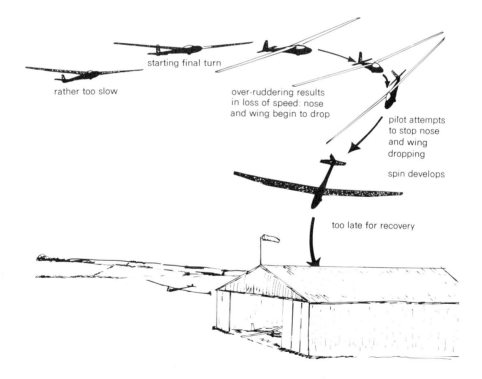

starting final turn

rather too slow

over-ruddering results
in loss of speed: nose
and wing begin to drop

pilot attempts
to stop nose
and wing
dropping

spin develops

too late for recovery

24 Spinning off the final turn. An attempt to increase the rate of turn by applying extra rudder instead of increasing the bank causes the glider to lose speed and begin to stall. The instinctive correction of easing back on the stick will stall it completely, and a full spin is almost certain to develop.

(i.e. more than about one-third of the total available movement) either the glider is flying dangerously slowly, or far too much rudder is being applied.

Excessive rudder also often results in a distinctive buffeting and a change in the sound of the airflow. The airflow breaks away from the canopy and any sharp edges of the fuselage and the change in noise is easily recognised after a little experience. A skidding turn with the airbrakes open usually gives an even more distinctive buffet as the turbulent flow from the airbrakes hits the tail, shaking it violently.

As explained, extra rudder does *not* materially increase the rate of turn. If a tighter turn is required, more bank and more backward pressure are required to make an accurate, steeper turn.

Generally speaking, shallow turns are a snare and delusion. They lead to the temptation of trying to increase the rate of turn with the rudder and, because of the extra time taken to complete the turn, they often result in a much greater loss of height than a turn of 30°–40° of bank. This effect is best understood by considering a very gentle turn. It would take minutes to complete a full circle and hundreds of feet of height would be lost compared with a steeper turn which might only take twenty seconds to complete. The steeper turn may lose more height per second but this is far outweighed by the time taken for a shallow turn and the optimum angle is about 45° of bank.

Stalling in turns　A few simple experiments in attempting to stall most types of glider in a turn at 30° of bank or more will show that without a very violent backward movement of the stick, it is extremely difficult, if not impossible, to pull the wing up to the stalling angle. Most of the available elevator range has already been used up to produce the extra lift required for the turn, and the remaining small amount of backward movement is almost always inadequate to stall the aircraft. With a gentle turn, however, only a small amount of backward movement is needed for the turn so that there is plenty left to pull the wing to the stalling angle.

This result is largely due to the very small radius of turn when the glider is circling at steep angles of bank. In a tight turn the airflow is meeting the aircraft in a constant curve as in Fig. 25. The air is meeting the nose and tail at different angles and this reduces the effective difference in incidence between the wing and tail. This makes a much bigger backward movement on the stick necessary so that it is extremely difficult to stall the glider in the turn.

When the radius of turn is much larger, this effect is negligible. Stalling in a steep turn is, therefore, a very real hazard in most powered aircraft whereas in gliders it is virtually impossible to demonstrate.

When a steeper bank is applied quickly and at rather low speed, the usual result is an immediate slipping towards the lower wing, followed by an increase in speed as the nose drops. The steeper the angle of bank, the more likely this is to happen. A well-banked turn is itself, therefore, a good insurance against the risks of stalling in a turn. Investigations after accidents

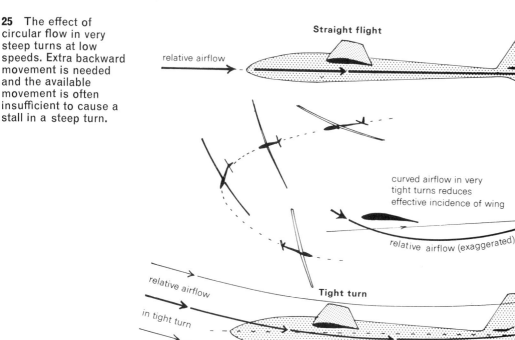

25 The effect of circular flow in very steep turns at low speeds. Extra backward movement is needed and the available movement is often insufficient to cause a stall in a steep turn.

Straight flight

relative airflow

curved airflow in very tight turns reduces effective incidence of wing

relative airflow (exaggerated)

relative airflow in tight turn

Tight turn

often show that when a glider appears to have spun off a steep turn, eye-witnesses saw the machine in a steeply banked position and assumed that it had been turning steeply when it was stalled. In all probability the pilot had lost control of a much more gentle turn some seconds before and the steep bank was the start of the incipient spin from which he failed to recover.

Very few glider pilots ever spin accidentally from a well-banked turn, whereas it is not uncommon to hear of people spinning from a gently banked turn, particularly if too much rudder was being used.

Cultivate the habit of using plenty of bank for turns. Avoid gentle turns and you will not be tempted to over-rudder!

As with other manoeuvres, when the loading is increased by turning, the stalling speed is raised. Fortunately the lift increases with the square of the speed so that a small increase in speed gives a considerable increase in the lift. The result of this square law is that the stalling speed for any manoeuvre can be calculated easily if the loading is known. The new stalling speed is just the normal stalling speed times the square root of the loading. For example, if the turn involves a loading of 4g, the stalling speed will be twice normal. This loading will occur in an accurate turn of 75° of bank. Fig. 26 shows the results of this theory in terms of the stalling speeds at various angles of bank – this is for reference, and is not worth memorising.

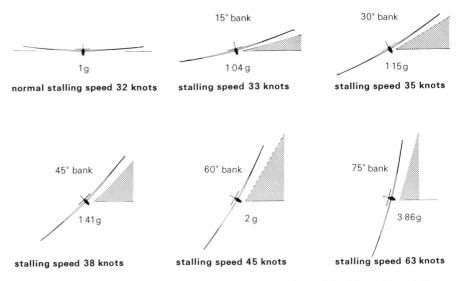

26 The increase in stalling speed in turns. Up to about 45° of bank the stalling speed increases gradually. Steep angles of bank do not alone raise the stalling speed but it is only when the correct backward movement on the stick is applied for an accurate turn to be made that the loading and stalling speed increase to the amounts shown here.

It is worth mentioning at this point that most pilots have a greatly exaggerated idea of the angle of bank which they use when thermalling in tight turns. 50°–60° of bank is a very steep angle indeed and most pilots do not exceed much more than 45° of bank.

However, if you fly as a passenger with a really skilled glider pilot you will probably be concerned to see that he flies his steeply banked thermalling turns at what at first seems an alarmingly low airspeed. Although he is turning steeply he has only increased his flying speed by 2 or 3 knots. This is not as dangerous as it looks for various reasons. If we take a training glider such as a Schweizer 233, Blanik or ASK 13 with a stalling speed of, say, 32 knots, a speed of about 40 knots would be adequate for gentle turns of about 20° of bank. At this angle the stalling speed would be raised by the increased wing loading to about 33 knots so that there is a margin of 9 knots. In a steeply banked thermalling turn it may prove perfectly practical to circle at 43–45 knots, although the stalling speed for that turn may have increased to 40 knots. (In a 45° banked turn the stalling speed would be increased by over 19 % to 38 knots).

This is largely because the safe minimum speed for turning depends not only on the margin above the stall, but also on the control response or handling. In this case, at speeds below about 40 knots the glider would become almost unmanageable because of the sloppy controls. Also any stall recovery would involve regaining speed which takes time and height.

In steeper turns, however, even at the point when the initial stall buffet begins at 43 knots, there is still 43 knots of airflow over the controls and good response. The wing will unstall instantaneously when the backward pressure on the stick is reduced and full control will be available immediately because of the much higher speed. Unless one wing happens to drop, little or no height will be lost in the recovery.

It is, therefore, quite practical to fly the glider to within 3 or 4 knots of the stall in steeper turns and still have good control. If the glider has an aerofoil which can work at relatively large angles of attack without incurring large drag losses, turning steeply at low speed will give a much smaller turning radius and enable the pilot to make better use of the strong narrow cores of the thermals. Some of the laminar flow aerofoils suffer very large drag losses unless they are operated at relatively small angles of attack, and gliders with these wing sections must be flown well above the possible minimum speeds. This problem is usually made apparent when these machines are outclimbed consistently by relatively low-performance designs. The pilot may also notice the distinctive change of noise at low speed and the slight but noticeable pre-stall buffet as the airflow near the wing root begins to separate and break away, causing loss of lift and higher drag.

With most gliders, the optimum speed for circling is the minimum speed at which good control is maintained at all times and at which no pre-stall buffet can be detected. This will always be a lower speed in smooth con-

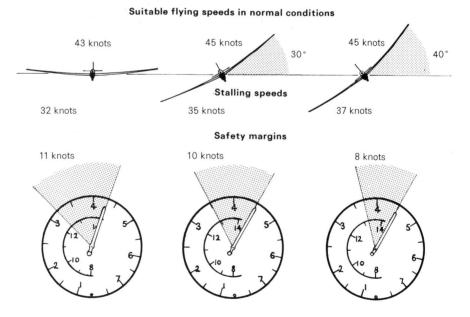

27 Practical thermalling speeds showing the reduced margin of speed above the stall required for steeper turns in a training two-seater such as an ASK 13.

Going into a turn to the right

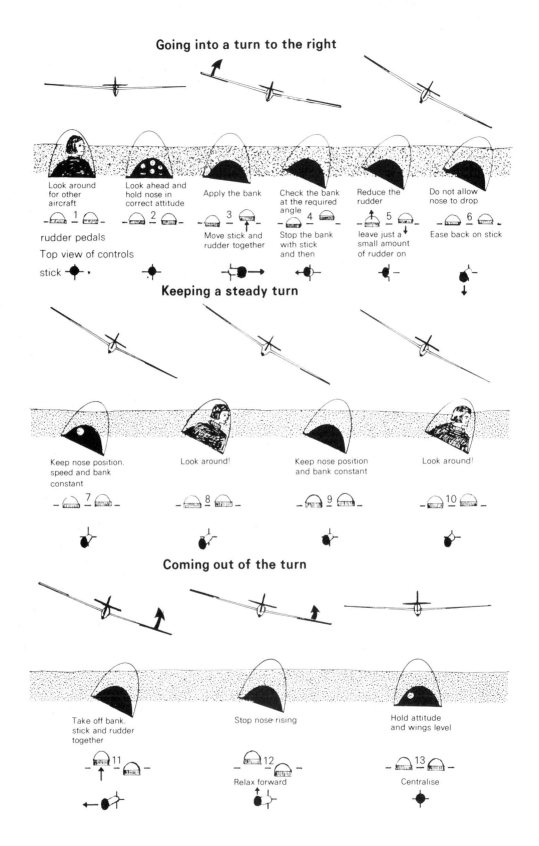

Look around for other aircraft

Look ahead and hold nose in correct attitude

Apply the bank

Move stick and rudder together

Check the bank at the required angle

Stop the bank with stick and then

Reduce the rudder

leave just a small amount of rudder on

Do not allow nose to drop

Ease back on stick

rudder pedals

Top view of controls

stick

Keeping a steady turn

Keep nose position, speed and bank constant

Look around!

Keep nose position and bank constant

Look around!

Coming out of the turn

Take off bank, stick and rudder together

Stop nose rising

Relax forward

Hold attitude and wings level

Centralise

28 (opposite) The control movements for a turn. After a few flights the beginner ceases to think about the exact movements on the controls.

ditions than in rough air. This speed is not safe for hill soaring and other turns at low altitude since it does not allow enough margin for the effects of an unexpected increase in turbulence.

One further point needs an explanation. A steep bank alone does not raise the stalling speed. If only the bank is applied, the aircraft will not have sufficient lift to make a steady turn and therefore it will start to sideslip towards the lower wing. The nose will soon drop and the aircraft will dive away, gaining speed rapidly. In this situation the loading on the aircraft has not been increased and the angle of attack of the wing has not changed appreciably. The stall turn and wingover are cases where the aircraft is banked over very steeply for a few seconds while the inertia carries the machine round the top of the manoeuvre at speeds well below even the normal stalling speed. A stone describes a nicely shaped trajectory at the top of its flight if you throw it up nearly vertically. In both cases the force of gravity changes the direction of flight of the stone and the aircraft.

It is only when the aircraft is changing direction as a result of variations in the lift from its wings that the stalling speed is affected. Apart from inverted manoeuvres, this only happens as the pilot pulls back on the stick and changes the direction of flight. Only then are the wing loading and stalling speed increased. Furthermore, it is only in an accurate turn that the loading and stalling speed increase as shown in Fig. 26 on page 52.

Control movements in turns

Summarising the control movements needed to turn a glider or powered aircraft, the bank is applied by using the ailerons to increase the lift on one wing and to decrease the lift on the other. At the same time, sufficient rudder is applied to prevent any tendency to swing off in the opposite direction, since the wing developing extra lift must also create extra drag. As the desired angle of bank is reached, the ailerons have to be more or less centralised to equalise the lift and hold the bank steady. (Usually on *gliders* the stick has to be held off a little, since there is a tendency for the bank to go on increasing with the stick central.) From this moment the rudder movement is no longer needed to overcome the aileron drag and as soon as the ailerons have been centralised the rudder is reduced to leave only the very small amount required in the steady turn. (A small amount in gliders and next to nothing in most other aircraft.) Immediately the bank has been established, a backward movement is needed to increase the angle of attack of the wings and so provide the extra lift required for the turn. The amount will depend upon the angle of bank – a small movement for a shallow bank, and a movement which becomes progressively larger as the angle of bank increases. In the case of gliders, no extra speed will normally be needed for turns of up to about 40°. Beyond this angle extra speed will be needed, and this can be obtained during the turn by leaving a slight delay before applying the backward movement. Small corrections may be needed during the turn to counteract the effects of turbulence. The bank is controlled with the ailerons, the attitude and speed with the elevator, and the rudder is only used in conjunction with the ailerons to overcome any aileron drag, or to correct any slight inaccuracies which cause slipping or skidding.

Coming out of the turn, the stick and rudder are again used together so that no adverse yaw occurs as the wings are brought level. At the same time the backward movement on the stick is relaxed to keep the glider in the normal attitude. The ailerons and rudder are then centralised together just as the wings are coming level.

Stalling, the link between normal flight and spinning

In order to understand stalling and all the situations when stalling may occur, it is worth emphasising again that it is a matter of the angle of attack getting too large and not just of flying at a low airspeed. A pilot needs to understand how the angle of attack can be dangerously large when the attitude of the aircraft looks quite safe (Fig. 9 on page 31).

The real danger of stalling in the air is that the pilot may fail to realise what is happening until it is too late. If the nose starts to drop because the wing is stalled and the pilot does not recognise the symptoms, he will instinctively pull back on the stick to stop the nose dropping, as he would in normal flight. This will worsen the stall and delay the recovery. If the aircraft is not very high this alone could result in a nasty accident because of the rapid loss of height.

Recognising the onset of the stall, and preventing it from developing, always seem a simple matter in a glider. The stall is very gentle and the nose drops slowly. There is usually what appears to be a very obvious warning that the aircraft is at the point of the stall which is the distinctive buffeting (vibration) which can be felt through the stick. This is the result of the airflow breaking up over the wing root and striking the tailplane and elevators. However, above 600 or 700 feet, the loss of height is hardly noticeable, and it is surprisingly easy to be distracted by something in the air or on the ground and not notice that the nose is just a little higher than normal, or that you have been easing further and further back on the stick. Once in this situation, any severe gust or further backward movement on the stick can result in an inadvertent stall.

Unless the glider is flying absolutely straight with the wings level, they will not stall evenly and one wing will stall a little before the other, causing it to drop. This situation is known as an 'incipient' (or undeveloped) spin, and is really only a stall in which one wing has dropped. At this stage the proper recovery action will prevent any possibility of the stall developing into a full spin. However, if the pilot does not realise what has happened a full spin can result causing a very large loss of height (Fig. 29).

The motion of an aircraft in a full spin is not easy to describe accurately and it is sufficient for the average pilot to understand why it happens, how it starts, and what it looks and feels like. He must also, of course, be able to stop a spin promptly. Spinning can be dangerous because it can mean losing a lot of height in a very short space of time. To stop, and recover from a

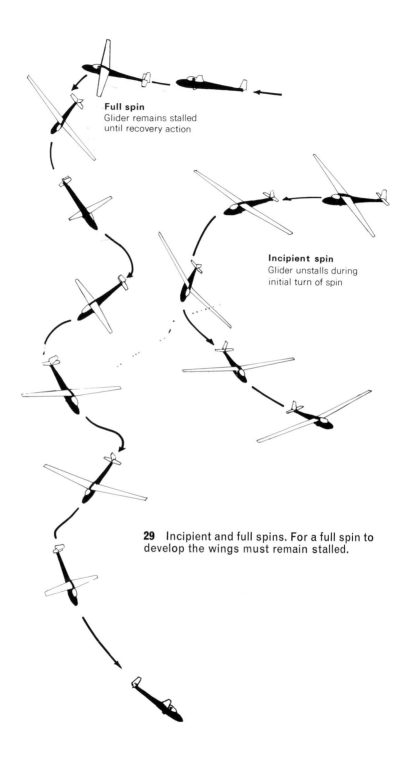

Full spin
Glider remains stalled
until recovery action

Incipient spin
Glider unstalls during
initial turn of spin

29 Incipient and full spins. For a full spin to
develop the wings must remain stalled.

fully developed spin takes several hundred feet, even when the pilot is doing it deliberately and is ready to take recovery action.

When a spin occurs at low altitude even the most experienced pilot will have to force himself to take the correct recovery action. Against all his instincts he must resist the temptation to pull back on the stick until he has unstalled the wings. This is not easy if he is facing the ground in a near vertical position with only a few hundred feet to go. Of course, unless the pilot recognises that the glider is stalled, he is bound to try to raise the dropped nose by easing back, making the situation even worse.

There is no mystery about why an aircraft spins. A spin can only develop from a stall, and only then if one wing is allowed to drop and if the wings are kept stalled as the wing and nose drop.

In normal flight, all aircraft are stabilised against rolling movements by the 'damping' effects of the wings. If in flight the left wing starts to drop the direction of the airflow relative to that wing changes. As the wing moves downwards the relative airflow is moving up at a slightly larger angle than before, as in Fig. 30. Since a larger angle of attack means an increase in lift, the downward movement of the wing is soon stopped. Similarly, the right wing moves upwards and develops less lift, and this again tends to stop the rolling movement. This effect ceases when the banking movement stops.

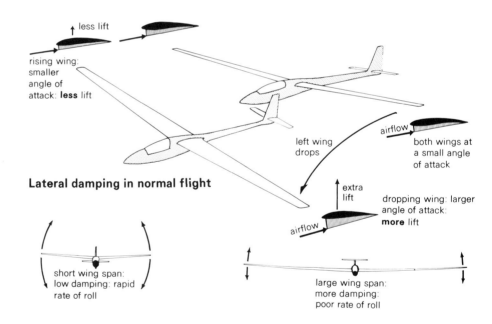

Lateral damping in normal flight

30 Lateral damping. In normal flight, if a wing drops the tip meets the airflow at a slightly larger angle of attack, resulting in extra lift which tends to stop the wing dropping any further. Similarly the rising wing has reduced lift and angle of attack. The ailerons have to overcome this damping effect to produce rolling movements and the rate of roll of a glider is therefore mainly dependent on the wing span.

However, this damping effect ceases to work when a wing is stalled. From that moment the aircraft becomes laterally unstable and tends to roll over further. This rolling tendency is called 'autorotation' because it continues automatically once it has started. Fig. 31 shows why autorotation occurs. Notice that the downward moving left wing meets the airflow at a larger angle than before the wing drop (just as it did in normal flight in Fig. 30). But this time, a larger angle results in that wing becoming *more* stalled. Instead of making more lift it makes less, and drops still further. Once a stalled wing starts to drop it tends to go on dropping since it becomes more and more stalled and loses more and more of its lift.

The upward moving wingtip has a reduced angle of attack, as it had in normal flight. This lessens the lift slightly if the wing was not stalled at the time of the upward movement. However, it can increase the lift if it was slightly stalled, and in this case normal lift is re-established because of the reduced angle of attack. The result is that the rising wing is always lifted further, helping the autorotation.

When an aircraft stalls, the nose drops, height is lost rapidly and the aircraft becomes laterally unstable, tending to drop one or other wing. If unchecked, this movement can develop into a spin.

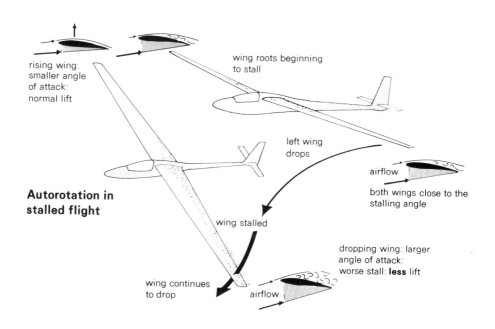

rising wing: smaller angle of attack: normal lift

wing roots beginning to stall

left wing drops

airflow

both wings close to the stalling angle

Autorotation in stalled flight

wing stalled

dropping wing: larger angle of attack: worse stall: **less** lift

wing continues to drop

airflow

31 Autorotation. When the wings are stalled, or very close to the stalling angle, any wing drop results in an increase in the angle of attack of that wing, stalling it still further. The aircraft suddenly becomes unstable, tending to roll into a spin. When the wing becomes unstalled this rolling stops immediately as the lateral damping (Fig. 30) comes back into play.

If – with a low-speed aircraft like a glider – a wing starts to drop at the stall, the machine will swing round in that direction so that a steep diving spiral begins. If this happens unexpectedly and the pilot does not realise that he is stalled, he will react instinctively and try to stop the wing and nose from dropping by using opposite aileron and pulling back further on the stick. This can only make matters worse because he will be pulling the wing to an even larger angle and so preventing a recovery. However, if he eases forward instead of pulling back, the wing angle will be reduced and the wing will unstall immediately. Then the autorotation or rolling motion will stop, and within seconds the glider will have gained normal flying speed and can be brought back to level flight again. In fact, with most gliders, it is only with very light pilots and the centre of gravity near to the aft limit, that a stall and wing drop can be made to develop into a full spin. With the C of G further forward, the wing tends to unstall itself as the nose drops during the first half turn or so, leaving the aircraft in a diving turn instead of a spin.

If the wings remain stalled as the aircraft drops into the downward spiral, the autorotation both continues and speeds up and a fully developed spin occurs. This is really just a very steep and rapid downward spiral with the wings stalled. The motion generally settles down to a steady rotation after two or three turns and height is lost very rapidly. In a true spin the aircraft does not gain speed although it is coming down very steeply, the descent looking almost vertical from the cockpit. In fact it is nowhere near as steep as that and both wings are usually meeting the airflow at very large angles, usually 20°–30°.

During a spin the speed is prevented from increasing by the very high drag created by the stalled airflow over the wings. This is far, far greater than the drag caused by flying with the airbrakes opened which, at the most, limits the speed on a dive to about 120 knots. Although the aircraft is descending very steeply in a spin, the speed is usually only about one and a half times the normal stalling speed. The airspeed indicator frequently gives false readings because of the large angle of yaw (see Fig. 22 on page 47).

Whereas in the incipient spin only one wing may be stalled, during the full spin both wings are usually stalled and the inner one will be at a much larger angle of attack, because it is moving down rapidly to meet the airflow. When both wings are stalled, the dropping wing is more affected than the other and develops less lift as a result. This keeps the autorotation going because in addition to losing lift the dropping wing has extra drag, and this helps to yaw the aircraft in that direction.

Why yawing makes things worse

When flying at low speeds, or when the aircraft is stalled, any yawing is of critical importance. The yaw speeds up the outer wingtip and slows down the inner one, so increasing the tendency to bank and roll in that direction. Quite apart from the situation when the aircraft is stalled, yawing always tends to result in a banking movement because of the effect of the dihedral (see lateral stability, page 177) and because the fuselage screens the wing root of the inner wing, spoiling its lift when the aircraft is skidding sideways through the air. Another detrimental result of this yawing movement is that the inner wingtip is operating as a wing with sweep back. This encourages the airflow to break away at that tip first. Conversely, the other wingtip has in effect sweep forward and this increases its resistance to tip stalling (Fig. 32).

Just slowing down one wing does not make it stall, but if the whole aircraft is losing height the slower wing will always meet the airflow at a bigger angle. This can be most easily understood by considering an imaginary aircraft in an extremely tight turn in which the inner wingtip is pivoting about a point. In one complete circle the whole machine loses the same amount of height, and, with no forward movement, the inner wingtip must be descending vertically. In other words, the relative airflow is coming up vertically to meet that wing. At the same time, however, the outer wingtip moves forward quite a long distance for the same loss of height. The relative airflow meets that

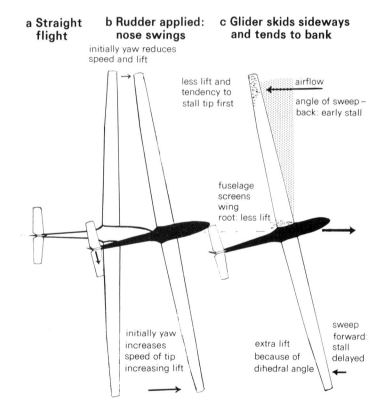

a Straight flight **b Rudder applied: nose swings** **c Glider skids sideways and tends to bank**

initially yaw reduces speed and lift

less lift and tendency to stall tip first

airflow

angle of sweep – back: early stall

fuselage screens wing root: less lift

initially yaw increases speed of tip increasing lift

extra lift because of dihedral angle

sweep forward: stall delayed

32 The effect of applying rudder at low speeds. Initially the yawing increases the speed of one wingtip, giving more lift. The dihedral results in a larger angle of attack on the forward wing and more lift. At very low speeds the contrast between the swept forward and swept back wing gives a tendency for early stalling on the swept back wingtip.

wingtip at a much smaller angle. This is a greatly exaggerated example and what happens in a normal gliding turn is shown in Fig. 33. Since there is always a difference in the speeds of the wingtips in a turn, and particularly when a yawing movement is taking place, the inner tip is always meeting the airflow at a larger angle and will, therefore, always tend to reach the stalling angle first. It might be thought that in normal turns the effect of the greater speed of the outer wingtip giving extra lift might be overpowered by the effect of the larger angle of attack of the inner wing, which would also result in extra lift. This does happen with faster, shorter wing span machines such as single-engined light aircraft, and there is usually a tendency for the bank to reduce itself in gliding turns. The very small difference in tip speed during the turn is far outweighed by the effect of the angle of attack. In a climbing turn under power, however, the outer tip has the increased angle and also the extra speed so that these two effects are combined. The result is a noticeable tendency for the bank to get steeper during climbing turns in powered aircraft. The important point is that with large span gliders any yawing when the aircraft is close to the stall is very critical since it tends to induce a rolling movement and increases the angle of attack of the dropping wing.

By limiting any yaw the difference in the angles of attack of the wings is evened out, so that the tendency to roll is reduced. This in turn reduces the

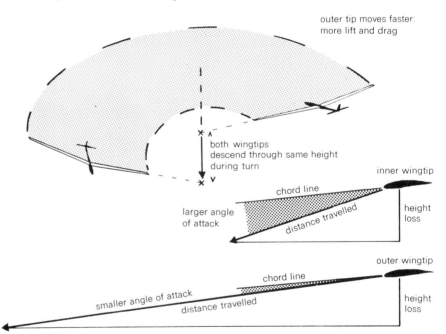

33 The influence of a large span and small turning circle on the handling of a glider. The outer wingtip travels further and faster but meets the airflow at a smaller angle. This results in extra lift and makes a glider tend to over-bank in turns. The inner wingtip will reach the stalling angle before the outer one, causing it to stall and drop if the glider is flown too slowly.

forces of autorotation. The rudder control is, therefore, a very powerful anti-spin control. However, it must not be forgotten that autorotation can only exist when the wings are stalled or partially stalled. This makes unstalling the wings even more important than preventing yaw.

How far the rolling-over movement goes depends largely on how promptly the wings are unstalled and on how far the machine is allowed to yaw. At the incipient spin stage the stick can be moved forward to unstall the wings, *at the same time* as the rudder is applied to limit the yaw. Any significant delay in easing forward after the rudder has been applied can sometimes result in only a partial stall recovery. Then a rather more violent flick into an incipient spin in the opposite direction is a possibility.

If the glider is turning in a well-banked turn, the stalling speed will be a little higher than in straight flight and, in consequence, any wing drop may be more violent. However, it will be more difficult to stall the aircraft fully because of the circular flow effect described on page 51, and the higher speed. Any reduction in the backward pressure on the stick will result in an immediate recovery and good control.

The need to avoid large aileron movements at or near the stall

When a wing drops at or near the stall, the pilot – unless he is deliberately practising stalls – is still almost certainly unaware that he is stalled and near a spin. He is therefore almost certain to use the controls quite normally to try to stop the aircraft from banking over. Because of the lack of immediate response he will find himself applying full opposite aileron and, momentarily, he will wonder why nothing is happening. This large deflection of the ailerons, used in an attempt to stop the wing from dropping at low speeds, can make matters far worse (Fig. 23). Since the downward moving aileron always has some extra drag (aileron drag) there will be a further yawing movement towards the dropping wing. This, as already explained in detail, will tend to increase the angle of attack of that wing and also increase the risk of causing, or intensifying a stall. In addition, the large downward deflection of the aileron may even induce the start of a stall at that wingtip. A large change in the camber may help the airflow to start to separate from the surface of the wing at the trailing edge so that it breaks away into the turbulent stalled flow.

It is, therefore, highly undesirable to try and stop the wing dropping at the stall with the aileron. Pilots should learn to avoid large aileron movements until they have unstalled the wing by moving forward on the stick. Once the aircraft is unstalled, however, the ailerons *must* be used, together with the other controls, in order to bring the wings level and return to normal flight. The rudder alone must *not* be used to attempt to level the wings. If the aircraft has become well banked during the incipient spin, applying full opposite rudder alone will generally only result in a continuous steep sideslip and a very large loss of height. It is only while the wings are stalled, or nearly stalled, that the aileron can have any adverse effect. Once the stall has been broken, and this usually only takes a few seconds when the stick is moved forward a little, the controls should be used quite normally to get the wings level – and the quicker the better as height will be lost very quickly while the aircraft remains banked.

The instinctive use of the ailerons when the wing drops at the stall is the main reason why accidental stalls often result in a much more violent incipient spin than usually occurs in training. The worst cases invariably result from gentle turns or almost straight flight and not, as is often thought, from steep turns. In fact, as stated earlier, it is comparatively rare in gliders for a spin to occur from a steep turn although it may appear to an eyewitness that this is what happened. In most cases the incipient spin started from a gentle turn and, as the bank increased, the eyewitness assumed that the pilot was steepening the bank deliberately when, in most cases, it was the beginning of the spin.

It is probably too much to expect that a pilot who has inadvertently allowed his machine to become stalled will realise what has happened in time to avoid using the ailerons to try and stop the wing from dropping. However, his training and experience of stalls and spins should enable him to realise what is happening within a few seconds. The all-important thing is for him to make the forward movement on the stick to unstall the wing.

Recovery from a fully developed spin

If the steady rotation stage of a full spin has already been reached, the order of movement of the controls becomes more significant. The most powerful combination of anti-spin forces is needed for a quick recovery. Full opposite rudder should be applied first as this will tend to reduce the rate of rotation and cause a nose down pitching effect which is often enough to unstall the wings and stop the spin. Conversely, any increase in the speed of rotation tends to flatten the spin and make recovery more difficult. These important effects are due to the centrifugal forces acting on the mass of the aircraft as it spins. The mass of the pilot in a glider or the mass of the engine in a light aircraft – both well ahead of the C of G – and the mass of the tail unit at the extreme end of the fuselage, both tend to be thrown outwards during the spin. (Fig. 34a and b.) This makes the spin flatten out as the speed of rotation is increased and helps the recovery by allowing the nose to drop when the rotation is slowed down by applying opposite rudder. On some aircraft there is a possibility that a downward movement of the elevator will have a blanketing effect on the rudder and reduce its effectiveness. Since any reduction in the yawing movement will have a marked effect on the auto-rotation, the rudder is always applied fully against the direction of the spin *before* the stick is moved forward in order to unstall the wings. This allows the rudder a brief moment to do its job before the elevator is moved progressively downwards into a position where it might, in some cases, reduce the effectiveness of the rudder by blanketing it. The rotation will usually stop very suddenly as the wings unstall and the aircraft becomes stable again. Then, without the turbulent flow from the stalled wings, the aircraft gains speed very rapidly. At this moment the rudder needs to be centralised and the

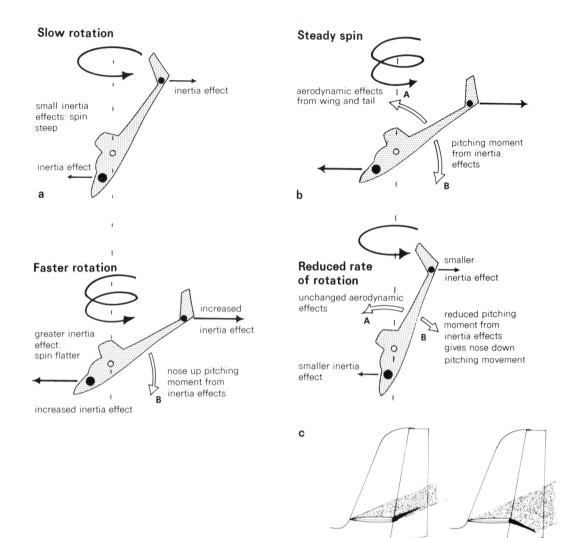

Slow rotation

inertia effect

small inertia
effects: spin
steep

inertia effect

a

Steady spin

aerodynamic effects
from wing and tail

A

pitching moment
from inertia
effects

B

b

Faster rotation

increased
inertia effect

greater inertia
effect:
spin flatter

nose up pitching
moment from
inertia effects

B

increased inertia effect

**Reduced rate
of rotation**

smaller
inertia effect

unchanged aerodynamic
effects

A

B

reduced pitching
moment from
inertia effects
gives nose down
pitching movement

smaller inertia
effect

c

elevator up   elevator down

34 a Spinning. Increasing the rate of rotation results
in a nose up movement because of the greater centrifugal forces acting on the masses in the nose and tail.
b The effect of applying opposite rudder and reducing
the rate of rotation. The inertia effects are reduced,
allowing the nose to drop. This also reduces the angle
of attack of the wings, so helping the recovery from
the stalled condition in the spin. **c** During a full spin
recovery, apply full opposite rudder and then move
forward on the stick until the spin stops. Moving the
elevator down first may cause blanketing of the rudder
and the shaded area shows the extent of possible
blanketing.

65

aircraft is then in a diving position from which it can be levelled out to normal flight.

If the rudder is very powerful it may actually stop the autorotation by stopping the yawing movement, even though the wings may still be partially stalled. If the stick has not been eased forward by this time, a further incipient, or full spin may occur in the opposite direction. The aircraft is laterally very unstable until the wings are unstalled and only needs the slightest inducement to drop one or other wing. Since a large rudder movement has just been applied to stop the initial incipient spin developing it will – unless centralised very quickly – cause a further yawing and a second incipient spin. This risk of a second spin is completely eliminated by easing forward on the stick after applying the full opposite rudder so that there is no risk of the aircraft remaining stalled.

The standard method of spin recovery is as follows:

Full opposite rudder,
a slight pause and then with the ailerons central,
move the stick progressively forward until the spin stops.
Then
centralise the rudder
and
ease the aircraft out of the dive.

It is very important to learn the recognised method of spin recovery and to stick to it exactly. Many pilots who only fly one or two types of aircraft tend to get into the habit of making the movements which are just adequate to stop a practice spin in those machines. In fact the amount of forward movement required to stop a spin will vary considerably even with the same aircraft. The position of the C of G (i.e. the cockpit load in the case of most small aircraft) will make a very noticeable difference. The exact mode of entry and the position of the aileron control during the spin, together with the number of turns, may also affect the recovery. The forward movement on the stick should always be thought of as a progressive movement and *never* as a move to the central position, even if, in fact, that is all that is generally needed. If there is a case of an abnormally slow recovery from a spin it is invariably caused by a half-hearted or incorrect action. Perhaps in ninety-nine cases out of a hundred a particular aircraft will only require the stick to be moved to the central position before the spin stops, but on the hundredth the recovery might take several turns unless the stick was being moved progressively further forward *until* the spin stopped. The forward movement is used to pitch the nose downwards in order to unstall the wings. How much movement is needed will vary from spin to spin. If the spin does not stop, this movement must be continued until the stick is right forward. This might be necessary in a glider if it had been damaged, or was badly iced up.

During a spin the ailerons tend to be deflected by the airflow, so that unless the pilot holds the stick firmly it will move itself across in the direction of the rotation. The position of the ailerons can affect both the motion of the spin and the recovery. With most modern gliders the spin may stop after a turn or so unless the ailerons are held central. In any case, the ailerons should always be centralised during the recovery action.

The rudder tends to lock over in the direction of the spin because of the large angle of yaw. This makes the force required to apply the full opposite rudder *much* greater than it would be in normal flight.

Similarly, in aircraft which tend to spin in a rather flat attitude, the force required to move the stick forward may be several times greater than normal. It is therefore important to be really positive about the control movements for a spin recovery. It is the *only* time in flying when it is good practice really to bang on the full rudder and if the pilot does not make the progressive movement forward on the stick firmly the aircraft may continue spinning. However, excessive height will be lost if the forward movement is continued after the spin has stopped.

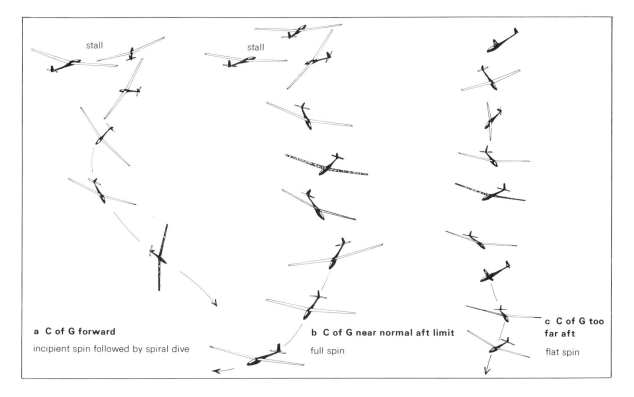

a C of G forward

incipient spin followed by spiral dive

b C of G near normal aft limit

full spin

c C of G too far aft

flat spin

35 The effect of the position of the C of G on the spinning characteristics of most gliders. **a** C of G well forward – continuous spinning is impossible as the wings unstall themselves and the spin develops into a diving turn or spiral dive. **b** C of G near the normal aft limit – a continuous spin is just possible but recovery is within half a turn. **c** C of G beyond the aft limit – a flat spin occurs which will be difficult, or impossible, to stop.

The effect of the position of the C of G on the spin

The position of the C of G has a very marked effect on the spinning characteristics of an aircraft (Fig. 35). In a glider this is largely a matter of the weight of the pilot because he sits out in the nose, well ahead of the C of G.

A heavy pilot will have difficulty in making most gliders even begin to spin since there is insufficient elevator control to keep the wings stalled for more than a few seconds. Even for cruising flight he will need the stick well back, leaving very little further movement to induce a stall.

A light pilot flying the same machine would find a totally different situation. It would be far easier for him to stall and spin, and instead of the aircraft tending to make its own recovery the pilot would need to take positive action to prevent or stop a full spin. As the C of G is moved further back behind the normal limit, the spin recovery becomes progressively less positive, until it is impossible to stop a spin. In some types of glider this may be matter of being only a few pounds under the minimum cockpit load shown on the cockpit placard. Provided that the C of G is kept within the correct limits, the standard method of recovery will *always* be effective and stop the spin within a few seconds.

Inverted spins

Pilots are often curious, or worried, about what may happen if they stall while they are upside down at the top of a loop. Have no fear, the last thing which is likely to happen is an inverted spin. In most aircraft it is practically impossible to enter an inverted spin deliberately. The wing must be kept

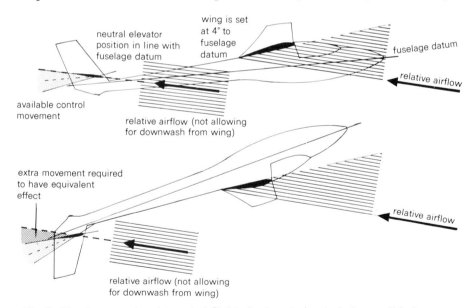

36 Stalling in normal and inverted flight. An inverted spin is impossible because the elevator range is inadequate to keep the wings stalled continuously. The Rigger's angle of incidence gives a difference of about 4° between the wing and tail which necessitates an extra 8° of movement for the effect to be the same as in normal flight. Note the extreme nose high attitude required to stall when inverted.

stalled by holding the stick right forward, and this is not sufficient to prevent the nose from dropping so that a spiral develops. The reason for this is that the effectiveness of any forward movement on the stick is greatly decreased by the Rigger's angle of incidence when the aircraft is upside down. Fig. 36 explains the situation.

In the case of a loop, a very low airspeed does not necessarily result in the wings becoming stalled. Gravity is helping to pull the aircraft over the top so that the load factor may be almost zero and the loop may still be completed normally, even if the speed is by then only a few miles an hour. If the stick is pulled back too harshly at the top of a loop the aircraft will either flop over the top normally, or it will flick over as one wing stalls a little before the other. It will usually just roll over to a normal position, unstall itself, and be left in a gentle dive. If the stick were held right back the flick might develop into a normal, upright spin (Fig. 37).

If the stick was moved right forward at the top of a loop an inverted or negative 'g' stall might occur. This usually results in a rolling motion, because one wingtip has stalled first. Any washout at a wingtip becomes an increase in incidence when the machine is inverted and this will encourage the tip to stall first. However, the inverted spin cannot develop because the wings become unstalled within a few seconds. Gliders which will not spin continuously in the normal attitude will never spin inverted.

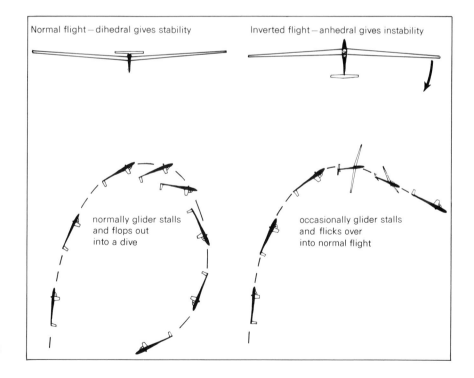

Normal flight — dihedral gives stability

Inverted flight — anhedral gives instability

normally glider stalls and flops out into a dive

occasionally glider stalls and flicks over into normal flight

37 The result of stalling at the top of a loop.

3 The effect of the wind

This chapter is also in *Beginning Gliding* because wind is a subject about which many pilots have misconceptions. Additional information on wind, weather and soaring is to be found in my book *Understanding Flying Weather*.

It is simple enough to appreciate how an aeroplane or glider flies, but in trying to understand the effect the wind has on them it is easy to become confused or misled. So far all our explanations about flying have assumed a no wind situation in order to avoid complications. The all-important relative airflow is then only the result of the aircraft's movement, and is moving at the speed, and in exactly the opposite direction, to the direction of flight.

Anyone who has been involved in flying model aircraft is almost certain to have watched the influence the wind has on the models and probably come to erroneous conclusions about its effects. Some of the likely causes of these misunderstandings will be discussed later. Similarly, without a clear and logical explanation of wind effects the average glider pilot would be lucky to reason the truth out for himself.

Because 'seeing is believing' and some things which appear to happen do not seem to agree with theory, a very large number of experienced pilots have muddled, and often completely false ideas about the effect of the wind on an aircraft.

If you want to hear some really confused thinking and hare-brained theories, try introducing this subject in the bar at your flying club.

One common misconception is that since the aircraft has a very high speed over the ground as it flies downwind all that energy has to go somewhere when it makes a turn into wind. Pilots will often claim to have had this increase in speed as they turn into the wind, particularly when hill soaring.

Other pilots, and even some instructors, on powered aircraft may comment on the dangers of losing speed when turning downwind at low altitude and on the loss of climbing rate going downwind.

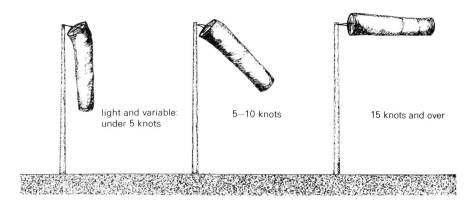

38 Judging the wind speed from the wind sock.

light and variable: under 5 knots

5—10 knots

15 knots and over

In these instances there often *appears* to be evidence to support the contention that an aircraft is affected by even a steady wind. The real causes of changes in airspeed in these circumstances are difficult to identify, and even more difficult to prove.

The wind and the weather map

Once you are learning to glide the strength and direction of the wind will become very important to you. Until you are fairly experienced your solo flying will be limited to days on which the wind is relatively light and blowing in directions which do not create any hazards at your particular gliding site.

For instance, if you are flying from a hilltop site, the turbulence and curl over in the lee of the hill may be severe when there is a 'ridge' wind. With a site in a valley, certain wind directions will produce very tricky conditions requiring a high degree of skill and experience for the approach and landing. After even a few disappointments, when you have been unable to fly because of the weather, you will begin to look more closely at the weather forecast charts in the newspapers and on the television. These charts will not mean much to you at first, but soon, even with a smattering of knowledge, you will find yourself able to tell whether the weather is likely to be suitable for flying, and, with more practice, whether the conditions will be soarable.

The main features on a good weather map are the pressure contour lines known as isobars (Fig. 39). These are lines drawn through the points which, at the time of the observations, have equal atmospheric pressure. If the pressure is changing very rapidly from place to place these lines will be close together and the winds will be strong. When the isobars are widely spaced, as is common in an anticyclone or high pressure system (known as a 'high') the winds will be much lighter. Without the rotation of the earth the air from a region of high pressure would flow directly towards a low pressure area until the pressure was equalised. However, the earth's rotation, combined with the centrifugal force which occurs as the air circulates round a pressure system, deflect the wind at height. Instead of flowing directly from high to low pressure areas it flows around the system, blowing almost exactly along the isobars. The tendency for the wind to blow in towards the centre of a

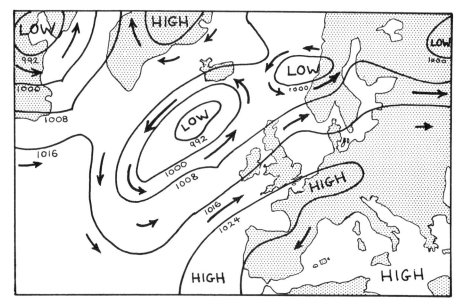

39 A weather map showing the isobars, or lines joining places with equal pressure. The gradient winds are parallel to the isobars.

low pressure area (known as a depression or 'low') and fill it up, is balanced by forces which are caused by the earth's rotation together with the centrifugal force created as the air moves round. The effect caused by the earth's rotation is known as the Coriolis effect, and this determines the direction of rotation of the airflow around a low and high. In the northern hemisphere the wind always blows anti-clockwise round a low and clockwise round a high. (The opposite direction if you are in Australia or New Zealand, or anywhere south of the equator.) This is usually similar to the direction in which the water revolves as it drains out of a bath and also the rotation of the air in a dust devil. However, in these cases the Coriolis effect is very slight and the direction of the rotation depends on the initial movement of the water or the air, so that it is possible for it to be in either direction. However, the tendency will always be towards an anti-clockwise movement in the northern hemisphere.

Below 2000 feet the wind speed is reduced by the friction of the ground slowing down the lower layers of the air. This reduction in wind speed in turn lessens these effects so that the lower winds tend to blow in more toward the centre of the low (Fig. 40). When the wind strength is high this change of angle may be 20°–30°, whereas in light winds it may only be a few degrees.

There will be a bigger difference first thing in the morning between the strength and the direction of the wind near the ground and the wind at 2000 feet. Then, as the heat of the sun starts convection and the thermals begin to mix up the lower winds with the much stronger upper winds, the surface wind becomes somewhat stronger and the direction changes a little. This is a useful fact for the Duty Instructor to remember as he wonders where to

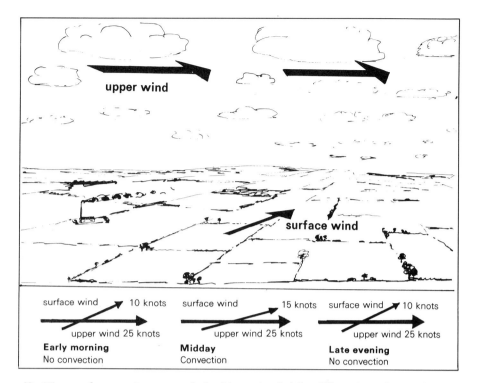

surface wind 10 knots   surface wind 15 knots   surface wind 10 knots

upper wind 25 knots   upper wind 25 knots   upper wind 25 knots

Early morning   **Midday**   **Late evening**
No convection   Convection   No convection

40 The surface and upper winds blow at slightly different angles and vary throughout the day. Mixing of the upper and lower winds results in an increase in surface wind and a veering as the thermal activity intensifies. As thermal activity dies out the surface wind backs and decreases.

site the winch early in the morning. The wind will normally veer and strengthen a little during the morning as the thermals start. In the late afternoon and evening, as the thermal activity dies out and the air becomes more stable again, the surface winds will usually drop and back. (Fig. 41 explains the terms veering and backing.)

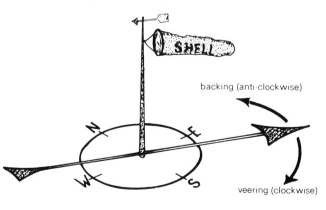

41 Changes in the wind direction – veering and backing.

backing (anti-clockwise)

veering (clockwise)

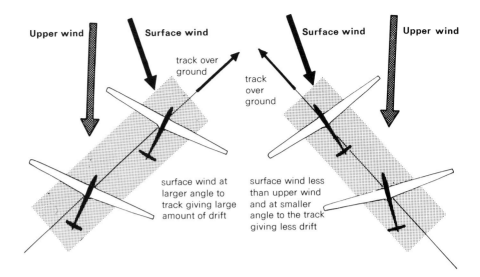

42 The effect of wind shear on crosswind landings. There may be more drift when landing with the wind blowing from the left in the northern hemisphere.

The change of wind direction with height is also significant when landing across the wind in strong winds. There is a difference between the effect on a glider of a crosswind coming from the left or from the right. In each case the wind strength becomes less as the glider approaches the ground, but the change in wind direction when the wind is from the left increases the crosswind component. With the wind from the right, however, both the wind speed and the change in wind direction are helping to reduce the drift (Fig. 42).

Usually the wind direction is marked on the newspaper and television charts but if it is not shown it can be determined very quickly by looking at the isobars and the pressure pattern. Fig. 43 explains how to do this using what is known as Buys Ballots law. This simply states that if you stand with your back to the wind then low pressure lies to your left and high pressure to your right (the opposite in the southern hemisphere). Since the low and high pressure areas are marked on the map, the direction of the airflow along the isobars can be found by seeing that the low pressure is to the left.

The wind which blows along the isobars at about 2000 feet is often known as the 'gradient wind' because its strength depends upon the pressure gradient or spacing of the isobars. By using a special scale to measure the spacing the speed of the wind at a given place can be estimated (Fig. 44). Note that the 'gradient wind' is nothing directly to do with the *wind gradient* which refers to changes in wind speed with height.

43 Buys Ballots law – in the northern hemisphere low pressure is always to your left if you stand with your back to the wind.

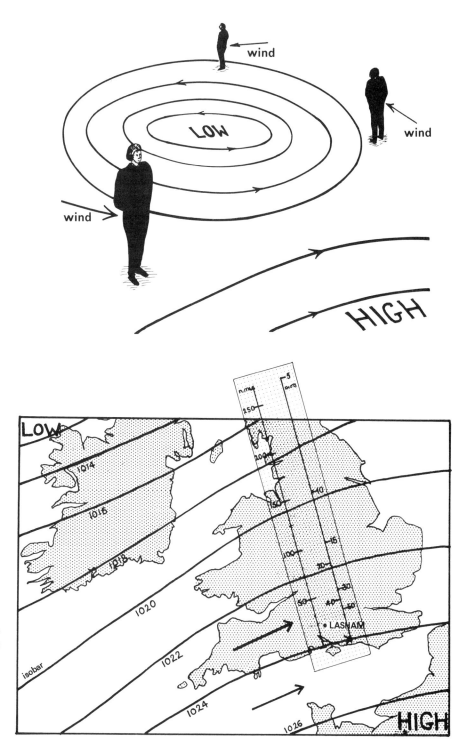

44 Measuring the gradient wind speed by means of a geostrophic wind scale. The closer the isobars, the stronger the wind. In this example, the gradient wind at Lasham is just over 20 knots.

Flying in a steady wind

The first important *fact* is that if the wind speed is constant the only effect on any kind of flying machine, be it balloon, airship, glider or jet, is to drift it away in the direction of the wind. However strong the wind there will be no changes in *airspeed* as the machine turns into or downwind. In fact, above a layer of fog or cloud the pilot of a glider or other aircraft would have no idea in which direction the wind was blowing.

In effect, it is as though the aircraft circles or flies all the time inside a huge block of air. On a still day the block is stationary, whereas on a windy day, the block is drifting across the countryside (Fig. 45). Another way of thinking of this is to think of the aircraft circling in its block of air while the earth below moves off steadily with the speed of the wind.

A few examples of similar situations in other walks of life may help to clarify this concept and make it more credible.

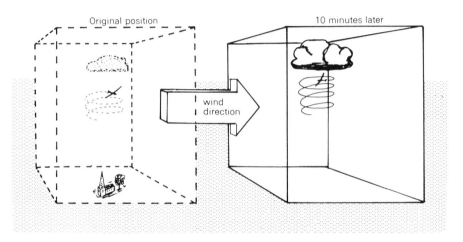

45 Circling in a strong wind. The glider circles under the cloud while the block of air is moved over the ground at the speed of the wind.

Think of the position as you walk to the dining car of an express train. Providing that the train is travelling smoothly, we have a situation similar to flying in our block of air in a steady wind. It is as easy to walk either up or down the train or across the carriage. We are inside the train, just as we are inside the block of air when we are flying. However, if the train is accelerating or braking, or taking a sharp bend, the situation is very different. In the same way the aircraft is affected by gustiness or sudden changes in the wind.

To take another example, imagine yourself about to swim across a wide river on a day with patchy fog. Standing with your feet on the bottom you can feel the current trying to sweep you downstream. As soon as you start swimming you cannot feel the current and can only see that to reach the landing stage on the far side you will have to aim upstream of it to allow for the effect of the current. If you stop swimming and float you would start to drift along with the river within a few seconds. You would feel no movement and there would be no 'slip' between you and the water. You would move at exactly the speed of the river and if the fog came down you would have no idea which way to go to reach a bank. It would not be any easier to swim downstream rather than upstream and *never is* except when you can see the bank and want to reach a particular point on it. If the current is strong and we do not make much progress it will be harder work if we swim faster to go upstream against it. However, if we swim steadily the swimming itself is just as easy heading in one direction as another – regardless of the strength of the current.

A flight in a balloon is a wonderful experience which has some unexpected pleasures. There is absolute silence in level flight because the balloon is floating stationary in the air, although the air is moving all the time at the speed of the wind. It is as though the basket were suspended, stationary, while the earth moved along below! The only wind that can be felt in a balloon is caused by any up or down movement as it gains or loses height. The effects of severe gusts may be felt very occasionally but most of the time you sit virtually stationary while the earth moves silently along.

Ground speed and airspeed

The lift from the wings depends solely on the angle of attack of the wing and the airspeed. It is nothing whatever to do with ground speed, or what is happening down below on the ground.

The airspeed is a measure of the speed of the air as it meets the aircraft and in still air this is the same as the speed over the ground.

If the aircraft is flown steadily at the same airspeed but against a strong wind, the speed over the ground will be reduced.

If flying downwind at the same airspeed, although the speed of the airflow over the wings is the same, the speed over the ground is much higher. For a given loss of height, therefore, the glider will always fly much further downwind. The glider pilot cannot afford to ignore the effect of the wind or he will soon end up too far downwind of the landing field to be able to get back against the wind. This is probably the most common cause of landing *aux vaches* (with the cows) as the French would say.

Taking a rather extreme example, if the wind is 40 knots and the glider is flown at an airspeed of 40 knots against the wind it will have no forward movement over the ground. However, by increasing the airspeed to 60, or even 80, knots against this very strong wind, the glider will begin to penetrate and make progress. This is a very important principle to remember if you allow your machine to be drifted back too far behind the airfield. Of course, flying at the higher speed uses up the height more rapidly, but if it gets us back to the field safely and spares us the wrath of the C.F.I. who cares?

The rate of descent of the glider is unaffected either by flying into wind or downwind and only varies if rising or sinking air is encountered, or if the airspeed is varied.

Flying downwind with a 40 knot wind the speed over the ground would be

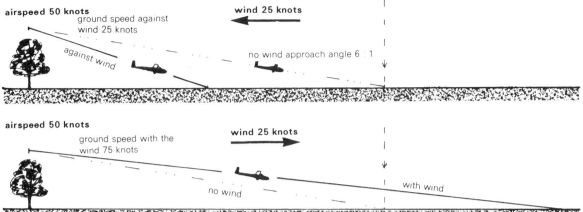

46 The effect of the wind on the approach angle and ground speed. Into wind the approach angle is much steeper and the touchdown speed much lower. Whenever possible, landings are always made into the wind.

80 knots. Whatever happens the pilot must not be influenced into attempting to slow down because of this high ground speed. The normal airspeed must be maintained or the aircraft will be in danger of stalling.

Fig. 46 shows how the flight path of a glider can be changed by the wind. It is not unusual on a windy day to be able to slow down to the point when the glider is drifted backwards across the countryside. It is also possible to 'kite' on the winch cable to a phenomenal height in strong winds. (Fig. 47.) This is done by launching normally and then slowing the glider down to its minimum flying speed so that it drifts backwards while the winch cable is paid out again. A further launch can then be made to a much greater height and this process repeated several times, in the same way as the string is let out on a kite. (The maximum legal height in most countries is 2000 feet but heights of almost 5000 feet have been recorded.) Unfortunately, there is not much point in trying for great height in strong winds because, having released, one circle will take the glider out of reach of the field! Also, if the cable breaks, or the winch driver cannot wind it in quickly, it will fall across every power and telephone line downwind of the field, besides being a serious hazard to motorists on any nearby roads.

Circling flight in a strong wind (Fig. 48.)

A steady circling flight results in a gradual drift downwind, so that each circle becomes an oval in relation to the ground. Whereas at height it is difficult to see any effect of wind as the glider circles, at low altitudes the aircraft appears to slip sideways as it turns across the wind. It is very tempting to try and stop the apparent slipping with the rudder, but this will only result in a bad turn with very much higher drag. This can cause serious trouble, particularly in a rather low final turn or when hill soaring at low altitudes. Always try to ignore this apparent slip and skid if you are turning

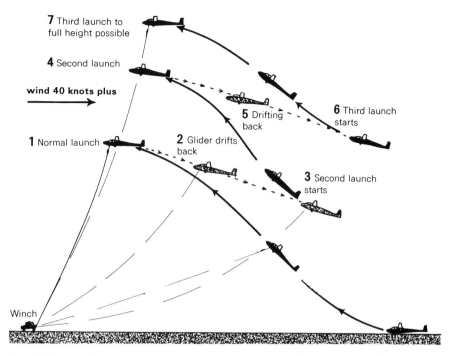

47 Kiting on a winch launch.

7 Third launch to full height possible

4 Second launch

wind 40 knots plus →

1 Normal launch

2 Glider drifts back

5 Drifting back

6 Third launch starts

3 Second launch starts

Winch

in a high wind and concentrate on using the controls quite normally to make an accurate turn.

However, the actual drift must never be ignored, particularly at low altitudes. A common cause of low-flying accidents with light aircraft is forgetting to allow sufficiently for drift. All the time an aircraft is turning it is being drifted by the wind and, once the turn has been started a little too late, even tightening it cannot save the machine from being drifted into trees or other obstructions. While the radius of turn may be very small as the aircraft turns into the wind, it will be much, much larger turning from downwind to crosswind. This must always be allowed for, particularly when turning onto the base leg of the circuit in windy conditions (see Fig. 49).

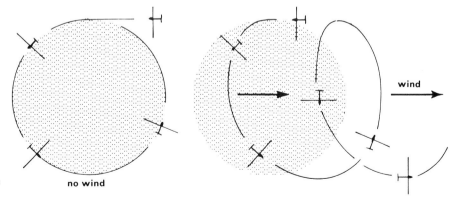

48 Track over the ground while circling.

no wind

wind →

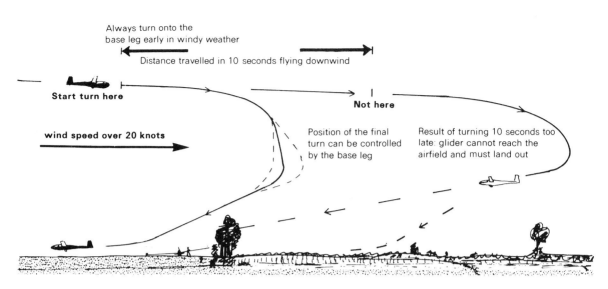

Always turn onto the
base leg early in windy weather

Distance travelled in 10 seconds flying downwind

Start turn here

Not here

wind speed over 20 knots

Position of the final
turn can be controlled
by the base leg

Result of turning 10 seconds too
late: glider cannot reach the
airfield and must land out

49 In strong winds, turn onto the base leg before reaching the downwind boundary and stay within easy reach of the field.

Flying across the wind
(Fig. 50.)

Again, all that is necessary is to fly the aircraft normally and take no notice of the apparent slipping across the ground. In order to arrive at a certain point over the ground, therefore, a normal turn is made to point the aircraft in the direction needed, so that, allowing for the drift, it will arrive there. Any corrections should be made by using normal co-ordinated turns and never by means of the rudder alone.

Even experienced pilots find that they must check the accuracy of their flying when hill soaring at low altitude because of the tendency to correct this sideways motion quite unconsciously with a little rudder.

To summarise the effects of a steady wind:

1 The airspeed is unaffected by circling.
2 The ground speed *is* affected and this in turn affects the gliding range, reducing it drastically when flying into a strong wind.
3 The drift must be allowed for by turning and heading the aircraft into wind a little when flying across wind.
4 At all times the aircraft must be flown normally and accurately at a safe airspeed.

The effects of variations in the wind

Even as glider pilots we have surprisingly little detailed knowledge about the fluctuations and eddies in the atmosphere. There are so many variations caused by thermal activity or disturbances from hills and other obstructions that it is practically impossible to predict, or account for, changes in wind, particularly near the ground.

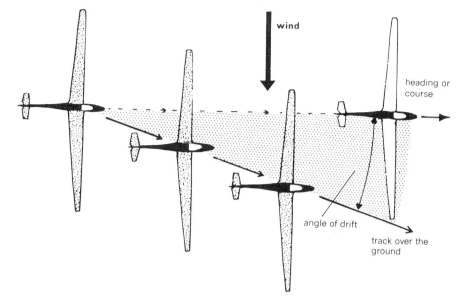

50 Drifting across the wind.

Because these variations break up the steady movement of the air they *do* have an effect on all aircraft. Gliders are particularly affected because of their low flying speed and relatively poor control response.

In some conditions there may be quite significant changes in the wind speed and direction where two distinctive masses of air are moving at different velocities. This will sometimes occur at a front, or where there is a very strong temperature inversion, or a stable layer of air which prevents the usual mixing of the air.

These variations can sometimes be detected in a glider during a winch or car launch. At low levels the air is cold and often hazy with a light wind. Then, at a certain height, a change of wind strength makes itself felt by a jump in the airspeed as the glider climbs. At precisely the same height near the top of each launch, there will be a jump of 5–10 knots in the airspeed as the glider hits the stronger wind.

During the glide down into wind there will be a noticeable drop in airspeed and a sudden sinking feeling as the glider flies into the lighter wind again. After a few seconds the rate of sink and airspeed will return to normal. These effects will only be felt if the change in wind speed takes place in a very shallow layer of air. Had the same change been spread over a depth of several hundred feet it would have been virtually undetectable. The glider would have regained any lost speed almost immediately and the only change that the average pilot would notice would be a slight increase in the rate of sink for a few seconds.

When a large change of wind speed occurs in a layer of air only 50 or 100 feet deep the glider moves from the top to the bottom of this layer in a very short time. Due to its inertia the aircraft tends to resist any change in its speed or flight path, and, therefore, the drop in wind speed *does* affect the airspeed. One moment the aircraft is flying steadily into a strong wind and a few seconds later this wind has dropped. Had the change been gradual, the aircraft would have just lost height a little more quickly for a few moments until it regained its former speed and settled down to a steady glide again.

This recovery will be automatic providing that the drop in speed is not sufficient to leave the aircraft stalled. As the speed is reduced by a change of this sort in the wind the glider sinks more rapidly because of the immediate reduction in the lift and at the same time the normal stability comes into play and lowers the nose a little. Then, as the speed increases, the stability results in a return to the original attitude and a steady glide again.

If the pilot reacts instinctively and tries to stop the sinking by raising the nose a little there is a very grave risk of stalling. The rapid sinking increases the angle of attack as the air comes up to meet the wing and any raising of the nose may pull the wing beyond the stalling angle. This is a special hazard if the glider is near the ground.

Squalls Very rapid changes in wind speed and direction occur near heavy showers and thunderstorms and extra care is needed both when flying and on the ground. While large clouds of this kind are developing there are very strong

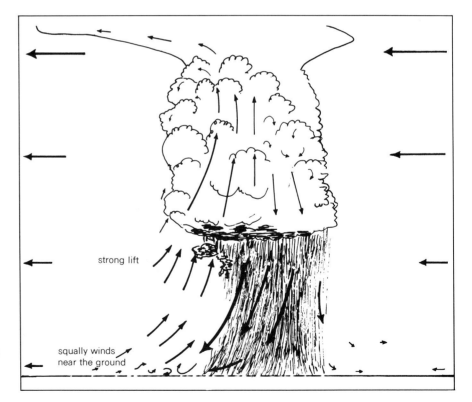

strong lift

squally winds
near the ground

51 Squally conditions can be expected close to heavy showers and thunderstorms.

upcurrents, and air is being swept up from all directions causing changes in the surface winds. The wind may drop temporarily, or may swing right round and become strong and gusty. This makes landing tricky and also means that it is most unwise to leave gliders unattended in the open unless they are picketed down and secured against a wind from any direction. A few tyres on the into wind wing are *not* adequate since the wind may swing right round and the glider may be blown over by a strong gust from any direction. There is a great temptation for people to go inside for a cup of tea when a shower is imminent and this is just the time when such squalls occur and gliders get blown over. Getting wet is a small price to pay for saving a valuable glider and avoiding an expensive repair.

When heavy rain begins to fall from shower clouds the air cools rapidly and descends very quickly often forming a wedge of cold gusty air travelling ahead of the rain. The cold wedge produces a wonderfully powerful updraught, often extending into the rain itself. But beware! Gusts of 30–40 m.p.h. can be expected and the wind direction may also vary from minute to minute making a landing extremely difficult. However, once the rain starts falling the situation is even worse, since it will then be difficult to see ahead. It is prudent to get down before heavy rain arrives since you cannot slow down or stop as you would in a motor car if the windscreen wipers fail to keep your windscreen clear.

The wind gradient The wind at two or three thousand feet is almost entirely governed by the variations in the atmospheric pressure which are associated with changing weather situations. Below this height the airflow is slowed down by the friction between the air and the surface of the earth and it is also deflected by high ground and other local influences. Since the friction is greatest close to the ground, the biggest change in wind speed occurs in the first few hundred feet. Fig. 52 shows the changes in wind speed with height on a typical windy

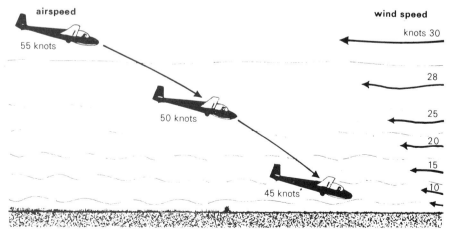

52 The wind gradient. Friction between the ground and the air slows down the airflow near the ground.

day. Notice the very rapid change close to the ground. There is an almost insignificant rate of change above about 500 feet.

The severity of the wind gradient depends upon several factors. Obviously, if there is only a very light wind at 1000 feet, any change in wind speed lower down will be insignificant. A steep wind gradient can only occur in a fairly strong wind. The amount of friction between the air and the ground is also important and the wind gradient will generally be worst in the lee of rough country, and less severe near the sea or to the lee of flat, open country where the surface friction will be low. This is demonstrated by the very strong surface winds experienced on the coast, where winds of 60–70 m.p.h. are quite common. Inland, only 20 miles away, such winds are rare although the strength of the upper winds is much the same.

Fairly obviously, if there is only a very light upper wind there will be very little friction effect and very little change in the wind speed with height. In strong winds the reduction in the wind speed near the ground will be considerable, even over open ground.

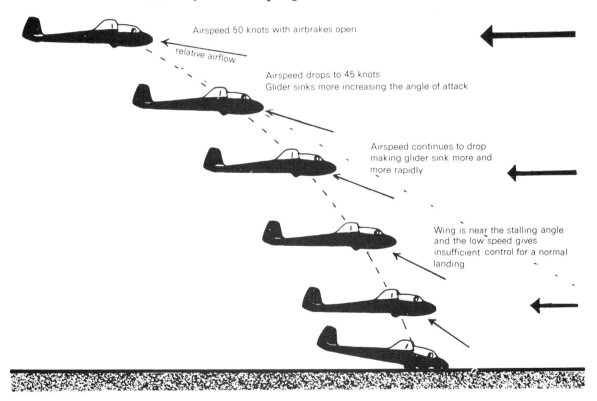

53 The effect of the wind gradient. The increase in the rate of descent when the glider loses speed because of the wind gradient means that at one moment it may be flying against a 30 knot wind at 70–80 feet and only 3–4 seconds later it may be flying against a wind of only 15 knots. This causes the sudden loss of airspeed which can leave the glider semi-stalled.

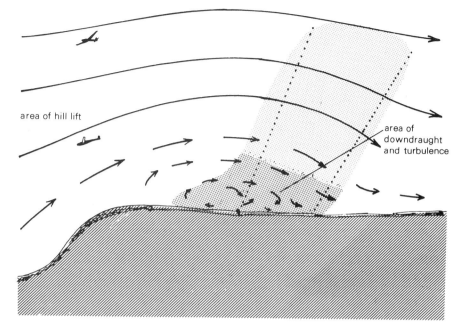

54 The 'clutching hand' effect in the lee of a hill top is an area of severe downdraughts and turbulence behind the hill top.

area of hill lift

area of downdraught and turbulence

The wind gradient can have a very significant effect on a glider during take off and landing. During a landing for instance, it only takes a few seconds for the glider to descend the final hundred feet or so. One moment it is gliding down against a strong wind and a few seconds later it has lost height and is against a wind which is 10 or 15 knots lighter. This sudden change causes a drop in airspeed which reduces the lift and results in a much higher rate of sink. Unless the approach has been started with extra speed in hand to allow for this loss there may then be insufficient speed or control to round out properly for a normal landing. There will also be a tendency to undershoot the landing area (Fig. 53).

Once the speed begins to drop even slightly, the glider sinks more, going down through the steepening gradient more quickly and experiencing an even more rapid loss of speed. This effect escalates and there is seldom sufficient height or time to regain the lost speed and make a safe landing.

A high proportion of heavy landings is due to this effect for which there is no absolute cure. It is important, therefore, to take the precaution of choosing an adequate speed for an approach in windy weather. Alternatively, the approach must be progressively steepened during the last hundred feet or so to maintain a safe speed for landing.

The higher rate of sink must also be allowed for by aiming the approach further into the field than usual. The glider reacts in the same way as when it flies into sinking air and, in extreme conditions, it seems almost to drop out of the air. This effect is often referred to as a 'clutching hand' because it is waiting there all the time for a chance to clutch at, and bring down, any unwary glider pilot who is foolish enough to make a slow approach or go too far behind the boundary fence.

Some of the worst conditions are found on gliding sites at the top of hills. The wind may form a continuous eddy, so that the surface wind may even be reversed in some places. Very high approach speeds are essential to cater for this kind of wind gradient and the loss of height during an approach can be very severe, sometimes reaching 2000 feet per minute! (Fig. 54.)

The effect of the wind gradient is much more marked if the approach is very steep because the aircraft moves more rapidly from strong to lighter winds. However, in windy weather it is just not safe to make a flat approach in a glider since sudden unpredictable losses of height can occur in turbulence near the ground. Powered aircraft making shallow approaches are hardly affected by the gradient but they still need a little more speed to give better control in the gusty air.

In windy weather it is wise to keep plenty of extra height in hand until the final turn into wind and then use a lot of airbrake to lose the height on the final approach. By using plenty of airbrake the glider has a certain amount of stored energy in reserve and if the speed does begin to fall off and the glider starts to sink too rapidly, the airbrakes can be closed in order to counteract the loss of speed and height.

If the initial approach speed is rather low, a steep wind gradient may, in an extreme case, cause sufficient loss of speed to leave the aircraft stalled. The only symptoms may be the rapid loss of height and the lack of response to the backward movement on the stick as an attempt is made to stop the nose dropping or to round out for landing. In this case the nose of the glider will not be high and the stall may occur in an attitude very close to that of normal cruising flight. What has happened is that the glider has lost speed, making it lose lift and sink rapidly. The high rate of sink has made the relative airflow come up towards the wing at a steep angle. A further loss of speed has repeated this process and the airflow has finally reached the stalling angle so that a stall occurs too near the ground for any hope of recovery.

This kind of accident used to be very prevalent in the early days of gliding when all the basic training was carried out on open Primary gliders by the solo method. By first making ground slides, and then progressing to low hops and high hops, the pilot taught himself with a few hints and tips from the instructor. Since he would often have had only a few minutes actual flying by the time he started circuits and hill soaring flights in quite windy weather, he had never had any practical experience of stalling. It was not uncommon for a beginner to fly a little too far downwind of the landing area and then try to get back by 'stretching' the glide. Unless specifically and repeatedly warned, most inexperienced pilots would instinctively fly a little too nose high in an attempt to glide further. Once at low speed, even a comparatively mild wind gradient would cause a further loss and the chain of events would then lead to a stall. All the pilot would know was that he had apparently flown into strong sinking air and that the nose had begun to drop inexplicably until he hit the ground. Fortunately, unlike modern machines, the gliders were very light and flew at low speed so that the pilot would usually scramble out of the wreckage unhurt. He would often be quite convinced that the cause must have been a broken elevator cable because of the sudden loss of control, whereas, as every pupil now knows, the primary symptom of the stall is that the aircraft will not respond to a further backward movement on the stick and drops its nose or wing.

It is very important to realise that, because of the effect of the wind gradient, recovery from a stall flying into wind at low altitude will take much more height than from one at circuit height. Similarly, a cable break on a wire launch is much more serious in windy weather than at any other time. In both cases the glider descends steeply through the gradient as the nose is lowered to regain speed. Whereas during practice at height only 50–70 feet may be lost in a full stall and recovery, two or three times that height might easily be lost close to the ground. In spite of lowering the nose, the speed may, in fact, be decreasing because of the effect of descending through the steep wind gradient.

Once the speed has dropped below the normal flying speed in such situations there can be little hope of recovery.

Remember this when learning to drive the winch or tow car and launching in windy weather. Give the glider a good clean take off with maximum acceleration until it has reached about 50 feet. This will ensure that, if the cable breaks, the glider has plenty of speed for a safe approach down through the wind gradient again. Above all, do not attempt to provide only just enough speed to get the glider off the ground, or it will accelerate very slowly and be left at a rather low speed for the initial climb.

Many people are rather surprised to learn that when a glider approaches the ground and meets the decreased headwind, it does not just glide further and float a greater distance. This does happen to some extent, but the loss of speed and height on the approach is usually much more serious than any gain in float near the ground. Once the airspeed has fallen much below the normal approach speed, the glider will not penetrate very far against even the lighter surface winds. Furthermore, once the speed is low, the aircraft is at the mercy of any turbulence and the airbrakes cannot be opened without the risk of a heavy landing.

Unfortunately the wind gradient is not constant for even a few seconds because there is always additional turbulence and a risk of gusts which vary the actual wind strength. Again, the seriousness of these effects will depend on the strength of the wind and the size and shape of any obstructions upwind of the landing area. It will also depend on the stability of the air at the time.

These additional factors effects are often much more hazardous than the gradient itself and it is worth discussing them in detail.

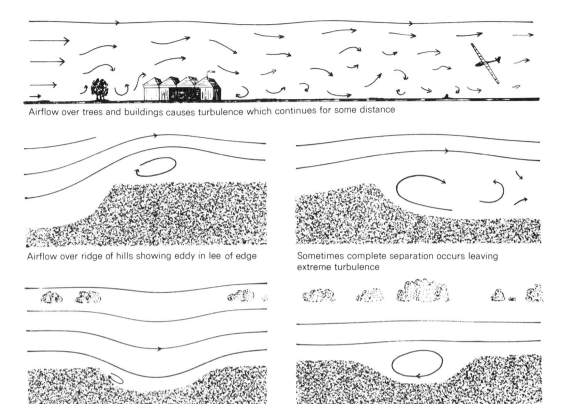

Airflow over trees and buildings causes turbulence which continues for some distance

Airflow over ridge of hills showing eddy in lee of edge

Sometimes complete separation occurs leaving extreme turbulence

Airflow across a valley. Separation has occurred but smooth flow has been re-established. Little or no cloud forms over valley because of descending air

Complete separation has occurred leaving a standing eddy in the valley. Upper airflow is unaffected

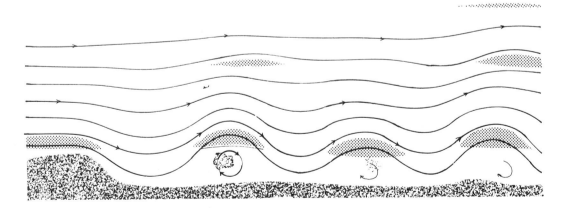

55 When favourable conditions exist, standing or lee waves form downwind of a ridge of hills or mountains. Violently turbulent rotor flow often occurs below the crest of a wave. Lenticular, or lens-shaped, clouds mark the position of a wave.

Surface obstructions

The air within two or three times the height of even small obstructions, such as trees or buildings, is seriously disturbed and turned into a mass of unsteady swirls and eddies of various sizes. Depending on their direction and strength these add to, or reduce, the effect of the wind gradient so that at one moment it is increased and at the next, perhaps, there is hardly any gradient effect at all. Whereas these fluctuations have very little effect on a Jumbo Jet, they can be critical to a glider, and disastrous to a model aircraft coming into land.

The general effect of the wind blowing over a ridge of hills is to give an area of rising air ahead and over the crest of the ridge. In the lee of the hills or near an isolated hill many different variations in the airflow can occur. These may range from the formation of a steady pattern of lee waves as in Fig. 55, to a complete breakdown of the steady flow. These variations usually upset the normal wind gradient for several miles to the lee of the obstruction (often 20–30 miles in the event of a wave system). The pilot should expect extra turbulence in the lee of a line of trees or a wooded area even though it is two or three fields away upwind.

Stability of the air

As every glider pilot quickly learns, the stability of the air will vary from day to day, if not from hour to hour. It is not possible to soar in thermals unless there are thermals to be soared in! If the air is too stable the experts will be at home gardening, or 'hangar flying' in the bar at the club.

When the air is unstable, any air which is disturbed and starts to move upwards will tend to continue to move upwards. In stable conditions, this movement would be damped out almost immediately.

The effect of air flowing over obstructions tends to be amplified if the air is unstable and produces tricky conditions for gliding in strong winds, with occasional violent turbulence and the risk of large areas of strong sinking air at unexpected moments.

The effects of changes in airspeed

If it were possible to have a perfect, dragless glider, height and speed would be exchangeable with no loss. A given amount of speed could be turned into a definite gain of height as in Fig. 56. In real life, however, there is drag even with the best machines and if, for example, slowing down from 80 knots to 40 knots gives us a gain of height of x feet, accelerating from 40 knots back to 80 knots will use up x, plus perhaps an extra 50 feet. Height energy (potential energy) is being exchanged for speed energy (kinetic energy). The effect of the wind gradient, or any loss of speed due to a sudden change in wind speed, is a loss in total energy possessed by the aircraft. It is therefore bound to cost either height or speed.

There are other causes of changes in airspeed which must be considered if an attempt is made to analyse any particular situation. Perhaps we have just experienced a case when the airspeed has repeatedly increased each time we have turned into the wind. Since this should not have happened in steady wind conditions, it is interesting to try and understand how the speed could have increased.

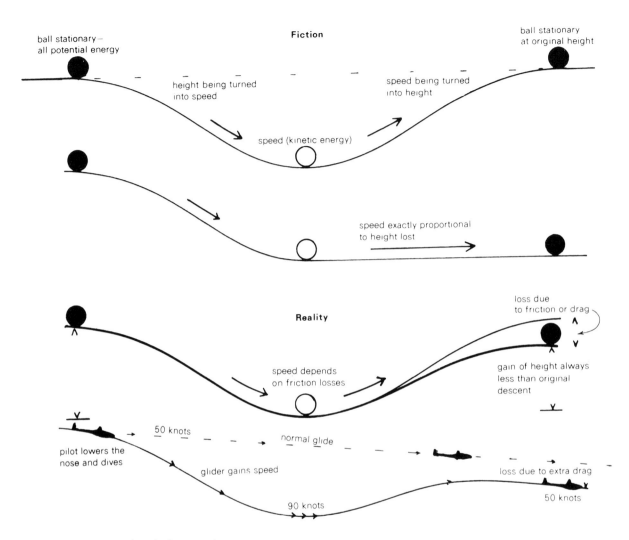

56 Exchanging height for speed.

As the aircraft flies into a region of rising air there may be a definite gain in airspeed of the order of 3 or 4 knots, caused by horizontal gusts or gradients near the thermal. This is only a temporary effect and the speed will then settle down again if the glider is allowed to carry on flying steadily. Similarly, a loss of speed may often occur when flying into sinking air. If it so happens that the glider is circling half in and half out of lift, there *will* be a gain of speed each time that it turns into wind and meets the lift.

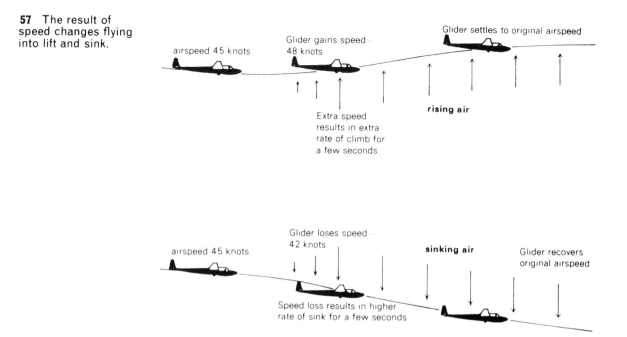

57 The result of speed changes flying into lift and sink.

airspeed 45 knots

Glider gains speed – 48 knots

Glider settles to original airspeed

Extra speed results in extra rate of climb for a few seconds

rising air

airspeed 45 knots

Glider loses speed – 42 knots

sinking air

Glider recovers original airspeed

Speed loss results in higher rate of sink for a few seconds

Movements of the air in thermals

Further changes in airspeed may occur close to, and in, thermals. If the thermal has a strong circular movement (like a dust devil in the desert) there will be a significant change of speed as the aircraft meets this flow. The result may be either a gain in speed and reduced sink, or a drop in speed which would cause a much higher rate of sink, or perhaps even an unexpected stall. However, except in the deserts, dust devils are uncommon and thermals tend to break away from the ground in huge bubbles instead of continuous streams. Once the thermal has left the ground, the circular movement tends to stop quite quickly. There is seldom any noticeable rotation above about 2000 feet and any attempt to change the direction of a turn to see if it results in an improvement in the rate of climb is most likely just to have the result of losing the thermal altogether. However, it can be seen that a definite advantage will be gained by turning against the circular flow so that the ground speed is lowered. This results in a lower angle of bank being required for the turn and therefore an increase in efficiency (Fig. 59).

Thermal bubbles are thought to have an internal circulation rather like a smoke ring (see Fig. 60). Near the top and bottom there can be horizontal movements of the air of 3–4 knots. These, like any other sudden changes in the wind speed, cause changes in airspeed and, therefore, variations in the rate of climb or descent of the glider.

The effects of these horizontal gusts, together with the changes in speed as the glider flies into rising or sinking air, account for most of the difficulties

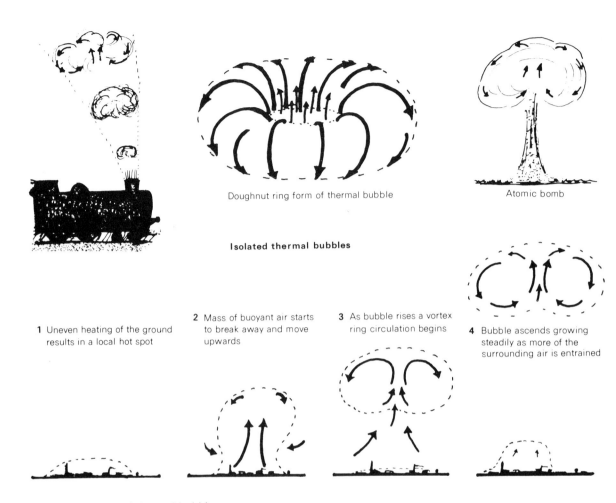

Doughnut ring form of thermal bubble

Atomic bomb

Isolated thermal bubbles

1 Uneven heating of the ground results in a local hot spot

2 Mass of buoyant air starts to break away and move upwards

3 As bubble rises a vortex ring circulation begins

4 Bubble ascends growing steadily as more of the surrounding air is entrained

58 The formation of thermal bubbles.

which even an expert pilot experiences when trying to get centred in a thermal. It is difficult to tell if a surge of extra lift is caused by an increase in speed due to a gust or horizontal flow, or whether it is due to flying into stronger lift. It is important to realise that if the horizontal gusts are sufficient to change the airspeed by a few knots, the resulting change in the rate of sink of the glider may make the variometer indicate a false position for the best lift. (This may be further accentuated by any total energy device fitted to the variometer.)

Near the cap of the thermal, flying from **a** to **b** in Figs. 60 and 61, the glider will meet the outflow, so that the variometer will show less sink and the pilot may interpret this as the beginning of the lift. (A total energy variometer may even show a high rate of climb here because of the gain in speed.) This

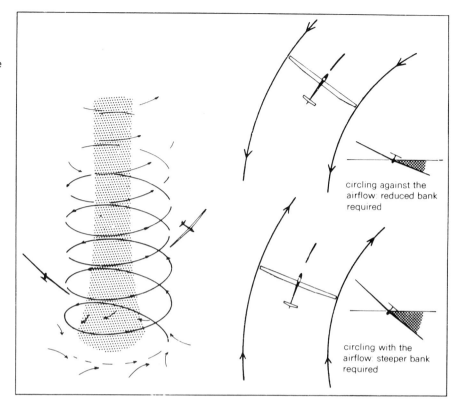

circling against the
airflow reduced bank
required

circling with the
airflow steeper bank
required

may be the explanation for the many occasions when the glider pilot is convinced that he has hit strong lift and circles, only to find he was mistaken. Further along the same track he will meet the real lift but it will probably turn out to be weak and rather broken. Flying on still further, out of the lift, there will be a momentary loss of speed as the glider encounters the outflow. This will result in a few moments of rapid sinking indicated on the variometer, although the air itself may not be sinking at all.

These effects can make the problems of centring in a thermal very difficult because the horizontal gradients and gusts give such misleading impressions. The gusts near thermals are particularly confusing on windy days when many of the thermals are narrow and impossible to use except in a slow glider turning very steeply.

Flying through the base of the thermal can be very confusing and the situation is more critical here because a failure to centre quickly may result in a limited climb in ever worsening lift as the glider subsides gently out of the bottom of the thermal. However, if the pilot centres quickly, the lift will strengthen almost immediately and a high rate of climb may be obtained. Moving from **e** to **f** (see Fig. 61 again) the glider may lose speed at first and sink abnormally as it flies into the inflow. After a few seconds it will reach the main area of lift but this may seem disappointingly weak. However, as the glider leaves the rising air it meets the inflow head on and the surge of extra speed combined with the indication of a surge of lift on the variometer may mislead the pilot about the real position of the best lift. In this case the variometer will cause the pilot to attempt to centre his glider beyond the best lift.

The effects of circling to one side of the main area of lift in the base of a thermal are of particular interest. The variometer will generally indicate two cores of stronger lift, one caused by flying into the inflow and gaining speed and the other, the real centre of the lift. The pilot will usually tend to choose the wrong core because the gust effects give momentary high readings on the variometer compared with the initially rather unimpressive result of flying into the area of smoothly rising air of the thermal proper. It is sound advice to the beginner that if there seem to be two cores no recentring move-

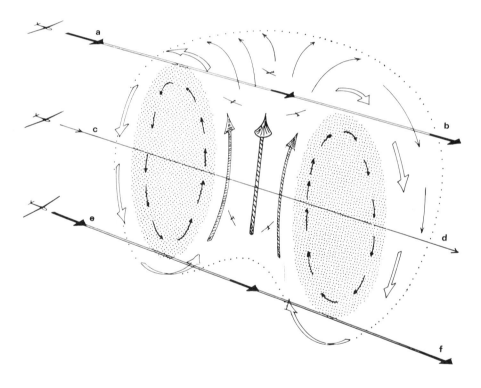

60 A cross-section of a thermal bubble showing the horizontal and vertical movements of the air inside the bubble. Practical experience shows that on many occasions these movements do exist and greatly influence soaring techniques.

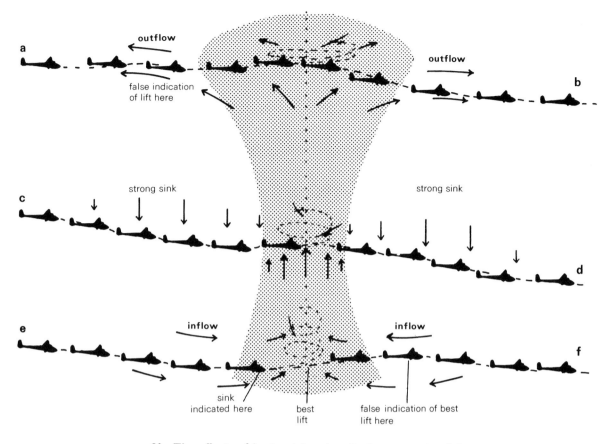

a outflow

false indication
of lift here

b outflow

c strong sink

strong sink **d**

e inflow

inflow **f**

sink
indicated here

best
lift

false indication of best
lift here

61 The effects of horizontal and vertical movements of the air on the glider as it flies through the thermal at various levels.

ments should be made for three or four turns. If the inflow is significant a glider in a well-banked turn will be automatically centred by its effects and the second area of false lift will disappear. On the other hand, any reduced rate of climb due to circling three or four turns can result in no permanent loss if the glider happens to be in the cap of the thermal. In the cap, the mean rate of climb settles down the rate of ascent of the whole bubble (about half the best rate of climb found in the core) and the glider is, in effect, bouncing on the top of the thermal rather like a ball on top of a fountain at a fairground. The lift in this region tends to be broken, with the glider being pushed away from the best lift by the outflow.

If the thermal bubble has this smoke ring type of circulation there will be a region in the base of the bubble where the air is moving inwards horizontally from all directions as in Fig. 62. A glider circling concentrically in this region will be flying with a steady inflow of several knots pushing it towards the centre of the turn. This could be thought of as an infinite number of gusts striking the glider as it turns.

It can be shown that the result of this inflow on a glider banking at an angle of 45° is a gain of an additional rate of climb equivalent to the speed of the inflow. For example, with an inflow of 2 knots the glider would have a bonus of 2 knots to its rate of climb. Even greater increases may be gained by the use of more bank and these may offset the normal loss of efficiency in a steeper turn. Normally, of course, a very steep turn results in a consider-

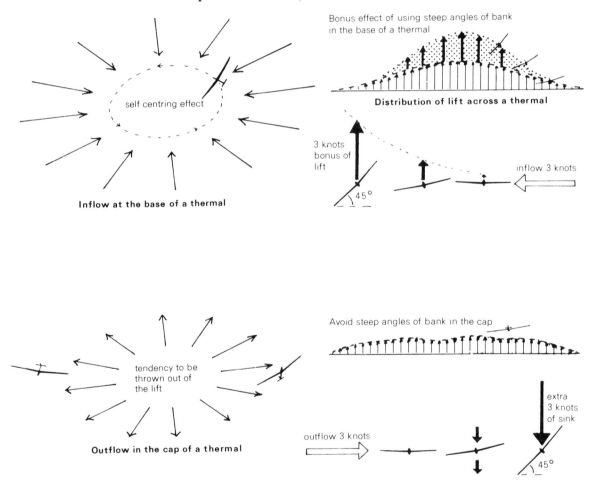

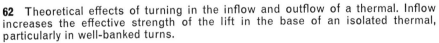

62 Theoretical effects of turning in the inflow and outflow of a thermal. Inflow increases the effective strength of the lift in the base of an isolated thermal, particularly in well-banked turns.

able increase in the rate of sink. However, experience shows that there are many occasions when the best results *are* obtained by using the steepest possible angle of bank for a few circles. The most likely explanation for this is that there is a strong inflow helping the rate of climb. At other times the glider may be flying in zero sink, which immediately turns into a positive gain when a turn is commenced. On some occasions this may also be due to the effect of inflow.

In the cap of the thermal the air is flowing radially outwards so that a glider in circling flight is far less efficient than usual. Here a gently banked turn would be most advantageous.

These effects help to give us an appreciation of the complexity of the motions of the air and of the never-ending opportunities for learning more about them so that we can improve our soaring techniques.

It should be understandable by now why pilots can so often produce instances of gaining speed when turning into the wind. There are so many possible reasons for this that it would, in fact, be very surprising if it did not happen quite frequently.

One situation when it very often occurs is close to a hillside when a glider is hill soaring. There are several likely causes here. Close to the hillside, the glider will be flying out across the wind gradient and also, since the wind strength is increasing, out into stronger lift (Fig. 63). Unless the pilot is very careful the glider may start to oscillate slightly nose up and down and as the

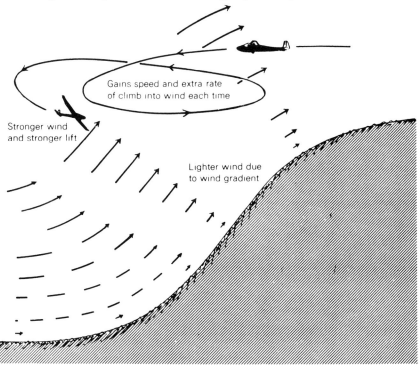

63 When circling close to a hillside, some of the changes in airspeed may be caused by the wind gradient.

natural frequency of this kind of oscillation is usually about 15–20 seconds, it may easily coincide with facing into wind during each circle. It is not easy to rule this out as a possible cause because, near the hillside, it is very difficult to be sure that the attitude is constant with the horizon ahead at one moment and the hilltop the next.

Away from the ground, the cause is more likely to be poor centring in a thermal so that the glider is moving in and out of the lift with resulting changes in speed. Alternatively it may be the effect of the inflow and outflow close to the thermal bubble, again most noticeable when the glider is not centred accurately.

Perhaps one significant point is that these changes in speed when turning into wind seldom, if ever, occur except in or near lift. A steady turn in non-turbulent air, however windy, always gives a steady airspeed!

Turning downwind at low altitude
The dangers of turning downwind at low altitude are very real, whether you are flying a glider or any other kind of aircraft. Any turbulence or loss of height is bound to be serious and at heights of less than 200 or 300 feet there is a high degree of probability that there will be adverse conditions in windy weather. The real hazard for the glider at low altitude is the final turn back into the wind. In a light aircraft there is also the very poor *angle* of climb while flying downwind to be taken into account and the risk of being drifted into an obstruction. The actual rate of climb is normal, but, with the wind behind, the distance covered is much greater, giving far less chance of clearing obstructions. The rate of climb will be affected by any wind gradient, and climbing downwind there will be a loss of speed and therefore a loss in rate of climb. (In effect the aircraft is climbing into an ever decreasing wind speed when it is climbing downwind near the ground.)

In windy or turbulent conditions, *any* turn at low altitude can be dangerous. With their large wing spans and rather low rate of roll gliders are particularly vulnerable during a low turn into wind. The upper wing may be as much as 30 feet above the level of the lower wing during a well-banked turn and this means that the speed of the airflow meeting the upper wing may be 10 or 15 knots higher than that of the lower wing because of the wind gradient. This causes a serious overbanking tendency, making it difficult, if not impossible, for even full aileron to be effective in bringing the wings level. This loss of control is nothing to do with stalling and can occur at any airspeed. In effect, the rate of roll becomes too poor to overcome what the pilot would almost certainly consider to be a gust (Fig. 64).

Some years ago I had an extremely lucky escape at Lasham from this type of situation. The student had made a very sensible final turn at several hundred feet and was approaching with plenty of speed. At a height of about 50 or 60 feet, the glider unexpectedly banked over in a sudden gust. He immediately applied full aileron and rudder to bring the wings level, but with no effect at all. A few seconds later it was 'You have control, Derek, I can't hold it!' (Quite what magic he thought I could do, I can't imagine.)

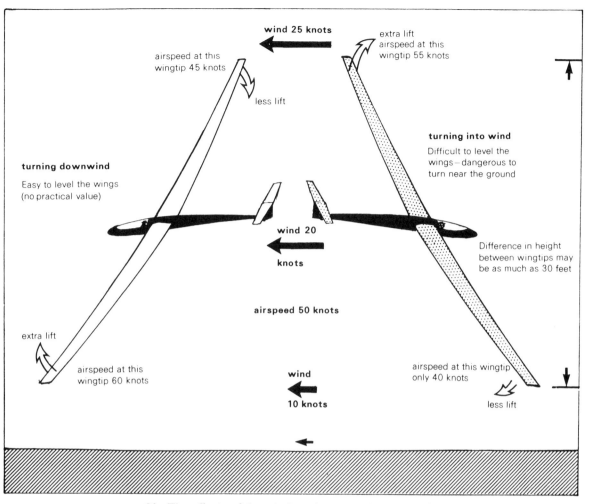

64 The effects of the wind gradient on a low turn. Always complete the final turn into a strong wind with extra height.

By then the glider was sideslipping down towards the ground, still with no signs of any response to the ailerons, and it was pretty obvious that we were going to crash. Fortunately, we had plenty of speed and so I abandoned the attempt to get level and changed the sideslip into a tight turn by pulling back on the stick. To my amazement, we completed the turn through 180° with the wingtip just clear of the ground. The wings suddenly came level and we arrived on the ground in a surprisingly gentle landing facing downwind. Luckily we rolled through a very convenient gap in the boundary fence and stopped with no actual damage, except to our morale and pride. Needless to say, on the next flight we landed back at the hangar and resolved to be a little more careful about the maximum wind strength we would fly in. At the time my reactions were almost instinctive and it was sheer luck that we had not written the glider off.

It is interesting to analyse what probably happened, and to learn some lessons from it.

Firstly, the rolling over was caused by some turbulence. This could have been catastrophic if it had happened during a low final turn as it probably would have rolled the machine past the vertical. Since the final turn had been completed nice and high this risk was minimised. A high straight approach is usually sufficient to ensure that the glider is not tipped over too far by a gust. There was no question of the glider being stalled, or even at a low airspeed. The controls were just inadequate to overpower first the gust and later the wind gradient effect. Unless it is turning, an aircraft cannot fly steadily in a steeply banked position without sideslipping, and therefore it started to slip down towards the ground. The effect of the wind gradient was then reinforcing the effect of the initial gust by giving the upper wing much more speed and lift than the lower one. At this stage a crash seemed inevitable. However, by pulling back on the stick, the slip was immediately changed into a steep turn and the speed was sufficient to allow the turn to be made for a short time without any loss of height. Whereas while facing into wind the effect of the wind gradient had prevented any levelling of the wings, now that the glider had been turned downwind, the effect was reversed and the rate of roll was much higher than normal. This had the nearly magical result of levelling the wings almost instantly. Facing downwind, any wind gradient now caused a *gain* in airspeed, and, together with a slight cushioning ground effect, this saved the glider from a heavy landing.

I learnt quite a bit about wind gradients that day!

The double gradient effect It would be criminal not to mention another special situation which has brought me, and many others, close to disaster.

Most gliding clubs have an Open Day, or assist in entertaining the public occasionally by giving a glider aerobatic display. The pilot usually manages a few practices beforehand and he chooses nice calm conditions for his rehearsals if he can.

Inevitably, when the actual day comes, it is either wet or windy, or both, and of course the show must go on. Most pilots plan to end their display with a steep dive at high speed going downwind just in front of the spectators, followed by a pull up into a final chandelle or steep turn before coming in to land.

Usually the aerobatics go well, except for a tendency to drift downwind all the time. This makes it a little more difficult to get into an ideal position just upwind ready for the final dive. The pilot will probably manage to get into position, but with a little less height than on the rehearsals, with the result that the dive does not give him as much speed as he would really like. Possibly the audience is rather more spread out than he visualised on his practice flights, with the result that he is tempted to fly low for a few seconds longer.

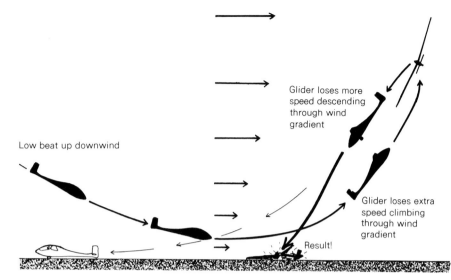

65 The double wind gradient effect – to be taken into account by display pilots.

Glider loses more speed descending through wind gradient

Low beat up downwind

Glider loses extra speed climbing through wind gradient

Result!

The pull up begins, therefore, quite a few knots slower than in the rehearsals, but, compared with normal gliding speeds for steep turns and the like, there is obviously plenty in hand. Suddenly, the pilot senses that all is not quite as it should be. All that speed has disappeared remarkably quickly so he starts the turn early. Just as he thinks he is round safely (although by now the speed is desperately low) he feels that terrible sinking feeling as the wind gradient begins to snatch away the speed on the final approach . . . crunch into an obstruction just short of the landing area (Fig. 65).

What went wrong?

Whereas on the rehearsals in calm conditions the initial speed for the beat up was near the maximum permitted, on the display – through bad planning – the pilot failed to get into position at the required height for his dive. Even if he had done so, he might have deliberately limited the speed because of the gusty wind. Perhaps he started to pull up after a rather longer low run and therefore with a lower speed. (It is always a great temptation to give the public its money's worth and stretch things a little more when there is an audience – something the experienced display pilot will never do.) During the pull up, the glider was climbing downwind through the wind gradient and therefore losing speed and energy unexpectedly quickly. Then, after the turn, the glider was descending through the wind gradient flying into wind, and losing energy yet again. These two gradient effects plus the slightly slower speed at the start, resulted in a completely unpredicted situation which led to a nasty accident.

The importance both of understanding and of having a healthy respect for the effects of turbulence and the wind gradient cannot be over-emphasised. The glider pilot must accept that there are still many situations where even skill and good equipment are not enough. There is a time to put the aircraft away in the hangar and this should be *before* these limits are reached.

Dynamic soaring   No account of the effects of gusts and turbulence would be complete without some comment on dynamic soaring. This is the art of making use of the energy in the gusts and wind gradient. At first sight it smacks of perpetual motion and of trying to get something for nothing but *all* soaring is a matter of exploiting the movements of the air, and using the energy in gusts is really a similar principle.

It has already been explained how, near the ground and when there is a steep wind gradient, descending downwind and climbing into the wind can give the glider extra energy. Since the lift of the wing varies with the square of the speed, even small gains in speed can result in a significant increase in the lift. Simple arithmetic shows that much more is to be gained from an increase in speed of, for example 5 knots, than is lost by a similar decrease in speed.

If the glider is cruising at 45 knots and meets a sudden change of wind speed of plus 5 knots and, later, minus 5 knots, the variations in lift will be in proportion to $50^2:45^2:40^2$.

$$50^2 - 45^2 = 475 \text{ whereas } 45^2 - 40^2 = 425.$$

It should, therefore, be possible to gain more in the gusts than is lost in the lulls! This would certainly increase the efficiency of the glider and result in a reduction in the rate of sink.

In order to achieve this the glider must be pulled up slightly as a gust gives an increase in airspeed, while still maintaining a reasonably efficient speed during the lulls. In practice, this is very hard and exacting work for a very small advantage. Some energy will be gained even without pulling up, and the best hope is for the glider to be slightly unstable so that it reacts automatically to the gusts. The principle of pulling up to take more advantage of any increases in airspeed which occur in soaring is generally accepted, since it keeps the glider down to an efficient speed and the radius of turn small. It also ensures that the glider stays in the area of lift longer – if flying into lift is the cause of the increase in airspeed.

Some birds have evolved ways of using the wind gradient to save their energy. However, in order to do this they have to be flying very close to the ground, or water, where the gradient is steepest. A glider pilot trying to imitate the birds would find it a difficult and arduous kind of flying with a constant risk of hitting the ground in an unexpected change of wind. The birds nearly always seem to combine dynamic soaring with the use of slope soaring or wave lift and perhaps this is what we should do in our much larger and clumsier flying machines.

Fig. 66 shows two patterns which are efficient ways of using the wind gradient for dynamic soaring. Point **a** shows the bird diving downwind until it is very close to the water to gain speed and to take energy out of the gradient. It then makes a climbing turn into the wind and climbs up through the gradient until it is nearly stalled. (By doing this the bird will be able to continue climbing much higher than in still air. The gains of speed due to

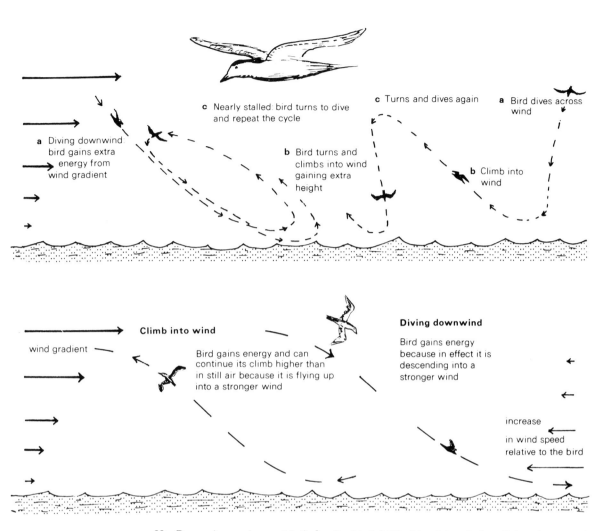

66 Dynamic soaring – strictly for the birds! Climbing into wind or diving downwind in a steep wind gradient the bird (or glider) gains energy compared with normal conditions.

climbing up into a stronger and stronger wind tends to reduce the normal loss of speed due to climbing.) The bird then makes a further turn and dives down again to repeat the process. If the wind gradient is steep, the energy extracted from it by the bird may be sufficient for continuous flight without flapping. Many sea birds use this technique, together with a little hill soaring along the sea waves, for transoceanic flights, apparently soaring for days on end with scarcely any wing flapping to help them.

In the early days of soaring there were many attempts at dynamic soaring in hill lift with varying degrees of success. The discovery of thermals and wave lift soon made the gains possible in dynamic soaring so insignificant in comparison that almost all attempts were abandoned. However, now that glider performance has reached such a very high level that even the slightest gain is a triumph, perhaps pilots and designers will take a new look at this interesting subject. It would not take much improvement to turn a gliding angle of 1:40 into no loss of height at all!

The behaviour of model aircraft in a wind

The model, like a full-sized aircraft, should be unaffected by a steady wind as it circles round and round. However, anyone who has watched, or flown, many model aircraft will realise how model behaviour appears to contradict theory.

For example, it is very noticeable that the model will almost always tend to stall as it turns into wind, as if in doing so it has gained extra speed so that the nose has come up automatically and precipitated the stall.

In order to explain this apparent anomaly, it is necessary to plot the path of the model in still air and then in a wind. Fig. 67**a** shows the model after it has been disturbed by a bump, so that it begins to oscillate slightly nose up and nose down. Only in absolutely still air and in perfect trim would it glide perfectly smoothly without any phugoid of this kind.

Figs. 67**b** and **c** show the same gentle oscillation plotted into and downwind in a wind of 15 m.p.h.

Notice how the model scarcely seems to oscillate at all as it flies downwind, whereas into wind the flight path is so foreshortened that it appears to be stalling quite sharply. If we plot the same model when it is slightly over-elevated and stalling gently, again it seems to be hardly stalling at all flying downwind, whereas into wind the stall appears sharp.

This simple example shows how deceptive the movements of a model can be. In fact, much the same impression will be made on the observer of a full-size aircraft or glider in a strong wind. The pilot, watching the horizon well ahead, will be quite unaware of the apparent difference between the flight into and downwind as seen from the ground.

If the effects of the wind gradient are added to the plot of the model's flight path the loss of height in any stall into wind is increased by the loss of airspeed as the model drops into the lighter winds and is decreased as the model stalls and loses height as it flies downwind.

Since the wind speed forms such a large proportion of the model's flying speed these effects make it difficult to analyse what is going on by just watching the model in flight, unless the wind is very light and the air is smooth.

Models, just like full-sized machines, gain and lose speed as they enter rising and sinking air and either result will start a phugoid so that a series of stalls occurs.

Thermals tend to stop rotating once they have become detached from the ground and, therefore, the glider pilot will seldom find much evidence of rotation at the height he flies. However, the model flier frequently sees a model swept into a turn by the rotation of a thermal, and in some cases even being upset from a well-trimmed circle into a vicious spiral dive.

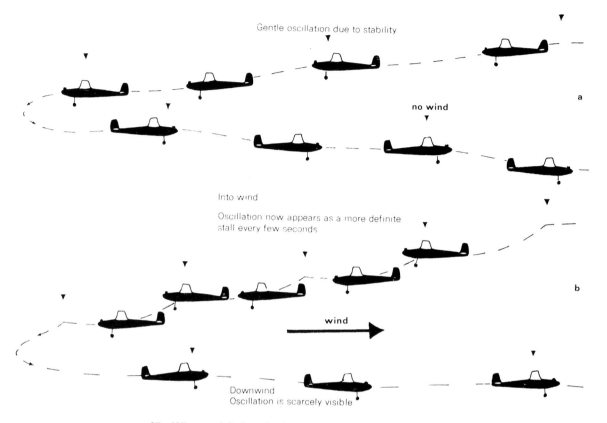

Gentle oscillation due to stability

no wind

a

Into wind

Oscillation now appears as a more definite stall every few seconds

b

wind

Downwind
Oscillation is scarcely visible

67 Why model aircraft always seem to start stalling as they fly into the wind. Any oscillations appear as a definite stall when the model flies into wind.

All these factors make it very difficult to be sure why a model behaves in a certain way. It is not surprising that few modellers understand the real effects of the wind and most of them do not believe, and cannot be convinced, that a steady wind can have no effect whatever on a circling model, apart from drifting it away out of sight.

4 Design for performance

Performance The performance of a powered aircraft can easily be defined in terms of speed, rate of climb, stalling speed, payload etc. Apart from the salesman, no one is very much concerned about the exact speed because no two engines give identical power and each machine will vary slightly. These variations can be smoothed out in cruising flight by using just a little more, or less, throttle.

The glider pilot needs much fuller information about his machine's performance. In fact he may want to know how the gliding angle and rate of sink will vary at all the speeds at which he is likely to fly. However, even in this age of computers, it is impossible to calculate the performance of a glider really accurately. There are so many unpredictable little drag variations that the best the designer can do is to estimate them, based on his experience of previous designs.

Even trying to measure the performance of a modern glider is very difficult and expensive, and at best only gives approximate results. The usual method is to tow the machine up to about 5000 feet on a dead calm morning and find the rate of descent by measuring the loss of height at each speed. This has to be done many times to get reasonably accurate results. These results are then corrected for height and temperature errors and after averaging out and discarding any obviously erroneous readings they can be plotted to show graphically the performance of the glider. This is known as a 'polar curve'.

This kind of test flying can only be done in the calmest of weather because the slightest turbulence or thermal or wave activity will completely distort the results. For example, if the glider has a gliding angle of 40:1 at an airspeed of 50 knots, the rate of sink is only 25 inches per second. If the air was descending at even 2 inches per second the measurement would show the gliding angle as 38:1 instead of 40:1, an error of 5%. Since it is very difficult to be sure whether such up and down movements of the air are occurring or not, the exact gliding angles of the best gliders can never be known accurately. Fortunately, we very seldom need to know the exact figure for a machine's best gliding angle except for trying to compare one with another for sales purposes. The modern pilot is much more concerned with the performance over a range of speeds. Even then it is largely a matter of 'it's all according to how you like it'. A competition pilot who is thinking of flying on the continent may be prepared to sacrifice some low speed performance for a better performance at high speeds. This will mean that on some occasions, when the thermal lift is very weak, he will have a problem in keeping airborne. In good conditions with strong lift the slightly lower rate of climb will be offset by the faster cruising speeds and better gliding angles at those speeds. He is prepared to gamble on the competition being abandoned on poor days in hope of better conditions the next day. In England the same type of glider might find itself committed to an early landing because of a temporary area of poor thermal activity, while other gliders might be able to stay up.

For less experienced pilots flying in weak lift conditions a lighter and slower machine may be better. It will probably circle at a much lower speed, which will enable it to make use of smaller thermals. Of course, it will not have the good performance at high speeds, but that is not important for local soaring or short cross-country flights. It will also be a good deal less expensive since it can have a smaller wing span and does not need to be quite so perfectly streamlined.

Fig. 68 shows the designer's estimate for a high-performance machine. These estimated polars are usually checked by tests at one or two points and then amended to make them more accurate. If the manufacturer over-estimates the performance the word soon gets round that it is far worse than claimed. On the other hand, if he is honest and states a performance which is not as good as that claimed by a rival manufacturer, no one buys his glider! (It's a hard life with little profit, and most manufacturers just enjoy the challenge of producing a good machine, hoping to recover their costs and make a profit on some other product such as furniture.)

The rate of sink of the glider in Fig. 68 at a certain speed, say 60 knots, is found by measuring down to the curve at the 60 knot point and reading off the rate of sink against the side scale. If compatible units are used for both scales, for example the airspeed in knots and the rate of sink in knots (1 knot is almost exactly equal to 100 feet per minute) the actual glide may be found by simply dividing the speed by the sink rate. I have done this for the whole polar and the lower curve shows glide angles against the speed.

For our purposes the actual figures do not matter but it is very important to understand a little about gliding performance. Any glider pilot may need to know how to get the best out of his glider in order to get back to the field safely if he has allowed himself to drift off too far downwind. Most importantly, he must know what *not* to do in these circumstances.

First of all a general look at the two curves. Near the top of the curve there is quite a wide range of speeds where the rate of sink only varies a little. Then, as might be expected, as the speed is increased by lowering the nose of the glider, the rate of sink and the glide angle get worse and worse. The performance deteriorates at lower speeds also. Although the nose position is high and it may look from the cockpit as though the glide is flat, the glider is in fact mushing down with a high rate of sink. The curve stops

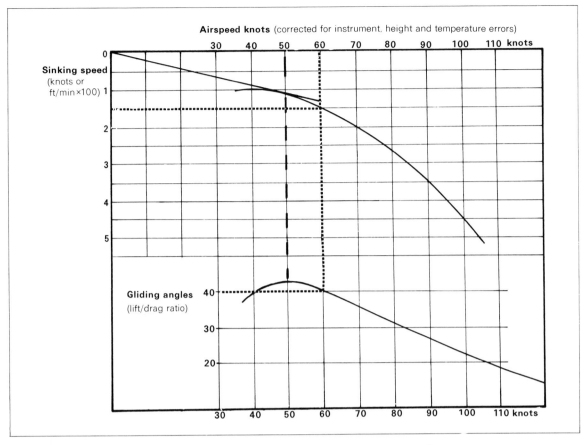

68 The polar curve may be used to calculate a performance curve showing the gliding angle (L/D ratio) achieved throughout the speed range. In the graph above the rate of sink at 60 knots is 1.5 knots and therefore the gliding angle is 60 ÷ 1.5 = 40:1. Small errors caused by slight vertical movements of the air during tests can give misleading results.

abruptly at about 35 knots as the glider cannot be flown steadily below that speed without stalling. It does not, therefore, pay to fly at the slowest possible speed.

When it is necessary to make progress against the wind and travel the maximum distance for a given amount of height, it pays to increase the speed to well above that found from the polar curve for the best gliding angle. This is most easily understood by thinking of a glide against a very strong wind. In this instance the glider would make little or no progress over the ground if it was flown slowly. However, by increasing the speed the glider penetrates the wind and goes further. The optimum speed for penetration in these circumstances can be found from the polar, but for practical purposes it is good enough to fly at the best gliding angle speed plus one-third of the wind speed and to increase the speed still further in sinking air.

The polar curve is also used to calculate the best speeds for cruising between thermals, and most experienced pilots carry a simple pocket computer in order to estimate how far the glider will go from any given height and the optimum speed for the conditions. (This 'speed to fly' computer is simply explained in my first book, *Gliding*.)

The gliding angle and the lift/drag ratio

The glide angle in still air depends only on the proportion of lift to drag. It has nothing to do with the weight of the aircraft. In steady flight the weight has to be balanced by the combination of the lift and the drag but the glidepath will depend on the proportion of these ingredients only. Fig. 13 on page 36 showed some examples of the balance of forces in a glide at various angles.

It can be proved very simply that the glide angle is always the same as the angle in the triangle formed by the lift and drag. This angle is always proportional to the magnitude of the lift and drag. (If it is a long time since you were at school and you have forgotten about force diagrams and the balance of forces, they are simply explained in Appendix B.)

Extra weight does affect the airspeed required for steady flight, but because both lift and drag increase with the square of the speed the best glide angle is unchanged, provided that the glider is flown at the correct speed. If the speed is increased by the right amount for the extra weight, the lift and drag remain in the same ratio because the glider is still meeting the air at the most efficient angle. The extra speed needed for an increase in weight is very small, but since the machine is going down the same slope at a higher speed the rate of descent is higher. A heavily loaded glider flown correctly will glide just as far when flying between thermals but will always be outclimbed by a lighter machine.

If the speed of a heavily loaded glider is not increased the extra lift can only come from the wing meeting the air at a larger angle. This angle will then be too large for efficiency and the gliding angle will suffer.

A heavily loaded glider will normally keep the same glide angle at a higher speed and this fact is used to advantage in good conditions by many competition gliders. If the weather is good enough to be sure of strong lift in the thermals, the gliders are loaded up with water held in rubber bags or suitable tanks in the wings. An extra 200 lb (90 kilos) of weight may increase the cruising speed by 4 or 5 knots and this increase will be well worth while for a flight of several hours' duration, particularly if it happens to be against the wind. Now that gliding angles of over 40:1 are not uncommon, any further improvement in performance is becoming very difficult to obtain and even slight design changes can make a significant difference. One surprising bonus can come from carrying extra weight, as we have seen. Far from spoiling the gliding angle it may, in fact, improve it. The rather small chord of the wingtips on some machines is actually more efficient at the slightly higher speeds needed with extra weight. For example, the theoretical performance curves for the Kestrel show an improvement in the best gliding

69 Aspect ratio. The induced drag is inversely proportional to the aspect ratio. For maximum efficiency a glider needs a high aspect ratio as this reduces the wingtip vortexes by improving the lift and reducing the drag.

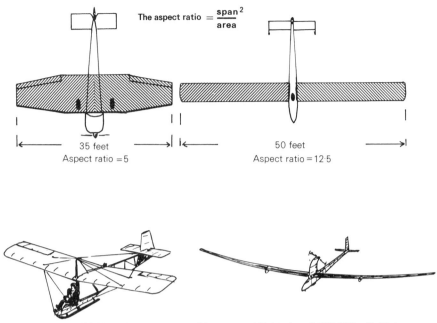

The aspect ratio $= \dfrac{\text{span}^2}{\text{area}}$

35 feet
Aspect ratio = 5

50 feet
Aspect ratio = 12·5

Primary glider (SG 38) with low aspect ratio (Gliding angle 12 : 1)

Manpowered flight aircraft (SUMPA) with high aspect ratio (Gliding angle 38 : 1)

angle from 43:1 at 48 knots, when it is flown at an all-up weight of 880 lb, to over 44:1 at 53 knots with an extra 160 lb carried. This extra efficiency tends to offset some of the increase in the rate of sink normally associated with a higher wing loading and extra weight. However, the penalty of a larger turning radius remains which is a handicap in small, weak thermals.

Since the gliding angle depends solely on the ratio between the lift and drag it can be improved either by increasing the lift or decreasing the drag.

The lift can be increased by the use of a more efficient aerofoil and by having a larger wing span for a given wing area (Fig. 69). The ratio of span to the area, or to be precise the span²/area is known as the 'aspect ratio' (A.R.). With a high aspect ratio (large span and small wing chord) a smaller percentage of the wing is affected by the airflow leaking around the wingtip from the higher pressure below the wing to the reduced pressure above it. The loss at the wingtips can be reduced by increasing the span and by using a tapered wing. The lift should ideally be distributed elliptically along the span of the wing as this reduces losses at the wingtips.

Obviously any leakage of air through the wing surface itself will ruin the lift in that area as well as creating extra drag. Every effort must be made to eliminate any leakage through the airbrake boxes and aileron and flap hinges and at the fuselage to wing junction. A poorly designed wing root fairing can seriously reduce the lift at that point and in many instances the success or failure of a particular type of glider can be traced to the design of the wing to fuselage junction. Wing root joins should always be sealed with adhesive tape – a simple and inexpensive way of improving performance.

Once there is a reasonably efficient wing to provide the lift, the all-important factor governing the performance is drag. A flatter gliding angle can then only be obtained by reducing the total drag. The drag of a glider may be considered as the total drag from various sources, and although some of these are inter-related it is easiest to take them one at a time.

Induced drag Some of the wing drag is inevitably created as lift is produced and this cannot be entirely eliminated. This is known as induced drag. There is always a bad area of turbulence at the wingtips where the effect of the wing pushing the air downwards suddenly stops. A wing with a high aspect ratio has better lift and far less induced drag than a stubby, wide chord one. A long wing affects more air in a given time and a much smaller proportion of the wing is affected by the vortex at the tip. This makes it more efficient.

If the airflow were visible it would be possible to see a definite vortex swirling back behind each wingtip. Fig. 70 shows why this happens. Above the wing the airflow has a slightly reduced pressure and below the wing the pressure is increased so that the air passing below the wingtip tends to flow out and round onto the top surface. This movement influences all the airflow below the wing and results in it flowing very slightly outwards. The flow

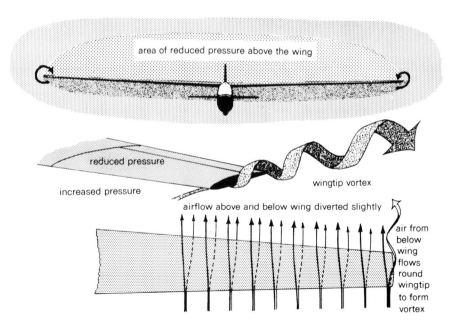

70 Induced drag. Because of the differences in pressure above and below the wing, air flows round the wingtips forming vortexes which create drag. These are worse when the wing is at a large angle of attack and at low speeds.

above the wing is also slightly affected so that it tends to flow inwards across the top surface. This results in the two airstreams meeting at an angle at the trailing edge of the wing causing turbulence and extra drag. These eddies are swept up together near the wingtip to form one large vortex. The vortex will be worst when the angle of attack is large, because that is when the difference in pressure is greatest. This normally happens when the aircraft is flying slowly but may also occur when the machine is turning very tightly or pulling sharply out of a dive. These wingtip vortexes can sometimes be seen at air displays when a high-speed aircraft makes a tight, steep turn. The reduction in pressure over the wing is sufficient to cool the air and condense the moisture out to form a trail of cloud for a few seconds. The cloud is limited to the extreme wingtips and shows the vortex clearly. It is sometimes possible to hear the noise made by this swirling air after the aircraft has flown low overhead.

When the wing is brought to a large angle of attack the difference in pressure above and below it is increased so that there is a strong tendency for the air from below to spill round the wingtip. In addition, at low speed there is more time for the airflow to be diverted. Induced drag is therefore greatest at low speeds and large angles of attack, and becomes less and less as the speed is increased and the angle of attack reduced.

A high aspect ratio is particularly important for gliders which need to be efficient at low speeds. It enables them to circle tightly with a low rate of descent to make the best use of thermals and to have a very flat gliding angle for maximum range. It is also an advantage for other aircraft where economy and long range are important since a better lift to drag ratio will reduce the power required for cruising flight and so save fuel.

Tapered wings   It should be fairly obvious that a short span wing of large constant chord will have a serious loss of efficiency at the wingtip unless something is done to reduce the differences in pressure above and below the wing at that point.

The best way of lessening the wingtip vortexes is to taper the wings towards the tips in order to reduce the amount of lift developed there. It can be shown theoretically that the best shape for lift distribution is elliptical (as in Fig. 71) and an elliptically shaped wing like those of the Battle of Britain Spitfires can be used but it is expensive and complicated to make and shows no improvement in practice over simpler forms of taper. With a high aspect ratio wing, as on a glider, an elliptical shape would give a negligible advantage and a straight wing with tapered portions towards the tips would almost certainly be better. This is because it is easier to keep a really accurate wing section on a straight taper and also because there is a serious loss of efficiency if the wing chord becomes too small. (Pointed wingtips are very inefficient.)

A small amount of twist or 'washout' at the wingtip to reduce the angle of incidence may also have much the same effect as taper in reducing the lift and therefore the wingtip losses. However, this is not efficient at higher

71 Wing shapes or plan forms. For maximum efficiency the lift distribution should be elliptical. Tapered wings are lighter and more efficient but cost more to produce.

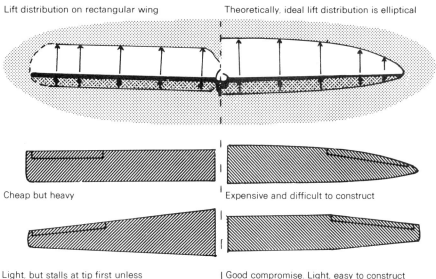

Lift distribution on rectangular wing

Theoretically, ideal lift distribution is elliptical

Cheap but heavy

Expensive and difficult to construct

Light, but stalls at tip first unless washout is used

Good compromise. Light, easy to construct and efficient

speeds when the wingtip may be meeting the air at a negative angle and producing a down load instead of useful lift. The effect of this may be seen when a large span glider with washout dives steeply at high speed. The wingtips are bent downwards by this negative lift, as in Fig. 72. (The more usual reason for using more than 1° or 2° of washout is that the test flights have shown the glider to have a rather severe wing drop at the stall. Washout reduces this tendency by keeping the angle of attack of the tips well below that of the main part of the wing which ensures that the wingtips do not stall first.)

The tapered wing has another important advantage besides reducing the induced drag. Since the lift is reduced towards the wingtips, the bending loads at the centre of the wing are also considerably reduced and this will make the tapered wing much lighter and stronger. With the maximum bending and shear loads at the wing root, the larger chord, and therefore deeper aerofoil section, at the wing roots of the tapered wing will leave more room for a good deep spar to provide plenty of strength where it is needed.

Tapered wings also give better control response. Less wing area at the wingtips reduces the resistance of the wing to rolling movements, and the fact that the greater part of the weight of the wing is nearer the centre reduces the inertia forces which the ailerons have to overcome. The net result is that a tapered wing will usually be more efficient, lighter, and have a better aileron response than the equivalent wing of constant chord.

The major disadvantages of tapered wings are the extra cost and complication, and the problems of stalling tip first. The tendency to stall tip first

72 The effects of washout at low and high speeds. At high speeds, wingtips may be producing negative lift and extra drag.

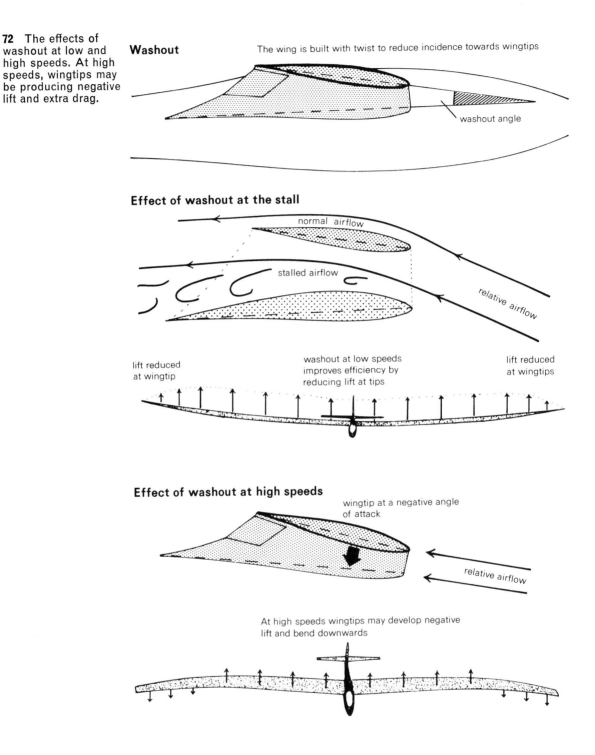

Washout

The wing is built with twist to reduce incidence towards wingtips

washout angle

Effect of washout at the stall

normal airflow

stalled airflow

relative airflow

lift reduced at wingtip

washout at low speeds improves efficiency by reducing lift at tips

lift reduced at wingtips

Effect of washout at high speeds

wingtip at a negative angle of attack

relative airflow

At high speeds wingtips may develop negative lift and bend downwards is caused by the smaller size of the chord at the tip. A shorter chord is always inclined to stall at a slightly smaller angle of attack. This tendency can be reduced by selecting an aerofoil which has a very gradual, gentle stall instead of a sudden complete breakaway, or by changing the aerofoil at the tips to one with a later stall. If this fails and test flights show that the stall is still unacceptable, the last resort, other than to build a completely new wing, is to use more washout. This will mean an inevitable loss in performance, particularly at high speed.

With smaller gliders the designer is faced with various possibilities. If he uses a tapered wing it will have a very small chord at the wingtip which may result in low efficiency and bad stalling characteristics. A wing of parallel chord and high aspect ratio may be more practical and just as efficient. It can also be considerably less expensive to produce, particularly with metal construction.

The shape of the wingtip itself can have an important effect on the total induced drag of the wing and much research has gone into trying to produce the best possible shape for high lift and low drag. The present trend is for wingtips to be almost square cut to keep an accurate wing section for as long as possible. The final few inches of wing is then often swept up towards the trailing edge. If the wingtip is well designed the airflow can be encouraged to peel off cleanly into the main wingtip vortex. Very short wing chords and rounded and pointed tips are not as efficient and the amount of taper is often limited on smaller gliders by the need to keep the chord at the wingtip a reasonable size.

A few gliders have small, streamlined shapes at the extreme wingtip but these are usually a practical device to prevent wearing away the wingtip or aileron on the ground, rather than an attempt to stop, or reduce, wingtip vortexes. Even if they do reduce the induced drag very slightly, the shapes themselves create extra form drag and so reduce the performance at higher speeds (Fig. 73). Other designs have the wingtips bent downwards.

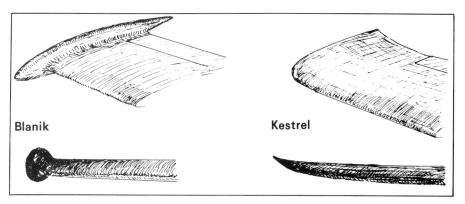

Blanik   Kestrel

73 Wingtip shapes.

Form or profile drag   The remainder of the wing drag, caused by the aerofoil shape and skin friction, is usually known as the profile drag. Similar drag created by non-lifting parts of the aircraft, such as the fuselage and tail, is known as form drag.

There is not much that the designer can do about the form drag of the wing except to select the aerofoil carefully and eliminate such things as poorly-shaped wing root junctions and control horns. However, the form drag of the rest of the aircraft can be reduced by having the minimum possible frontal area and by careful attention to the streamlining (Fig. 74). Even this can be taken too far, and many machines suffer from having uncomfortably cramped cockpits, some too small for even an average-sized pilot. This is ridiculous, as the lessening of drag resulting from reducing the cockpit by an inch or so can never offset the losses in performance caused by the pilot being uncomfortable. Except in training machines, when performance is of secondary importance compared with ease of operating, a main landing skid has become obsolete and the main wheel is invariably retractable for drag reduction.

Tailplane drag and the drag of the fin and rudder must be kept as low as possible by making them only just big enough to do their job of stabilising the aircraft. Since they both work like a miniature wing, a moderately high aspect ratio is preferable to very short, stubby surfaces. Unfortunately, whenever the tailplane is producing an up or down load there will be tip vortexes, as with a normal wingtip. In a modern glider this may be one of the largest sources of drag, particularly when the glider is badly out of trim so that the tail is having to produce a large stabilising force all the time. In this respect the glider with a minimum of fore and aft stability is more efficient since the tail loads are far less and therefore the induced drag of the tailplane is lower. Competition pilots frequently ballast their machines to bring the centre of gravity back to the rear limit in order to reduce the stability and minimise this source of drag.

A considerable amount of drag is also caused by the interference between the wing and fuselage and the fuselage and tail. This is one factor which

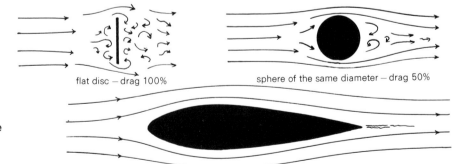

flat disc – drag 100%   sphere of the same diameter – drag 50%

74 The reduction of form drag with streamlining. Since the form drag increases with the square of the speed, streamlining is very important.

streamlined shape of the same diameter – drag 5%

usually upsets the calculations made of the performance of a proposed glider and is best studied in a wind tunnel. Very slight changes in a fairing at the wing root will often make an unbelievable improvement in the performance.

Skin friction Now that gliders are all very streamlined, one of the best hopes for more efficient performances lies in reducing the skin friction. This alone could be the subject of several volumes but the essential facts are fairly simple.

Skin friction is the drag caused by the airflow moving over the surface of a body. The layers of air close to the surface are slowed down by the friction in the same way as the wind near the surface of the ground is slowed down, creating the wind gradient described in Chapter 3. In general, the rougher the surface the greater the skin friction, which increases rapidly with speed like most other forms of drag.

The airflow is only slowed down in a region very close to the surface, known as the boundary layer. This layer is about 0.01 inches (0.3 mm) thick at first, but as the air moves further along the surface the thickness of the boundary layer increases many times until near the trailing edge of the wing

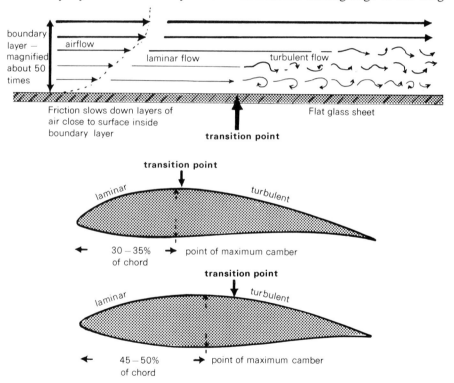

75 Laminar and turbulent airflow in the boundary layer. Even over a flat glass sheet the airflow in the boundary layer changes from laminar to turbulent after quite a short distance. The boundary layer starts very thin (about one hundredth of an inch) but becomes much thicker, until at the trailing edge of a wing it may be an inch or more deep.

it may be as much as an inch. The air inside this layer may be either laminar or turbulent (Fig. 75) and this has a significant effect on the amount of drag caused by skin friction.

Laminar flow   When the boundary layer has laminar flow, the layers of air slide smoothly over each other. The layer in contact with the surface is stationary and each successive layer above it is moving a little faster until, at the top of the boundary layer, the air is moving at the speed of the main airflow, i.e. it is not slowed down at all by skin friction. Unfortunately, it is difficult to keep the flow laminar for long. Even with air flowing over a perfectly flat glass surface, the boundary layer gradually thickens and then suddenly breaks up into very tiny eddies. The point at which this occurs is known as the 'transition point'. The total amount of skin friction depends upon the speed and on how much of the flow is laminar and how much is turbulent. For a high-performance glider it is very important to try and keep the flow laminar for as long as possible over *all* the parts of the aircraft.

Various factors influence how much laminar flow can be maintained before the inevitable change at the transition point. If the surface is rough or wavy the flow will only remain laminar for a short distance. The transition point is also affected by the pressure gradient over the surface. For example, the flow will remain laminar for much longer if the airflow is still accelerating, so that the pressure is dropping. If the airflow is slowing down the boundary layer gets thicker and stagnates so that it changes to turbulent flow. Fig. 76 shows various types of aerofoil including some specially designed to maintain laminar flow over more of the surface, which are known as laminar flow aerofoils. In reality, all aerofoils for gliders have some laminar flow. The modern, low drag sections are designed to keep much more laminar flow by shaping the section to give a more gradual acceleration of the airflow over the surfaces. The distinctive difference is that the maximum depth of the section is much further back, often at the 50% point of the chord. With each type of aerofoil section there is only a limited range of flying speeds and angles of attack within which a worthwhile amount of laminar flow will occur. At

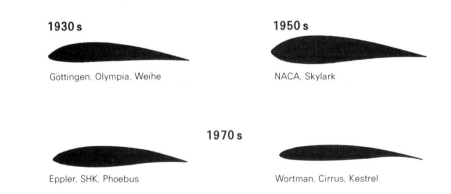

1930s

Göttingen, Olympia, Weihe

1950s

NACA, Skylark

76 Types of aerofoil. Examples of the common families of aerofoil section used on gliders.

1970s

Eppler, SHK, Phoebus

Wortman, Cirrus, Kestrel

118

large angles the flow is already slowing down much earlier along the wing surface so that the transition point is moved forward.

The glider designer tries to select an aerofoil which has the low drag range coinciding with the cruising speed range. Unfortunately, some of the lowest drag sections have only a narrow range of speeds, or else have poor characteristics outside that range. Others are hypersensitive to the surface finish so that the performance is completely ruined by the lightest drizzle or dust on the wing.

Some aerofoils which work beautifully in the low drag range suffer serious drag losses at lower speeds. Unfortunately, a laminar boundary layer does not adhere to the surface contours as well as a turbulent one and sometimes the flow will peel off, leaving a thick wedge of turbulent air. This will cause both a loss in lift and a serious drag rise, so that the glider may turn out to have a worse performance than one with an old-fashioned wing section. Laminar separation, as this is known, may be detected by premature pre-stall buffet or a change in the sound of the airflow. The loss in performance may not be very obvious except when the glider is being flown in close proximity to other machines, when the poor rate of climb may become obvious. Careful performance tests may also reveal this kind of trouble.

Whereas with most older sections the glider may be flown very close to the stall without significant loss, it is not advisable to fly the majority of modern machines in this manner. Any slight turbulence would result in separation and buffeting and would cost valuable height. Only careful experiments with various speeds and angles of bank while flying with other gliders will show whether there are serious losses on a particular aircraft when it is flown at low speeds. One absolute rule, however, is that modern gliders should not be flown at speeds where any obvious buffet can be felt or heard – extra noise is always an indication of extra drag.

With model aircraft it is quite common practice to use a turbulator to change the boundary layer flow from laminar to turbulent deliberately. This usually consists of a strand of cotton or wire mounted just ahead of the leading edge, or on the top surface of the wing in order to set up the tiny eddies. A turbulent boundary layer adheres to the surface much better than a laminar one and this delays the stall. The use of a turbulator enables the model to be consistently flown at lower speeds which in turn result in lower rates of descent. At model speeds, skin friction is usually less important than with full-sized machines.

On many modern designs the angle of the whole trailing edge section of the wing can be adjusted both up and down. This changes the camber, and thereby the lift of the wing, without changing the basic angle of attack of the all-important leading edge and front portion of the wing. The trailing edge is hinged into a simple flap and the ailerons are moved up or down a little with it to give the effect of changing the wing section along the complete wing span. A wider range of speeds is then possible over which the flow is kept laminar, as well as an increase in lift at low speeds so that both the thermalling and landing speeds are reduced. An added bonus is the maintenance at a wider range of speeds of more laminar flow over the fuselage nose, since the change of attitude of the fuselage is reduced.

In an effort to achieve the optimum performance a few designers have tried to eliminate the airbrakes from the wings and rely on a tail parachute or trailing edge flaps instead. It is virtually impossible to make the airbrakes fit perfectly without some imperfection or air leak and this will destroy any hope of keeping laminar flow behind them. The airbrakes are, therefore, usually fitted just behind the transition point in order to keep as much laminar flow as possible. Trailing edge flaps are also well behind the transition point but inevitably cause some increase in drag because they spoil the shape of the aerofoil slightly, and cause an extra loss if the air leaks through any gaps. Any leakage from the region of higher pressure below the wing to the area of reduced pressure above it will not only drastically reduce the lift but will also set up turbulence and cause a much earlier transition from laminar to turbulent flow in that area.

It may seem tempting for the designer of the ultimate sailplane to eliminate these losses by doing away with any form of airbrake and relying instead on a tail parachute. However, this would make landing in a confined space so worrying for the pilot that he might be forced to land prematurely rather than risk damage by flying on over bad field landing country.

Although the wing drag is a very significant factor because of the extremely large areas of surface involved, the designer of a really high-performance machine must also strive for the maximum amount of laminar flow over the nose of the fuselage. This is the main reason for the much cleaner modern shapes. Any joint or discontinuity over the first 4 or 5 feet of the nose and cockpit will result in a change from laminar to turbulent flow, with a consequent increase in skin friction.

Once the airstream has become turbulent the surface finish is far less important. However, the skin friction of the remainder of a fuselage, for example, can be reduced by slimming down the shape as far as possible in order to reduce the 'wetted' area. If the change in shape is too rapid the airflow may separate, leaving an extensive turbulent wake and very high drag. This can be a difficult problem to solve because of the need to keep the drag very low throughout a wide range of speeds when the fuselage meets the air at various angles. The wing root joint to the fuselage is a particularly important area since both lift and drag can be seriously affected by poor flow, or premature flow breakaway, in this area.

Since the total drag of a glider flying at 60 m.p.h. may be as low as 20–30 lb, unnecessary protuberancies such as nose skids, pitot heads and ventilators cannot be tolerated. The drag of a whip aerial about 2 feet long mounted on top of the fuselage is probably about 5 lb at that speed, reducing the gliding angle from 30:1 to 27:1!

Unless you actually own the glider it is difficult to change such fittings. However you can improve the performance, or rather get the maximum

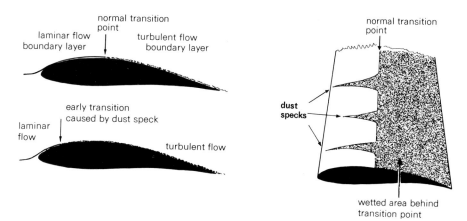

77 The effect of dust and dirt on the wing surface. Behind each speck of dust the airflow close to the surface becomes turbulent, creating extra skin friction. It is particularly important to keep the leading edge and first half of the wing clean and perfectly smooth.

performance that the machine can give you, by cleaning the surfaces really carefully. Any dust or fly dirt on the wings results in an immediate change to turbulent flow at that point. This can sometimes be demonstrated at the end of a day's flying if dew has fallen onto the wings just before the last flight. Fig. 77 shows what to look for. Behind each speck of dust, however small, the surface is wetted in the shape of a V where the flow has become turbulent.

The 'wetting' is rather similar to the result of drawing a finger over the surface of a mirror which has been misted over with steam. The turbulent flow is sufficient to stir up the tiny moisture droplets so that its extent may be clearly seen. The surprising thing is the very large area of spoilt flow behind the slightest speck of dust or dirt.

The position of the transition point further back along the aerofoil can also be seen clearly by this 'wetting'. On most training gliders, which are partly fabric covered, the cause of the change can be traced to a bump at the main spar, or a poorly finished fabric joint in that area.

Once you have actually seen this effect, the importance of keeping the wing surface absolutely clean is obvious. Never rest the leading edge, or any part of the wing surface, on rough ground during rigging and de-rigging. It only takes a moment to make a mark that will need many hours of careful work to fill and bring back to a perfect surface again.

Of course, the minute there is any rain or ice on the surface there is no hope of keeping laminar flow and the performance drops catastrophically. In flight, the pilot must avoid icing or rain like the plague. If there is any risk of icing only a very rapid gain of height can compensate for it. Unless the gain is likely to be an extremely large one or unless the prospect of any other lift is remote, it is usually better to stay out of cloud.

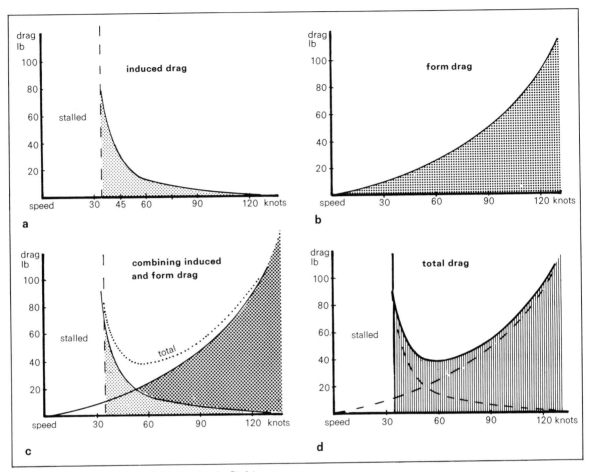

78 The drag curve for a glider in steady flight.

Total drag   Having discussed the various forms of drag it is interesting to see the way in which they influence the performance of an aircraft.

Form drag varies with the square of the speed and builds up very rapidly as the speed is increased (Fig. 78**b**). However, the induced drag behaves in a totally different manner. It is at a maximum at low speed when the wing is at a large angle of attack and decreases steadily, until at high speed it is almost negligible (Fig. 78**a**).

By combining these two drag curves (Fig. 78**c** and **d**), it becomes apparent that the total drag of an aircraft is at its lowest near normal cruising speeds. Much more power is required to fly it at either higher or lower speed. This explains why the glider has much higher drag and therefore a steeper gliding angle when it is flown too slowly *or* too fast.

In a light aircraft or motor glider there are two possible cruising speeds for each power setting, except the very minimum for level flight. One is at a very low speed with the aircraft mushing along in a nose high attitude with high induced drag, and the other is at a much higher speed in a normal flying attitude. A beginner will occasionally get his machine flying at the lower speed without realising how or why this has happened. It is usually the result of levelling out from a climb by reducing the power, instead of first lowering the nose to gain speed and then throttling back to cruising power. (See Fig. 138 on page 229.)

Boundary layer control

Recent experience and research has shown that many aerofoils have problems caused by laminar 'bubbles'. These are the result of the flow separating away from the surface and reattaching itself again a little further along the aerofoil. This has the same effect as a bulge in the wing section and causes a large increase in the drag.

Usually these bubbles occur towards the rear of the aerofoil. They can be eliminated by triggering the airflow in the boundary layer to change it from laminar to turbulent flow just ahead of the position where the separation is occurring. As a turbulent boundary layer adheres to the surface better than one with laminar flow, the bubble is elminated. In spite of the higher drag of the turbulent boundary layer, the overall drag is reduced by eliminating the bulge of the laminar bubble.

A simple form of turbulator is a self-adhesive plastic tape about the thickness of a postcard, cut in a zig-zag shape and running span wise along the wing. Another system is to blow air out through hundreds of tiny holes in the surface of the wing just ahead of the point where the laminar bubble forms. This has the advantage that the degree of blowing can be varied according to requirement at different speeds. However, it is a much more expensive method than adding on the tape.

The exact position of any laminar bubble must be found by experiment or very careful wind tunnel work. If the flow is changed too early, the extra skin friction caused by the turbulent boundary layer may be greater than the saving obtained by eliminating the laminar bubble.

This kind of technique is also useful for both stabilisers and fins and rudders, where the change in the control surface angle may cause early separation, making the control less effective with higher drag.

On some aerofoils, such turbulators have been used to advantage on both the top and bottom surfaces of wings. Probably no other form of aircraft uses such sophisticated means of drag reduction as the modern glider.

5 Airbrakes and other drag producing devices

Airbrakes and spoilers

The need for some kind of drag-producing device on a modern glider is obvious if we consider an approach to land in a field with trees on the boundary. With a gliding angle of more than 1:20 (and often nearer to 1:30) a modern glider crossing the boundary of a field at 50 feet would take more than 300 yards to reach round out height for the landing. Furthermore, it would then float several hundred yards before losing flying speed for the touchdown. This would obviously be quite unacceptable unless all fields were very large and completely unobstructed.

The solution is to use some kind of airbrakes or flaps for landing. The simplest kind of airbrakes are known as spoilers and consist of a hinged surface on the top of the wing which is raised into the airflow to spoil the lift and create drag over part of the wing. These can be quite effective with a low-performance glider but would not be of much value with a high-performance machine.

Airbrakes may be fitted to either the upper or lower surface of the wing, or more commonly to both. They are much larger and more effective than spoilers. The top surface airbrakes, like spoilers, result in a marked decrease in lift over that part of the wing, so that the stalling speed is usually raised by 2–3 knots. However, the main effect of airbrakes comes from the large increase in drag caused by the turbulence around and behind the airbrake paddles.

The opening of either airbrakes or spoilers results in a large increase in drag together with a decrease in the lift. This spoils the lift-to-drag ratio so that the gliding angle becomes much steeper. In order to maintain the same speed, the nose of the glider has to be lowered or the extra drag will cause a loss of speed. However, at any moment spoilers or airbrakes can, if necessary, be closed to restore the normal gliding angle. The increase in drag also shortens the distance which the glider will float after the round out, and, with skill, the touchdown can be controlled consistently to within a few yards by adjusting the airbrakes during the float.

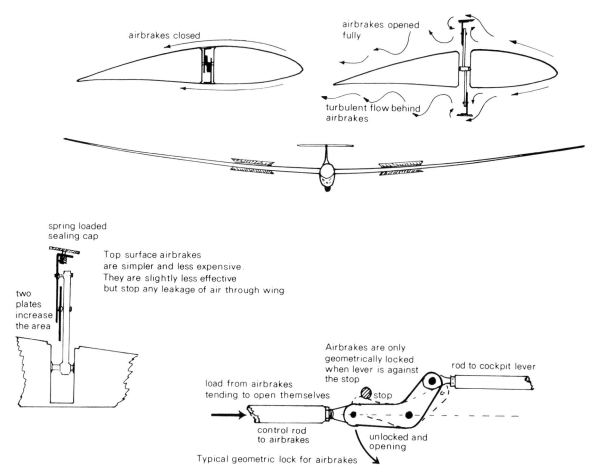

airbrakes closed

airbrakes opened fully

turbulent flow behind airbrakes

spring loaded sealing cap

two plates increase the area

Top surface airbrakes are simpler and less expensive. They are slightly less effective but stop any leakage of air through wing

Airbrakes are only geometrically locked when lever is against the stop

rod to cockpit lever

load from airbrakes tending to open themselves

stop

control rod to airbrakes

unlocked and opening

Typical geometric lock for airbrakes

79 Airbrakes. Unlike spoilers, these airbrakes tend to be sucked open in flight and a mechanical lock is essential to keep them closed. This is usually a geometric, over-centre lock as illustrated.

The small increase in stalling speed caused by the loss of lift when the airbrakes or spoilers are in use is not altogether a bad thing. It does result in a slightly faster touchdown speed, but at the same time it gives an added margin of safety. If the approach gets a little too slow, or the glider balloons up or undershoots the landing area, closing the airbrakes lowers the drag and increases the lift. This is almost equivalent to a burst of engine power and will often prevent an undershoot or a heavy landing.

The effects and limitations of spoilers and airbrakes must be clearly understood as their misuse will cause a heavy landing. The correct approach speeds are very largely a matter of opinion and vary with the type of machine and the conditions. Perhaps it is best to define the minimum approach speed for starting the round out in no wind and with full airbrake. This is the speed which allows the *round out* to be made without difficulty so that the glider

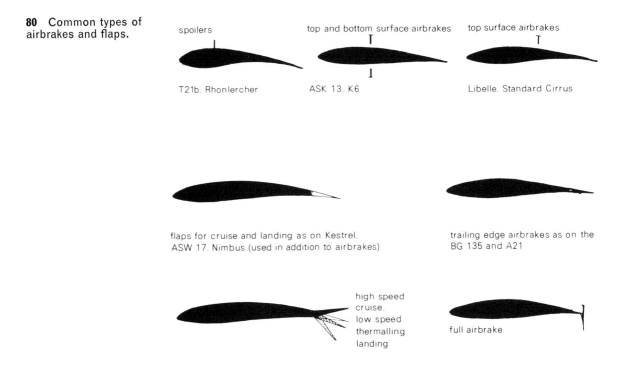

80 Common types of airbrakes and flaps.

spoilers

T21b, Rhonlercher

top and bottom surface airbrakes

ASK 13, K6

top surface airbrakes

Libelle, Standard Cirrus

flaps for cruise and landing as on Kestrel. ASW 17, Nimbus (used in addition to airbrakes)

trailing edge airbrakes as on the BG 135 and A21

high speed cruise. low speed thermalling landing

full airbrake

lands with a short float before touchdown. In winds of over 10–15 knots, this speed will need to be increased by about 5 knots or one-third of the wind speed, to allow for the effects of fluctuations in the wind near the ground, and the wind gradient.

A lower speed may be just adequate if less than full airbrake is used for the landing, because of the improved lift and lower drag. The reduction in drag is significant because of the lower rate of speed loss during the round out and hold off. Heavy landings often occur because there is insufficient speed to give enough control for a proper round out and hold off.

Inexperienced pilots are well advised to choose an approach speed a little above this minimum so that they can use full airbrake without fear of a bad landing. The only disadvantage of extra speed is the need to allow for the extra distance which the glider will float before touchdown. Below this speed, the amount of airbrake has to be restricted to avoid a heavy landing. It requires skill and experience to judge from the feel and response of the controls how much airbrake can be used at these lower speeds and whether the brakes can safely be opened further. Unless the speed is known to be adequate from having allowed extra speed on the approach, the beginner is advised to be prepared to reduce the setting during the round out and landing. Any sudden increase in the rate of descent near the ground is almost certainly a sign of loss of speed (perhaps caused by the wind gradient) and calls for an immediate reduction in the amount of airbrake. This will usually prevent a heavy landing but will also make the glider float beyond the intended touchdown point. Once the airbrake setting has been reduced the stalling speed is lower, so that a normal hold off and landing are usually possible.

If the airbrakes have been closed because of a high rate of descent on the approach, they must not be re-opened as the effect of doing this at low speed near the ground is immediate and often catastrophic. The glider sinks for a few seconds and unless the pilot makes a very quick backward movement on the stick it may hit the ground hard.

Whereas the airbrakes can be safely *closed* at any height or speed, extreme caution must be used when *opening* them close to the ground, particularly if the speed is marginal.

Once on the ground, opening the airbrakes fully will stop any tendency for the glider to leave the ground again in gusty conditions.

In order to understand this more clearly I will give the approximate speeds for a typical training glider such as the ASK 13.

Indicated stalling speed, airbrakes closed	32–33 knots
Indicated stalling speed, airbrakes fully open	35–36 knots
Normal cruising and thermalling speed	42–43 knots
Minimum full airbrake approach speed *in no wind*	50–52 knots
Normal full airbrake approach speed in light winds	55 knots
Normal full airbrake approach speed in strong winds	60 + knots

Note If the speed drops below the normal speed during the final stage of the approach the amount of airbrake being used must be reduced, as follows:

Speed 48–50 knots	Reduce to half airbrake or less
Speed 43–45 knots	Reduce to quarter airbrake or less
Speed 38–40 knots	Close the airbrakes completely

When the pilot is more experienced he needs to learn to adjust the amount of airbrake being used during the hold off. It is often necessary to close the brakes to float over some bad ground and then re-open them in order to land accurately on the remaining space beyond. As the airbrakes are opened the tendency to sink must be checked immediately with a small backward movement on the stick to prevent a premature touchdown.

Trailing edge airbrakes

Trailing edge airbrakes have the advantage of not spoiling the contour and surface of the wing over the most critical area where the airflow is laminar. They usually take the form of a flap on the trailing edge, hinged to open above and below the wing. The operating loads are small because the airload on one part is arranged to balance the airload on the other. They usually extend from the fuselage to the aileron roots so that their area is much greater than the average airbrake. However, because they do not affect the wing lift they are usually no more effective than top and bottom surface airbrakes.

While the approach and landing speed is a few knots lower than with conventional airbrakes and there is less tendency for the aircraft to drop rapidly if they are opened at low speed, there is no bonus of extra lift in hand if the glider balloons or the pilot suddenly realises that he is holding off too high for a normal landing.

Flaps Flaps can also be a means of controlling the approach and landing but their main use is probably for high and low speed cruising.

Efficient high speed cruising requires very low drag and an aerofoil with only a small amount of camber gives a distinct advantage. At low speed, extra camber is needed to produce high lift. Both these requirements can be met if the aerofoil has a flap at the trailing edge which can be raised or lowered in flight. Ideally the whole of the trailing edge of the wing should be adjusted in this way and many modern machines move the ailerons up and down in conjunction with the flap to produce the optimum result. With an efficient plain flap of this kind the effect of lowering the flap and ailerons is mainly an increase in lift for the first 10° of downward movement, and at low speed the total lift-to-drag ratio or gliding angle is almost unaffected by this amount of deflection. However, the stalling speed, and therefore the minimum circling speed, is reduced by 2–3 knots and this is a great advantage in a fast glider. Unfortunately, if the ailerons are drooped more than about 5° the aileron drag and adverse yaw become so excessive that they spoil the handling.

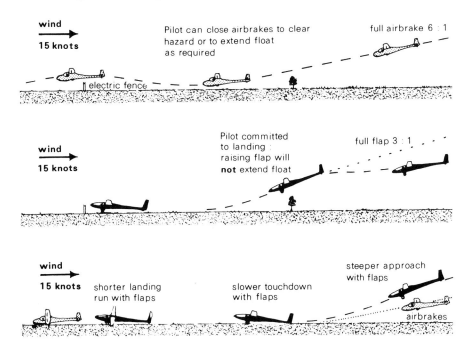

81 A comparison between the effects of airbrakes and landing flaps. Flaps can produce steeper approaches and lower landing speeds but airbrakes are more flexible and allow more accurate spot landings.

In gusty conditions poor handling may limit the amount of aileron droop which can be used to advantage. After about 10° of downward deflection of the flaps the increase in lift is offset by the much greater drag, and although the stalling speed is again reduced the gliding angle is much worse. After about 30° there is little further increase in lift but the drag increases rapidly so that the gliding angle becomes much steeper. The useful range of flap angles for efficient cruising and soaring is therefore very limited. Larger angles are needed for approach control but in this case the ailerons are not drooped at the same time.

The *lowered* stalling speed with flaps down allows a considerably slower approach speed than with airbrakes and, if the flaps can be lowered to more than 45°, the very large area of the flap surface makes even steeper approaches possible than with airbrakes. However, there are several snags with landing flaps. During the final stages of the approach and landing it is impractical to extend the float to clear a fence or rough ground by raising the flap because this would result in a loss of lift and sudden sinking. The pilot must, therefore, be absolutely certain of the landing area before committing himself by lowering a large amount of flap. The designer also has some difficult mechanical problems to overcome if the pilot is to be able to lower the flap quickly at fast approach speeds. The large area of the flaps results in much greater operating force than is necessary with airbrakes and therefore some kind of gearing is normally required.

When the flaps are lowered there is a considerable increase in the twisting load on the wing and speeds must be carefully limited or structural damage may occur. The longitudinal stability is also decreased because the more highly cambered aerofoil is less stable, but this does not normally cause problems.

Tail parachutes The tail parachute, or drogue, is another means of increasing the drag of a modern glider in order to steepen the approach and shorten the landing distance. The parachute is stowed in the rear of the fuselage or bottom of the rudder so that there is virtually no drag penalty when it is not in use. It is deployed by a toggle in the cockpit and, once opened, causes a very large increase in drag. This makes it essential for the nose to be lowered through a considerable angle to maintain the approach speed. The stalling speed is unaffected by the parachute and it would be logical to expect it to be safe to use a lower approach speed than with normal airbrakes. However, the very high drag gives a more rapid deceleration during the round out and hold off and therefore a little extra speed is needed to allow for this. In addition, the effect of the parachute drag at the tail is to increase the fore and aft stability slightly so that the elevator becomes a little less effective. As with all other forms of powerful airbrakes or flaps, a few knots of extra speed result in only a few yards of extra float, whereas a few knots too little means trouble.

Since the drag of the parachute increases very rapidly with extra speed,

82 The installation of a tail parachute.

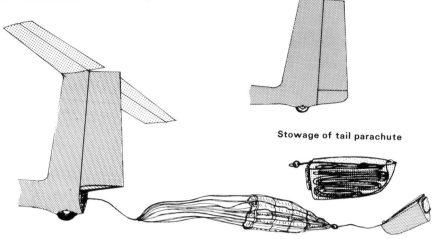

Stowage of tail parachute

any tendency to overshoot the landing area can be reduced by deliberately diving more steeply short of the aiming point. The excess speed will soon be lost during the hold off.

The very large increase in drag when the parachute is open means that the exact speeds and heights for deploying are rather critical. In general the parachute can only be opened safely:

1 at normal approach speeds when there is sufficient time and height to lower the nose to maintain the speed once the parachute is opened (approximately 100 feet or more);

2 at higher speeds when there is insufficient height and time before the start of the round out for the speed to fall below the normal approach speed;

3 very close to the ground when the glider will touch down almost as soon as it starts to decelerate.

If the parachute is deployed too soon and an undershoot seems possible, or if the speed does fall to a critical level, the only solution is to jettison the parachute immediately. However, unless the glider has some other form of airbrake, this may result in an overshoot into the far boundary.

The disadvantages of relying solely on a tail parachute, however effective, are obvious. It is very much a one-shot device and a high degree of skill is necessary for a landing in a really confined space.

In spite of the simplicity of the system, tail parachutes have a dubious reputation and it is not uncommon for them to fail to deploy correctly – such failures are usually the result of poor packing or of the fairing failing to fall away when the release is pulled. It is a wise precaution to make a sharp rudder movement at the moment of deploying the parachute to persuade the parachute container at the bottom of the rudder to free itself.

Sideslipping An alternative to using some form of airbrake on a low-performance machine is to sideslip and use the extra drag of the fuselage moving sideways through the air to spoil the gliding angle (Fig. 83). However, with any gliding angle better than about 16:1 some form of airbrake is really needed in addition to sideslipping.

Most gliders sideslip easily and the combination of full airbrake plus a full sideslip usually gives a high rate of descent. For sideslipping to be of any real use on an approach the glider has to be put into the sideslip very quickly the moment it is apparent that full airbrake is needed continuously and that there is a risk of overshooting.

The angle of bank is often very limited even with full rudder, and varies with the type of glider. The rudder loads usually become very light, or even reverse, during the sideslip. When they reverse, the pilot has to counteract the over-balance effect and use force to centralise the rudder in order to straighten up again (i.e. it will not centralise itself).

For each angle of bank, there is a certain amount of rudder required to hold a steady sideslip and prevent a turn. The airspeed indicator often becomes quite unusable at large angles of yaw so that the speed has to be

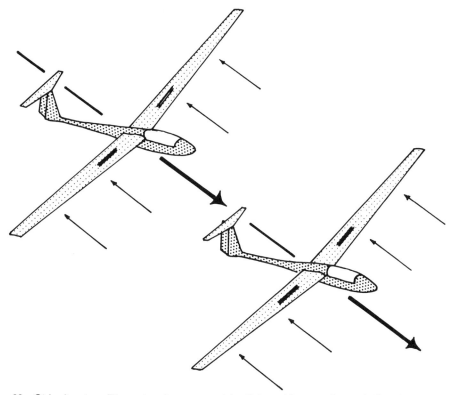

83 Sideslipping. The extra drag caused by flying sideways through the air results in a much steeper glide. The glider is banked to the right but is prevented from turning with left rudder.

guessed during a sideslip. Errors in judging the speed on an approach can be serious, particularly with a modern high-performance machine with ineffective airbrakes. Excessive speed will result in a long float, and possibly an overshoot into the far boundary in a field landing. Constant practice is required to judge the approach speed accurately and to control the glider so that it keeps its heading while sideslipping.

Unless there are high obstructions on the approach the need to sideslip should be taken as an indication that it has been badly mismanaged.

Limitations The normal requirements for gliders specify that drag-producing devices should be stressed for operating at up to the V_{NE} (Never Exceed Speed) and that the force required to operate them should not be excessive.

On most early designs the airbrakes were speed limiting to below V_{NE} in a vertical dive. However, the requirements have since been changed and more recent designs only restrict the speed in a dive of 45 degrees.

Experience seems to show that this is sufficient to limit the speed to a safe level if control is lost in cloud, although it may not be adequate to limit the speed in the event of falling out from inverted flight.

In addition, the airbrakes are required to reduce the gliding angle in the approach configuration to less than 6:1.

It is important to remember that, when the airbrakes are opened, the design load factor is only 3.5 g and not the normal full 5.3 g. (See page 203.)

6 Launching methods

Since many modern glider pilots only have experience of an aerotow launch it is worth describing winch and car launching.

The winch is a safe and efficient way of launching a glider to over 1000 feet in less than a minute but it is becoming less common because of the need to operate from smaller gliding sites and from active airfields. It is also noticeable that many modern glider pilots would rather pay extra to be launched by aerotow than contribute the effort needed to ensure an efficient winch or car launch.

The basic principle of winch or car launching is the same as launching a kite. The aircraft is pulled along the ground until it has sufficient speed to lift off and start to climb. The height it can reach depends mainly on the effective length of run and, in the case of the straight car launch, on the length of cable in use. When launching against a strong wind the glider does not have to be towed along so fast for the required flying speed and the take off is therefore much shorter and there is more time for climbing before the glider is over the winch or car. At the top of the launch the pilot releases the cable and starts his search for a thermal or hill lift. The cable parachute prevents the cable kinking and falling in a tangle after it has been released.

Winching The winch is a stationary vehicle with a power driven drum onto which the launching cable is wound. The cable, or cables in the case of a multi-drum winch, is normally towed out to the glider launching point by tractor.

Another method is for the winch itself to be taken to the launch point and for the cables to be laid by driving out across the field after securing the launching parachutes to suitable anchorages. This eliminates the wear on the cable while it is being laid out ready for launching. The cable may also be pulled out by a light cable with what is known as a retrieve winch. In this case the retrieving cable remains attached to the main cable and is paid out during the launch. Immediately the glider has dropped the cable the retrieve winch pulls it back to the launch point again. Retrieve winches of this kind

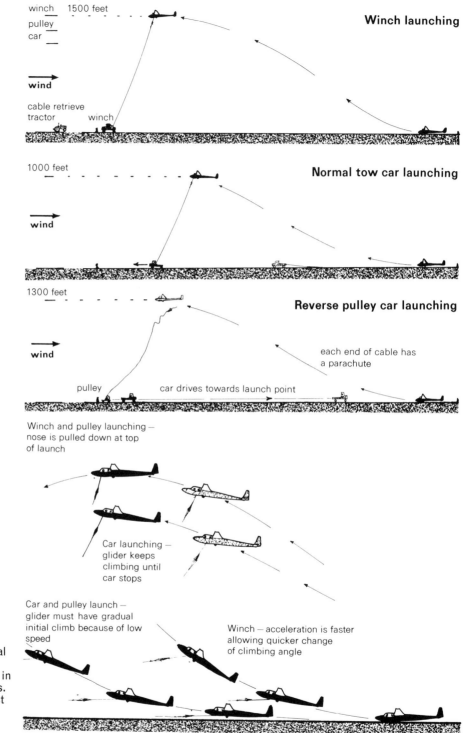

winch ___
pulley ___
car ___

1500 feet

Winch launching

wind →

cable retrieve
tractor   winch

1000 feet

Normal tow car launching

wind →

1300 feet

Reverse pulley car launching

each end of cable has
a parachute

pulley   car drives towards launch point →

Winch and pulley launching —
nose is pulled down at top
of launch

Car launching —
glider keeps
climbing until
car stops

Car and pulley launch —
glider must have gradual
initial climb because of low
speed

Winch — acceleration is faster
allowing quicker change
of climbing angle

84 Comparison
between winch
launching and normal
tow car and reverse
pulley car launching in
light wind conditions.
Winch gives the best
height because of
better acceleration.

are particularly popular on hilltop gliding sites where the ground is not smooth enough for rapid retrieving by a car or tractor, and where the reduction in launch height caused by the extra weight and drag of the retrieve cable is insignificant.

One of the main advantages of a winch is that the engine does not have to drag the weight of the vehicle along but only has to revolve the drum and pull in the cable. This gives it a far better acceleration than either a car or aeroplane.

The cable is usually a multi-strand steel cable similar to that used on glider controls and has 1–2 ton breaking strain. It is sometimes coated with nylon or plastic to reduce the wear.

Car launching

Car launching is only really practical if a smooth track or runway is available since on a calm day the tow car must reach a speed of 50–60 m.p.h. for the take off. The length of wire (which is usually either single-strand steel wire of about 12–14 s.w.g. or ex-service target towing cable) is normally about a quarter of the total available length of the runway for a light wind day. As with winching, an efficient drogue parachute must be used to keep the wire free of kinks as it drops after each launch.

The straight car launch is similar to launching a model kite, except that as the car nears the end of the available run, the driver slows down to signal to the pilot to release. The car is then driven on to allow the whole cable to drop to the ground under the tension of the open drogue parachute. The driver releases his end of the cable, drives back to the parachute, hooks it onto his car and tows the parachute and cable back to the launch point for the next glider. On a 4000–6000 foot runway the launch height should be between 1000 feet and 1500 feet and one tow car can launch 12 gliders an hour. This launch rate can be increased to about 20 an hour by using two similar wires and another car for retrieving. In this case, the arrangement is to ensure that the cable being retrieved is always on the way back as the launching car begins the second run. After the launch the car returns to the end of the first cable ready to launch another machine, leaving the retriever to collect the parachute end of the wire which has just been used.

Reverse pulley systems

Using a reverse pulley system, a large pulley is mounted at the far end of the runway and the launching cable has a drogue parachute at both ends. During the launch the tow car drives towards the take off point with the cable going round the pulley and back to the glider. After the glider has been launched and has released the cable, the tow car continues to the launch point to leave that end of the cable ready to be attached to the next glider. This is a very efficient system unless there are a number of cable breaks. The glider normally gets almost as high as on a winch launch and the skilled pilot can get very high launches indeed. With a winch or reverse pulley car system the reduced winch or car speed in a strong wind gives the glider a much longer wire to climb on and the optimum length of cable is always available regardless of the type of glider. (The cable length for a straight car launch is a compromise. A light, rapid climbing glider could make use of extra cable length whereas a very heavy two-seater would get highest with a slightly shorter cable. The optimum length allows the glider to reach an angle of $75°$–$80°$ to the car by the time it nears the end of the runway. With too much cable the car would reach the end of the run before the glider was anywhere near the top of the cable. With too short a cable the glider reaches the top of it long before the car is at the end of the run and potential height is lost. The exact cable length depends on the length of runway, strength of the wind and type of glider, and the height obtainable is then governed very largely by the speed of the launch and the piloting technique.) With a little practice, the tow car driver soon learns to judge the correct speed by the bow in the cable and the way in which the glider is climbing. The speedometer is not very much help because so much depends on the wind strength and the angle of climb achieved by the glider. An alternative is to have a tension measuring device on the tow car. In this case the pilot's technique is slightly different. The car driver increases speed if the tension drops below the best figure for the type of glider and the pilot adjusts his climb as he might on a powered aircraft, pulling the nose up if the speed is too high and lowering the nose if it is too low. This is contrary to normal practice, when the pilot has no control over the launching speed apart from giving signals to the car or winch driver to ask for more or less speed. A straight car launch in no wind will usually give a launch height of well below one third of the available length of run whereas a winch or reverse pulley can give a much higher launch, especially with a light glider.

Effects of the position of the release hook (Fig. 85.)

The balance of forces during the winch or car launch is not important, but there are various points which need explaining if the pilot is to understand how to make the most of the launch.

During the take-off run and initial climb any sudden load or snatching of the cable will tend to pitch the glider nose up because the cable is pulling through the release hook which is well below the centre of gravity.

If the hook is well *back* towards the centre of gravity, quite a large forward stick movement may be needed to prevent a dangerously steep angle of climb for the first few feet, particularly if the acceleration is fierce.

On gliders such as the Schweizer 222, Capstan and Skylark series, the design requirements stipulated that the hook position should be moved further forward to eliminate the need for this large forward movement on the stick which was considered unacceptable.

There are various arguments for and against the alternative positions for the hook. If it is well forward the pilot has deliberately to pull his aircraft up into a full climb and cannot inadvertently climb too steeply. However, as the glider gets above the first few hundred feet the downward pull on the cable limits the climbing angle so that less height can be gained. The tail loads are also very high and this may result in the need for additional strength and weight just to cater for this particular situation. One advantage is that the load

85 The effect of different release hook positions. The angle of climb is restricted when the hook is near the nose.

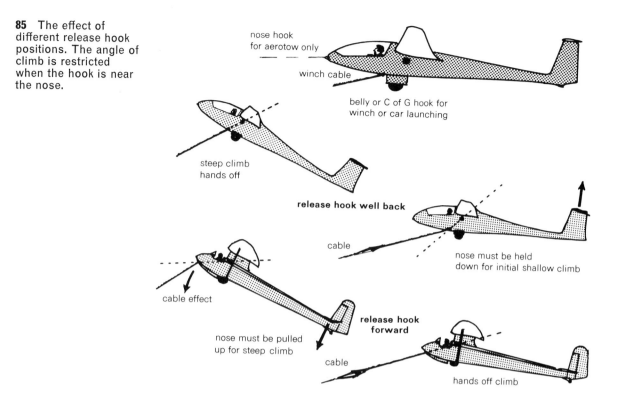

nose hook for aerotow only

winch cable

belly or C of G hook for winch or car launching

steep climb hands off

release hook well back

cable

nose must be held down for initial shallow climb

cable effect

release hook forward

nose must be pulled up for steep climb

cable

cable

hands off climb

on the launching cable can be easily gauged by the force on the stick so that there is less likelihood of the pilot unwittingly breaking the cable or weak link.

With a rather forward hook position the cable loads are balanced by the load on the tail, and near the top of the launch both loads are high and also in opposition. This can result in an unpleasant, and cable-breaking, pitching action or surging. Once this surging has begun, due to a gust or perhaps an inadvertent movement on the elevator, it becomes more and more violent unless the climbing angle is reduced slightly. With skill and practice it is possible to make a correction on the stick to stop this pitching but the beginner will often merely make things worse by attempting a correction and getting the timing wrong. Reducing the climbing attitude will normally prevent the next jerk of the cable and after waiting a few seconds to allow the cable to settle down and stop oscillating, the original climbing angle may be carefully resumed. However, if the nose is raised quickly a further jerk will occur and the pitching oscillation will start all over again.

This pitching only occurs near the top of the launch and is far less common with gliders which have the hook position well back towards the centre of gravity.

Launching speeds The optimum launching speed for most gliders in light winds is about 5–10 knots above normal thermalling speed. In windy conditions more height will be obtained at a slightly slower speed. The minimum cruising speed is also about the minimum safe launching speed for a limited angle of climb.

Above this minimum speed, and at a safe height, a little more speed will be gained by *steepening* the climb. This is explained in Fig. 86. For each foot of distance the tow car moves the glider flies further as it climbs more steeply.

However, if the launch speed becomes less than the minimum for safety while the glider is in, or near, the full climb, the pilot must act quickly to prevent the glider becoming stalled. Reducing the angle of climb will not necessarily result in more speed. Often a bow will develop in the cable, resulting in less, instead of more, speed.

If the speed is just acceptable, the climbing angle should be held and the pilot should be ready with a split-second response to lower the nose into the gliding position if the speed falls any further or if there is any sign of pre-stall buffeting.

If the speed is not sufficient for a safe launch, the nose must be lowered to at least the normal gliding position and the cable released immediately.

When using a winch fitted with a tension indicator or a governor restricting the cable load, the pilot simply pulls up steeper if the speed is too high and reduces the climbing angle to indicate the need for more speed. This greatly simplifies this form of launching.

With a more rearward position of the hook, a forward movement on the stick is essential if the initial climb is to be controlled. A dangerously steep attitude may occur in gusty conditions if the pilot mishandles the situation. However, if the cable does break. the forward position of the stick means that the nose will be lowered automatically when the cable load ceases. A quick reaction is, therefore, not as essential in continental gliders as in British machines where, due to the more backward position of the stick, the nose will be pulled up if the cable breaks.

An extreme position for the hook can be dangerous, since on some machines a backward movement of the stick will be necessary to get the front skid off the ground for take off and only a few seconds later a large forward movement may be needed to prevent a violent transition into a very steep climb. In gusty conditions the pilot must react very quickly or the glider may be left in a dangerously nose high position at low speed if the cable breaks.

A rearward hook position makes a considerably steeper and higher launch possible with a much lower tail load. However, in this case the danger is to overstress the wing, and the launching speed must be kept inside the prescribed limits to prevent structural damage in gusty conditions.

It is common practice, and mandatory in most countries, to incorporate some kind of weak link to limit the load which can be applied to the glider during a launch. This is important because a severe snatch on the cable could otherwise pull the release hook out of its mounting in the fuselage. It also provides some protection against overstressing the glider, either by pull-

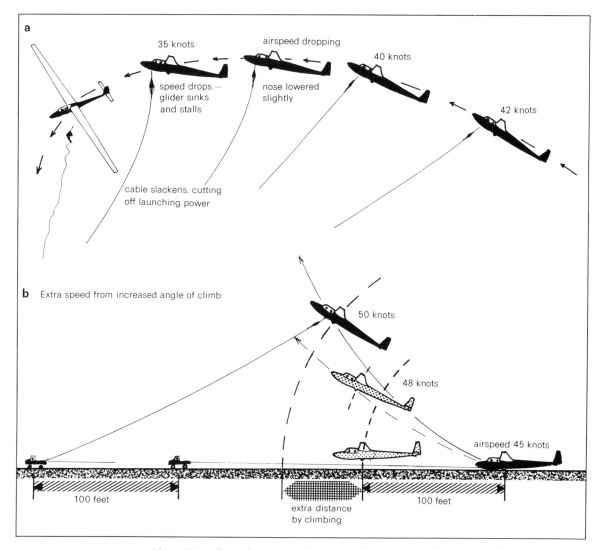

86 a The effect of reducing the angle of climb on a slow launch. **b** Increasing the angle of climb results in more, not less, airspeed.

ing up very steeply at an excessively high speed or from a severe gust. It is still possible to overload the glider momentarily, before the weak link actually fails, and therefore the pilot must be cautious when launching in gusty conditions. The main safeguard lies in limiting the launching speed and in turbulent conditions it is dangerous to exceed the cockpit placard speed for launching while climbing steeply.

During a car or winch launch the loads are very different from those in a steep turn or pull-out from a dive. The bending loads on the wing are greater since they are almost all reacted through the hook to the cable. Although the wing may be developing several times the normal amount of lift, as it does in a well-banked turn, there is no increase in the effective weight of the structure to help reduce the bending loads (see Fig. 87).

If the launching speed is increasing towards the placard speed, the pilot should try to signal immediately by yawing the aircraft from side to side with the rudder, keeping the wings level. Obviously if the glider is already in the full climb it will be wise to reduce the angle slightly to lessen the load in the cable before signalling. Otherwise the extra load caused by swinging the nose from side to side may overstrain the weak link.

During the past few years there has been considerable discussion about the use of a 'too slow' signal, since the glider is always very vulnerable when it is being launched too slowly. The signal used in England was to rock the wings gently if more speed was needed. This needs a stick and rudder movement to avoid any yaw which might be misinterpreted by an inexperienced car or winch driver as a 'too fast' signal. If the speed is really low when the wings are rocked, the movement could induce a tip stall and the glider would tend to spin. The signal certainly has to be used with extreme caution and many instructors now prefer to suggest that the launch should be abandoned by lowering the nose, releasing the cable and proceeding as if the cable had broken.

There have been a number of nasty accidents caused by slow launches – often because of the inborn optimism of the human pilot who expects the launch speed to increase at any moment, whereas it is just as likely to drop if there is a mechanical problem down below. There is a tendency for the pilot to lower the nose a little before signalling on the principle that this will reduce the risk of stalling. Unfortunately, it usually only results in the cable slackening so that the glider is still in a rather nose high position but with no power from the cable to help maintain speed. The additional weight of the cable will add slightly to the stalling speed.

If in doubt, lower the nose well down and release the cable. Do not risk stalling during the launch unless you already have a reasonable launch height. The better acceleration of the winch makes it safe to make the change in climbing angle much more rapidly than with a car launch. For safety, there must be enough speed and height at all times to recover into a normal landing approach without any risk of stalling if the cable should break or the winch or car fail.

With a winch or reverse pulley launch the cable and glider are actually pulled downwards near the top of the launch. This gives very high cable loads and excessive launching speeds unless the winch or car driver slows down correctly as the glider gets near the top of the climb. How high the glider gets depends mainly on the way the initial climb is made. If the glider is held down in too shallow a climb for too long, there is very little cable left to climb on!

With a normal car launch the glider is not pulled down in this way and the

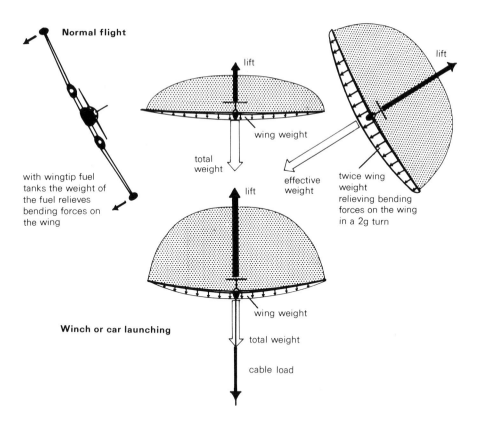

Normal flight

with wingtip fuel tanks the weight of the fuel relieves bending forces on the wing

lift

wing weight

total weight

effective weight

lift

twice wing weight relieving bending forces on the wing in a 2g turn

lift

wing weight

total weight

cable load

Winch or car launching

87 The stresses on the wing during a winch or car launch can be much higher than in normal flight at the same speed.

height obtained seems to depend more on maintaining a steady climb until the moment the car stops pulling, rather than on the initial climb.

With all wire launches, even in no wind, the driver has to make a reduction in speed as the glider steepens the launch to allow for the effect already mentioned in Fig. 86. However, in the straight car launch this effect is lost near the top of the climb and more speed is required from the car for the last few moments. In contrast, the winch must be slowed down near the top.

Of course any wind gradient has a large effect on the launching and in windy weather the car or winch speed has to be reduced even more during the initial climb in order to allow for the glider climbing rapidly into the much stronger headwind.

Safety Safe winch and car launching is mainly a matter of piloting technique and it is fundamental that at any stage of the launch the pilot must be in a position to make a safe approach and landing in the event of a power failure or cable break. This means that while the glider is climbing the first few hundred feet or so, the angle of climb must be limited so that at any time a recovery from a cable break can be made without stalling. The dangers of stalling at low altitudes are accentuated by the risks of spinning and by the far greater height loss in a stall recovery when there is a wind gradient and the glider is trying to regain speed near the ground.

If the acceleration is good, the angle of climb can be increased much more rapidly. The extra speed gives the pilot more time to react and lower the nose before the speed becomes critical. A slow launch, or poor acceleration, will make it dangerous to assume the full climb until a far greater height has been reached, since the glider could easily become stalled before the pilot was aware that the cable had broken.

Safety devices Safety is greatly increased by the use of the Ottfur type of cable release hook for winch and car launching. (The operation of the German Tost Combi E release hook is illustrated in Fig. 88 and is similar to the British Ottfur.) These hooks are designed so that the cable will release itself if there is a backward pull, i.e. if the pilot forgets to release and flies beyond or away from the winch at the top of the launch with the cable still attached. Without this device the glider could be pulled into a very dangerous ever-steepening dive if the pilot forgot or was unable to release.

The other excellent feature of the Ottfur type of hook is that if the cable is pulling to one side, the pull on the release knob to release the cable is unaffected. Some kinds of so-called 'safety' hooks tend to jam or require impossibly high forces to operate them when they are under side loads or while the cable is under full tension. Obviously the pilot should be able to release easily at any time and regardless of the direction in which the cable happens to be pulling.

The exact diameter of the smaller of the pair of rings which goes into the release is critical since it can jam if it is either oversize or elongated instead of being perfectly round. An elongated ring may wriggle round and lock itself above the spring-loaded automatic part of the release. **Never** use links of chain or non-standard rings for launching as they may distort or jam.

Cable weak links Some kind of a weak link is essential to protect the glider from excessive loads if the winch jerks the cable, or if the pilot pulls the glider up too steeply during a fast launch. Fig. 88 shows several types of weak link. In many countries a different strength of weak link is selected just before each launch according to the particular type of glider, i.e a weak link with a much lower breaking strain is used for a light solo machine than for a heavy two-seater. In England, until recently a 1000 lb weak link, which is suitable for all types of glider, was used. With the heavier gliders, this results in weak link failures which waste time and increase the risk of accidents. This is now eliminated by having weak links of various strengths available. With good cable and the correct weak link, the pilot can pull up steeper and get far higher launches.

A weak link is particularly important for aerotowing since aerotow release

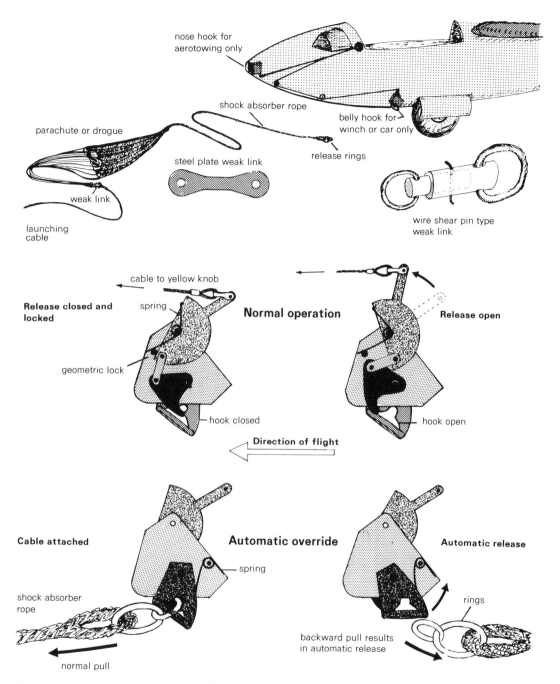

nose hook for aerotowing only

shock absorber rope

belly hook for winch or car only

release rings

parachute or drogue

steel plate weak link

weak link

launching cable

wire shear pin type weak link

Release closed and locked

cable to yellow knob

spring

Normal operation

Release open

geometric lock

hook closed

hook open

⟵ **Direction of flight**

Cable attached

Automatic override

Automatic release

spring

shock absorber rope

rings

backward pull results in automatic release

normal pull

88 Safety devices for launching. Winch and car launching cables have a cable parachute or drogue to prevent the cable falling in kinks. A weak link is incorporated in the cable to reduce the risk of damage if the pilot climbs too steeply or the cable is jerked badly. The automatic over-ride system on the release hook ensures that the cable will be released even if the pilot does not pull the yellow release knob in the cockpit.

hooks do not have an automatic release system. If the release fails, the rope must either be released by the tow plane, or the combination of glider and tug must make the landing together. Since the loads in the rope during a tow are usually less than 50 lb, a rope of 1000 lb breaking strain is ample for normal conditions. In very turbulent conditions it may be better to use a much stronger rope so that even if it gets a little worn it will be at least as strong as the weak link. In this case a weak link *must* be incorporated at the tow plane end of the rope. This will safeguard the glider but will also ensure that if the rope becomes entangled in an obstruction during a landing it will break before it pulls the tail off the tow plane.

Shock absorbers It is desirable to have some kind of rope between the glider and the main cable. This acts as a shock absorber and reduces the vibration and the minor jerks which otherwise would be unpleasant for the glider on the launch.

Cable parachutes or drogues The cable parachute is mainly used to protect the launching cable and prevent it falling too quickly after the release and becoming kinked or tangled. It is often a crude canvas parachute of about 4 foot diameter, or a surplus tail parachute from a military fighter aircraft.

Cable cutting or releasing device In the very unlikely event of a release failure, or the cable becoming tangled in the wheel or skid of the glider so that it cannot be released, there must be some way for the winch or car driver either to cut the cable free or release it. This usually takes the form of some kind of guillotine or cable cutter on the winch, or a release hook for the end of the cable on the car.

Good training and piloting technique, together with these safety devices, make winch and car launching surprisingly safe.

Aerotowing With an aerotow the glider is towed by a light aircraft until the glider pilot decides to release. Unlike all other forms of launch the height and position for the release are not restricted, except perhaps by the cost. The technique of aerotowing is fully explained in *Gliding* and advice on learning how to keep the glider in position on tow is given in *Beginning Gliding*. Unlike winch or car tows, however, aerotowing does require quite a high standard of flying and during early training flights the student will find that he needs help from the instructor. There is nothing technical about this method of launching – it is just a matter of keeping in formation line astern of the towing aircraft.

In smooth air the loads on aerotow are almost identical to those in straight flight and the glider will not be overstressed by towing at higher speeds than given on the cockpit placard. However, in gusty conditions the speeds should be limited to those on the placard since the combination of surge loads from the tow rope and the effects of gusts could otherwise cause overstressing.

7 Fore and aft stability and control

One of the most difficult things for the beginner to accept is that his aircraft is stable and that it is not about to turn over at any moment or fall out of the sky. In fact, if things are not going well in the early stages of training, it is usually because he is interfering too much and is not allowing the stability to do its job.

Stability and control are always a question of compromise. A very stable machine will be more difficult to manoeuvre quickly because the controls have to overcome the stability before the glider responds. Too little stability will necessitate the pilot making constant control corrections to fly accurately and steadily in turbulent conditions, but will give him a quicker response and better manoeuvrability.

Extra stability costs extra weight and drag because of the larger tail surfaces required and, therefore, most gliders are designed to have just sufficient stability to make them safe and pleasant to fly. Two-seater trainers and early solo machines are usually made more stable than high-performance gliders so that the controls have more feel and it is more difficult for an inexperienced pilot to overstress them inadvertently by over-controlling at higher speeds.

The wing is unstable

In very simple terms, the tailplane or stabiliser acts like the tail of a dart or arrow and corrects any pitching movements, nose up or nose down, giving the aircraft longitudinal stability (Fig. 89). In reality, most aerofoils are unstable and the stabiliser has, therefore, to be powerful enough to overcome the tendency for the wing to run out of control.

It is possible to have a stable aerofoil section, but this is usually at the expense of efficiency. The stable section will not develop nearly as much lift, the all-important lift/drag ratio is significantly worse, and performance will suffer.

In order to understand this instability of the wing, we must look at the distribution of pressure around the wing at various angles of attack. Fig. 90 shows a typical pressure distribution as the air flows over an aerofoil. The

Dart or arrow

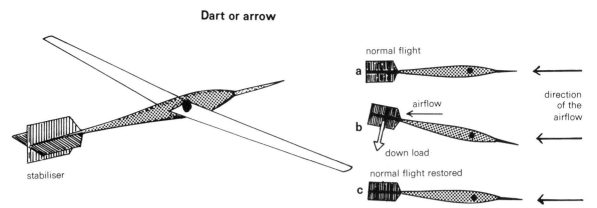

89 Fore and aft stability in its simplest form – the dart or arrow. When the dart pitches nose up or nose down the airflow meets the stabiliser at an angle producing a correcting force.

shape of the section, with its cambered upper surface, results in a decrease in pressure above the wing and an increase below it.

The sum of all these changes in pressure can be represented by one force, known as the 'total reaction' (TR), shown in Fig. 90 as an arrow acting upwards and backwards in relation to the direction of the airflow. This force is a combination of all the lift and all the drag of the wing and it acts through the point known as the 'centre of pressure' (C of P). If we consider a wing mounted in a wind tunnel so that the speed of the airflow can be kept constant, by changing the angle of attack of the wing the distribution of the pressure is modified so that the total reaction not only changes in direction and strength, but also acts through a different point. As the angle increases the total reaction gets larger with the resulting increase in lift and drag, and it also moves forward from a point about one-third of the way from the leading edge when at small angles, to the quarter chord point or even further

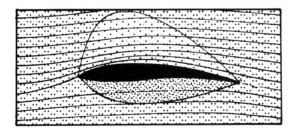 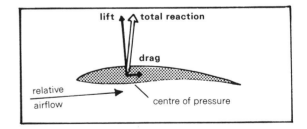

90 The forces acting on an aerofoil in flight. **Left** The pressure distribution round a typical aerofoil. Above the wing the airflow is accelerated and the pressure is reduced. Below the wing the airflow is slowed down and the pressure is increased. These changes result in lift. **Right** All the forces acting on the aerofoil can be considered as one force – the total reaction – acting at the centre of pressure. The total reaction may be split up into two components, lift and drag.

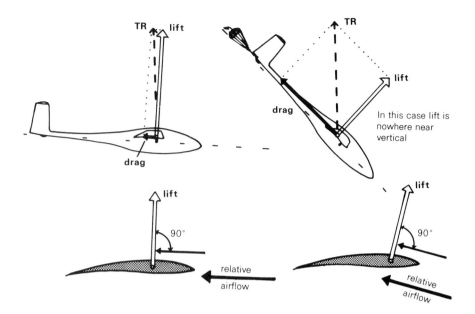

91 The total reaction (TR) may be considered as consisting of two components – lift and drag. Lift, by definition, always acts perpendicular to the relative airflow and not necessarily upwards. Drag acts along the direction of the relative airflow.

forward. This is an unstable movement because the larger force acting further forward tends to pull the front of the wing upwards. This in turn increases the angle still further giving even more total reaction even further forward as the centre of pressure changes with the increased angle. Without something to stop it the wing would topple over backwards. When the wing reaches the stalling angle, however, the lift is reduced by the turbulent flow over the top surface of the wing. The remaining lift and, therefore, the centre of pressure, moves much further back. This movement of the C of P is the main reason for the glider dropping its nose at the stall and its tendency to recover automatically.

As the speed is increased above the usual cruising speeds in normal flight the angle of attack of the wing gets less and less, and the point at which the lift acts moves back along the wing. Again, this is an unstable movement which helps to make the wing dive steeper and steeper. Most wing aerofoils behave in this way, i.e. they are unstable, and have an unstable movement of the C of P until they become stalled. Any attempt to make a simple flying wing or tail-less aircraft with these wing sections would result in longitudinal instability. They would tend to topple one way or the other as soon as they were disturbed (Fig. 92).

Streamlined, symmetrical aerofoils such as those used for tailplanes and the fin and rudder have no change of C of P at normal angles of attack.

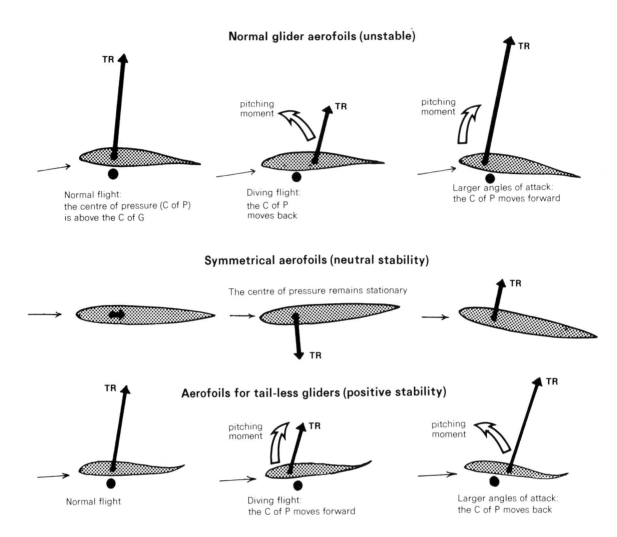

Normal glider aerofoils (unstable)

TR

TR

pitching moment

TR

pitching moment

Normal flight:
the centre of pressure (C of P)
is above the C of G

Diving flight:
the C of P
moves back

Larger angles of attack:
the C of P moves forward

Symmetrical aerofoils (neutral stability)

The centre of pressure remains stationary

TR

TR

Aerofoils for tail-less gliders (positive stability)

TR

pitching moment

TR

TR

pitching moment

Normal flight

Diving flight:
the C of P moves forward

Larger angles of attack:
the C of P moves back

92 Centre of pressure movements vary with the type of aerofoil. Normal aerofoils have an unstable movement but are more efficient when high lift and low drag are essential.

These aerofoils are neutrally stable while the control surface is in the central position. Unless the control surface is deflected to produce an extra upward or downward force, the C of P remains in a constant position close to the quarter chord point until the stall. Although they may have very low drag at small angles these uncambered aerofoils will not produce much lift and do not have a good lift/drag ratio. They are normally only used on tail surfaces, or for very high speed machines where low drag is much more important than lifting capability.

A further family of aerofoils has a stable movement of the centre of pressure, but once again they are not efficient lifters. Fig. 93 shows the layout of two tail-less or flying wing machines. The possibility of eliminating the weight and drag of the fuselage and tail unit seems to offer a chance of very high efficiency. However, the lifting capabilities of most stable aerofoils are only half to two-thirds of the unstable conventional ones. In other words, almost one and a half times the wing area is needed to carry the same load at the same speed. In addition, the drag of these aerofoils is considerably higher, so that the gliding angle suffers badly. These losses are so great that the conventional glider, even with a long slim fuselage, tailplane and fin and rudder, invariably has a better performance than any tail-less wonder. In addition to having lower performance, the control and stability of tail-less machines is never quite as good as a conventional machine and they all have their problems. Violent pitching is common when landing on rough ground.

With a normal aerofoil a tailplane or stabiliser is necessary in order to stop the tendency of the wing itself to pitch nose up or nose down when it is disturbed.

The stabiliser   Fig. 94a shows the position in a steady glide when the centre of gravity and the centre of pressure of the wing happen to coincide. In this case the tailplane is not required to produce any stabilising force. The wing is meeting the airflow at an angle of about 3° or 4° so that it produces the lift, and the tailplane is meeting the airflow at 0°, so that no force up or down is being produced. (This is a simplification of the exact situation.)

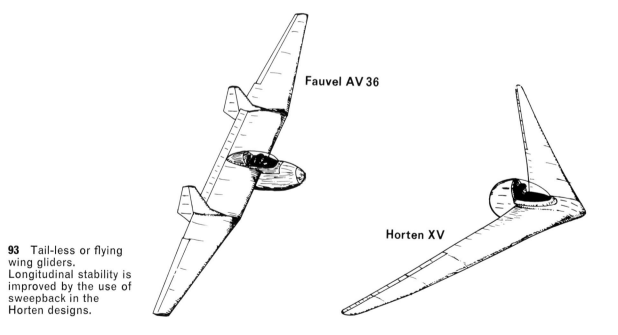

Fauvel AV 36

Horten XV

93 Tail-less or flying wing gliders. Longitudinal stability is improved by the use of sweepback in the Horten designs.

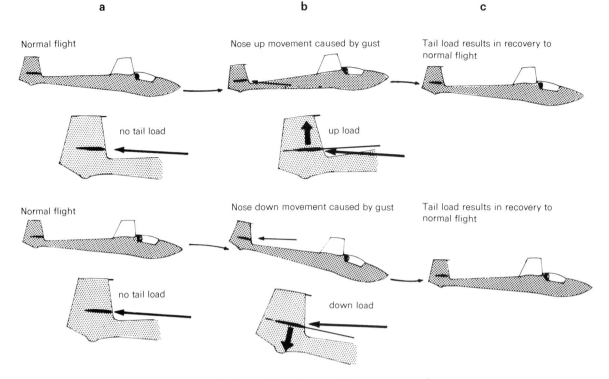

a   b   c

Normal flight   Nose up movement caused by gust   Tail load results in recovery to normal flight

no tail load   up load

Normal flight   Nose down movement caused by gust   Tail load results in recovery to normal flight

no tail load   down load

94 Longitudinal stability. The stabiliser produces forces to correct any nose up or nose down pitching movements caused by gusts.

Fig. 94**b** shows the situation a few seconds later, after the glider has hit a small up-gust. The inertia of the machine keeps it going in the original attitude so that the relative airflow has changed slightly. The wing meets the air at a larger angle so that more lift is developed. However, the position of the C of P moves forward a little so that the extra lift and the new position of the C of P produce a nose up pitching movement, tending to upset the machine still further. Meanwhile, back at the tail, the direction of the airflow has also changed so that the tailplane is meeting the air at a positive angle. This results in the tailplane producing an upward force. If the tailplane is large enough and the glider is stable, the nose up pitching caused by the wing is overcome by the stabilising effect of the extra lift from the tailplane, acting with its much larger leverage. This lowers the nose again. In the same way with a downward gust, the tailplane starts to generate a down load and this, with its powerful leverage, returns the aircraft to normal flight.

Similarly, if the glider drops its nose the action of the tailplane will bring it back to normal flight (Fig. 94). As the nose drops the angle of attack of the wing becomes smaller, so that the lift is reduced and the C of P moves back – both unstable movements. The tailplane, however, is also at a lower angle of attack to the airflow and develops a down load. After a few seconds, with no help from the pilot, the nose will rise. Because of the effects of inertia the aircraft will not return to exactly the original attitude without oscillating to and fro a few times as it overshoots a little. However, unless the disturbance is a large one, it will return to steady flight after one or two damped oscillations.

The degree of longitudinal stability depends on many factors.

1 **The type of aerofoil** and the direction and amount of movement of the C of P. Aerofoils with more camber are usually more unstable. For example, those using wing flaps will be less stable with the wing flaps in the full down position. The size of the chord is also important as a large chord will have a proportionally large C of P movement, making the aircraft less stable unless a proportionately larger stabiliser is used.

2 **Tail volume.** This is a measure of the power of the tailplane. It is determined by the size of the tailplane times the length between it and the centre of gravity, i.e. the tail moment arm. A large tailplane will need less moment arm, whereas a small tail area will need a much larger moment arm (longer fuselage) for the same degree of stability. The tail volume could be the same with both arrangements.

3 **The position of the C of G.** Once the aircraft is built this is usually the only factor which can alter from flight to flight. The glider will only be stable while the force developed by the tailplane times the moment arm to the C of G (the stabilising moment) is more powerful than the unstable pitching moment caused by the change in both lift and the C of P of the wing. This can only be so with the C of G close to the position of the C of P in normal cruising flight. At some point, when the C of G is further back than about half the wing chord (depending on the relative size of the tailplane and its moment arm) the glider will become neutrally stable. That is, it will not tend to correct any disturbance by itself. With the C of G further back still, the glider will be unstable and will tend to diverge further and further from normal flight. The instability of the wing will win over the stabilising effect of the tailplane because of the reduced moment arm between the tailplane and the C of G. In this case, the pilot will have to use the controls to stop the glider running away into an ever-steepening climb or dive. If the C of G is moved still further back the aircraft tends to diverge even more and, unless the pilot uses the controls quickly to stop this tendency, a state will soon be reached where neither the pilot nor the effect of the elevator will be capable of making the recovery at all.

At first it may seem strange that making the glider more tail-heavy will make it go out of control in a dive, whereas being too nose-heavy makes it more stable, but this is because the stability is determined by the moment arm of the tailplane about the C of G.

There are various forms of stabiliser or tailplane in use today. Whether they consist of a fixed tailplane and elevator, an all-moving tailplane, or a Vee tail, they are all controlled by forward and backward movements of the stick. Assuming a normal C of G position, so that the glider is stable, the tailplane and elevator combined provide the stabilising forces. If a glider drops its nose and goes into a dive, the wing angle is reduced and the C of P moves back. This is counteracted by the down load which is produced on the tailplane and elevator so that the glider will recover. To keep it in a dive, therefore, a small forward movement will be needed. This will reduce the down load so that, instead of recovering, the machine is held in the dive. If the aircraft has positive stability this forward movement of the stick will become larger and larger for an increase in the diving speed. On releasing the forward movement on the controls the stabilising effect of the tail will bring the nose up again.

Conversely, with a nose high change a progressive backward movement is required for lower and lower speeds until the stall occurs. The backward movement is reducing the upload on the tail and overcoming the normal stability.

It will come as a surprise to many pilots to realise that when they are pushing forward on the stick in a dive there is actually a down load on the tail! At high speeds, the down load is very large and, if the maximum diving speed (VNE) is exceeded in flight, there is a very real risk that the tailplane may fail before any other parts suffer damage.

Stability and trim   If the glider is longitudinally stable, it will tend to return to a steady glide after it has been slightly disturbed. It will settle down at a speed and angle at which the tail loads just balance out any unstable effect of the wing. However, only in one particular situation will the centre of pressure of the wing be immediately above the C of G so that the tailplane has no load. A heavy pilot will bring the C of G forward a few inches and this nose heaviness will result in the glider settling down at a higher speed than before. A lighter pilot will find the same glider settling down at a much lower speed than before. This is known as the trimmed speed, and it is the speed at which the glider will settle down if it is allowed to fly 'hands off'. The trimmed speed will vary with changes in the position of the C of G whether they are caused by variations in the weight of the equipment carried, or the weight of the pilot. Unless the aircraft is fitted with a trimming device to adjust for these variations, the heavy pilot will have to apply a constant backward load, and the very light pilot a forward load on the stick in normal cruising flight. This becomes very tiring and, therefore, all modern machines have some form of fore and aft trimming device. With gliders designed to be flown at speeds from 40–130 knots a trimmer is almost a necessity. If the glider happens to be in trim at, say, 50 knots the push force required to keep it in a gentle dive at 90 knots will be several pounds.

In a simple machine, such as the old T21b, with a very small range of efficient cruising speeds, an adjustable trimmer was not normally fitted. However, it was evident that the glider was a little nose heavy with almost all average pilots. This could have been corrected by adding lead ballast weights somewhere in the tail to move the C of G a little further back,

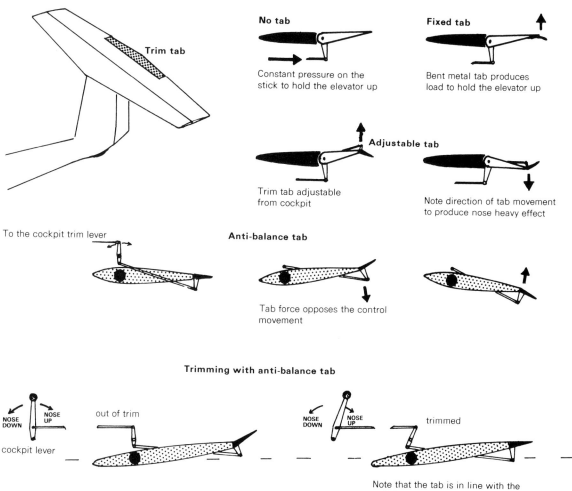

Trim tab

No tab

Constant pressure on the stick to hold the elevator up

Fixed tab

Bent metal tab produces load to hold the elevator up

Adjustable tab

Trim tab adjustable from cockpit

Note direction of tab movement to produce nose heavy effect

To the cockpit trim lever

Anti-balance tab

Tab force opposes the control movement

Trimming with anti-balance tab

NOSE DOWN   NOSE UP

cockpit lever

out of trim

NOSE DOWN   NOSE UP

trimmed

Note that the tab is in line with the stabiliser when glider is trimmed

95 Trimming and anti-balance tabs. With an elevator or all-moving stabiliser an anti-balance tab may be used to produce positive stick forces. As the elevator or stabiliser is moved, the tab also moves to produce an opposing force. Larger movements and higher flying speed produce higher forces and give good handling and feel. In addition, these tabs may be used for trimming by adjusting the neutral position as illustrated.

but instead of this a fixed trim tab of aluminium sheet metal was fitted to the elevator as in Fig. 95. When this tab is bent downwards it produces a small load upwards at the trailing edge of the elevator. This is sufficient to make the elevator take up a small angle and eliminates the need for the pilot to apply the backward pressure on the stick. In this way, the glider could be trimmed to fly 'hands off' at the desired speed, making it much easier and less tiring to fly.

Modern machines will always have some form of trimmer which can be adjusted over a wide range *during* flight. This enables any pilot who is within the weight limits laid down for the particular machine (in order to keep the C of G in a safe position) to trim the glider so that it will fly steadily, 'hands off', at any chosen speed throughout the normal cruising range.

It is important to understand that, once trimmed for a particular speed, the aircraft will always try to return to *that* speed after a small disturbance.

Discounting the effects of altering the position of camber changing flaps such as those fitted to the Kestrel and Nimbus, trim changes are normally made by an adjustable tab, or by applying a load to push or pull the stick by means of springs. In both cases the trim can be adjusted by the pilot in flight with a small control lever known as the trim lever. This is always arranged so that its movement is in the same 'sense' as the stick. A forward movement of the trim lever will help the pilot to push forward on the stick and will, in effect, make the aircraft nose-heavy.

From the manufacturers' point of view, the spring trimming is simple and inexpensive, since it does not involve control rods or cables from the cockpit back to the tail. However, it can only be used effectively when the stick forces to be trimmed out are small. An elevator tab, which is often used, is a more expensive but more powerful method. Inevitably it creates more drag, because of the discontinuity in the section when the tab is set at an angle to do its work (see Fig 95).

If we consider a tailplane and elevator in action, with a stable aircraft trimmed to fly with the elevator neutral and a speed of, say, 50 knots, the angle of deflection of the elevator required to hold the machine in a steady glide at 80 knots will depend on the degree of stability.

The tendency to return to 50 knots will be very marked with a stable machine, whereas it will be far less if the stability is marginal. A very stable machine will, therefore, require a much larger stick movement for a given change of speed. A measurement of the change of elevator angle (or from the pilot's point of view, the size of movement of the stick to produce the change of angle) for a change of speed, is a measure of what is known as the 'stick fixed' stability. In effect we are measuring the tail load needed to keep the aircraft from returning to its trimmed glide and speed. If the machine is stable, a larger and larger force is required with more increase or decrease of speed, above or below the speed for which it has been trimmed (Fig. 96).

If the C of G is moved further back, so that the stability is reduced, the amount of movement needed on the elevator will be less than before. Eventually when the C of G has been moved back to the 'neutral point', no progressive movement will be needed for an increase in speed. This situation is reached first of all at high speeds so that the aircraft may show a little positive stability by needing a forward movement at speeds up to, for example, 100 knots, followed by no further movement to, say, 120 knots. That is to say that, to go from 100 to 120 knots, a very small forward move would be needed to start the nose going down, but immediately afterwards the position of the stick, if measured, would be back to the original position again. At a higher speed still the glider would become unstable, so that to stop it diving still faster a backward movement on the stick would be required.

When flying a glider the pilot is scarcely conscious of the actual *size* of movement he makes on the stick, except perhaps during the take off and landing. However, without realising it, he soon learns to use the *feel* of the load through the stick to help him judge the size of movement he needs during manoeuvres. With a normal tailplane and elevator on a stable glider, not only does the stick movement increase for a progressive increase or decrease in speed away from the trimmed speed, but the stick force required for these movements will also increase progressively. Unless this is so the machine will feel very light on the elevator and will be difficult to fly at a constant speed. An aircraft is said to be stable 'stick free' when the loads increase progressively in this way. Stick free stability is a measure of the force acting on the elevator which tends to return it to the trimmed position, i.e. it is a measure of the stick forces (Fig. 97). Stick fixed stability, remember, is a measure of the need for a larger control surface movement to hold a change of speed and is a measure of stick movements.

Whereas a very stable machine will be rather heavy on the elevator control so that the pilot will need to retrim frequently, the less stable machines will be far lighter to handle, but will require much more care to fly accurately at a chosen speed. They will also be more difficult to trim exactly. The very stable machine will return to the trimmed speed by itself in a few seconds, while a less stable one will tend to oscillate to and fro for some time before settling down again.

Since the pilot is very aware of the stick forces he uses, but scarcely notices the actual size of movement, the degree of stick free stability is important. Providing that the control forces feel normal it may be quite acceptable for the stick fixed stability to be neutral – in other words for the stick movement to be small or non-existent for any increase in speed.

The stick free stability also becomes less and less as the C of G moves back, until it also reaches a neutral point beyond which the forces reverse. For example, when flying with the C of G at this point, and having applied a small forward pressure to increase speed, the speed will tend to increase more and more unless a backward pressure is held on the stick all the time. This will feel most unpleasant and twitchy. In an extreme case recovery from a steep dive at high speed might depend on whether the pilot was strong enough to pull out against the tendency for the machine to dive steeper and steeper.

Unless a pilot actually tries to measure the movement of the stick and the forces he is using, he may be quite unaware that his machine is unstable. A classic example of this was the Slingsby T21c, a special version of the famous old side-by-side trainer with the wings lowered and mounted either side of the fuselage to make it a shoulder, instead of a parasol wing. This change effectively increased the wing span by the width of the fuselage,

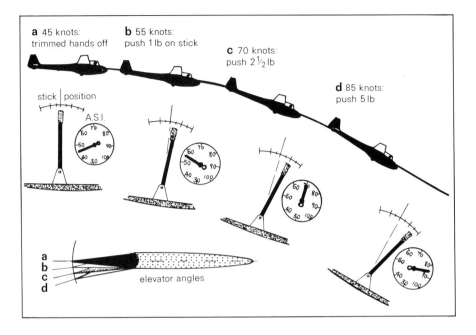

96 Stick fixed stability. The aircraft has positive stick fixed stability if it requires a progressive forward movement on the stick for higher and higher speeds. If the stick pressure is relaxed the aircraft will return to its original trimmed speed.

about 4 feet, which gave an increase in the effective wing area and efficiency. Because the tail area remained the same as before, the relative area of the tail to the wing was reduced and so the tail volume and stability was also lessened. During its debut the glider was flown by a large number of pilots before the formal test flying began and none of them noted anything abnormal in its performance, and many thought it excellent. On my first flight to assess the general handling as a matter of routine I gradually increased speed watching the position of the stick, only to find to my amazement that it was quite unstable. Since there was plenty of control power available this was not dangerous, but it meant sending the machine back to the works for a larger tailplane to cure it.

This situation was even more serious with a replica of a First World War fighter that I flew in several films. This was slightly unstable both stick fixed and stick free, but again none of the pilots had recognised it. Before I flew it I had been assured that it was quite all right, although, 'it took a lot of pulling on the stick to pull it out of a steep dive'. Again, it did not feel unusual in normal flight, but even a gentle dive showed that a pull force was required to stop it running away out of control. Landing was also interesting because, at low speeds after rounding out from the approach, it

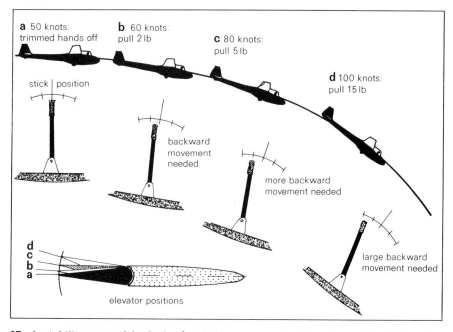

a 50 knots: trimmed hands off

b 60 knots: pull 2 lb

c 80 knots: pull 5 lb

d 100 knots: pull 15 lb

stick | position

backward movement needed

more backward movement needed

large backward movement needed

elevator positions

97 Instability caused by lack of stabiliser area or tail heaviness (C of G too far back). **a** Steady flight at 50 knots with no stick force. **b** Backward movement needed to hold constant speed if nose has dropped. **c** Larger backward movement needed at higher speed to stop nose dropping further. **d** In an extreme case a pilot's strength or range of control movement may be insufficient for recovery from a dive at high speed.

would continue the hold off by itself and just before touchdown a push force was being applied!

The cure for this kind of problem is usually either a larger tailplane, or a lump of lead ballast in the extreme nose in order to move the centre of gravity further forward. The average pilot should never meet this problem, because the minimum cockpit load on the glider, or the approved load distribution for powered machines, ensures that the C of G is within safe limits at all times. However, such blunders as taking off with the tail ground handling trolley still attached to the rear fuselage of a glider could easily result in serious instability.

Whereas the stick fixed stability is governed by the tail volume and the C of G position, the degree of stick free stability can be varied 'artificially'. Provided that a progressive movement is required on the stick (i.e., the stick fixed stability is positive) a simple spring will produce a progressive force and make a normal feel of sorts. Alternatively, a special elevator tab, known as an anti-balance tab, can produce a progressive force.

It is sometimes very desirable to be able to fly a glider with a very large range of possible C of G positions in order to cater for light and heavy pilots.

Normally the elevator control would be very light and twitchy at the aft C of G position but this can be partly overcome by using an anti-balance tab as in Fig. 95. This is used on the K8, K13, SHK, Dart and many other types of glider. The tab is actuated automatically by the movement of the elevator, so that as the elevator moves down the tab moves down at an angle to it. In this way the tab produces a force which is trying to push the elevator back to the original position, and this provides the feel on the stick. The larger the movement of the stick and elevator, the larger the tab angle and the greater the force opposing the pilot's hand.

Since the tab becomes more and more effective with an increase in airspeed, the stick forces will increase with speed even if the stick position is not changed. In this way it is feasible to have quite acceptable stick forces (positive stick free stability) with neutral stick fixed stability. This is quite common when the C of G is in the extreme aft position. In this case both the stick fixed and stick free stability would also be positive when the C of G was further forward, i.e. in gliders with a heavier pilot or ballast.

In addition to acting as an anti-balance or 'feel' tab, the same surface can be made to adjust from the cockpit, so that it acts as an elevator trim tab as well. (Fig. 95 on page 153.)

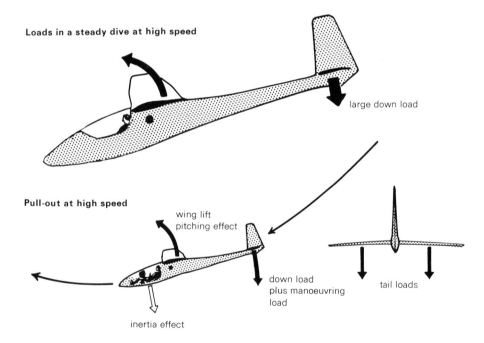

Loads in a steady dive at high speed

large down load

Pull-out at high speed

wing lift
pitching effect

down load
plus manoeuvring
load

tail loads

inertia effect

98 The most critical loads occur during diving and pull-up at maximum speed. At high speed the centre of pressure moves back, producing a large nose down pitching moment. This is counteracted by a large down load on the stabiliser. In a pull-up, the tail also has to overcome inertia effects.

The tailplane and elevator

The conventional tailplane and elevator already described has various advantages and disadvantages. The tailplane is really just a rather small wing designed for very low drag. Obviously any aerofoil with a broken surface at a hinge will have extra drag. The fact that it is of very small span and relatively large chord, giving it a low aspect ratio, will result in large tip losses and high induced drag whenever there is an up or down load being produced. The thin symmetrical aerofoil has low drag and is modified by moving the elevator so that it becomes cambered, but the wrong way.

If the glider is very stable a large deflection is needed on the elevator at both high and very low speeds. Since the total load in a steady dive is a large down load, the most efficient shape is a section with its lower surface cambered. But the tailplane with an elevator deflected at an angle in fact becomes a very inefficient aerofoil with high drag because the resulting camber is the wrong way to produce a down load (Fig. 98). Notice also the effect of a trim tab deflected to trim out the load on the stick. Again the shape of the aerofoil is spoilt by the angle of the tab.

Tailplane drag like this can be reduced by avoiding too much stability and, at times when any additional drag is a severe penalty, for example when gliding at high speed between thermals or on a final glide, it can be further reduced by leaving this kind of trim tab in the neutral position and accepting the extra load on the stick. This is probably worthwhile on machines such as the old Skylark 3 and 4, if they are being flown in long straight glides.

The 'all-moving' tailplane or stabiliser

An alternative to the tailplane and elevator is the 'all-moving' tailplane. Since one of the properties of a symmetrical aerofoil is the constant centre of pressure at all normal operating angles, it will require no force to move it if it is pivoted at the C of P. All-moving tails are always hinged at the quarter chord point. If the hinge was further back, the pilot would have difficulty in preventing it snatching hard over, in one direction or another (Fig. 99). Notice also that if the hinge was too far forward we would get the wrong feel. For example, having put the glider into a dive the surface would tend to trail along the line of the airflow in a zero angle position, and instead of developing a down load it would allow the unstable wing to run away into an ever-steepening dive. This means that in a dive the pilot would need a backward pull on the stick all the time and the aircraft would always be unstable in the stick free sense. (The Scud glider of the 1930s had the hinge at the leading edge and no fixed tailplane.)

An all-moving tail correctly hinged at the C of P has no feel whatsoever and neutral stick free stability at all speeds. This is not desirable, as it feels terribly twitchy and unstable – rather like being balanced on a knife edge. Since it requires no real effort to move the stick at any speed it would be very easy to damage the glider by using a large movement at a high speed.

An all-moving tail should, therefore, have either springs or anti-balance tabs to provide some feel and enable the machine to be trimmed to definite speeds (Figs. 95 and 100).

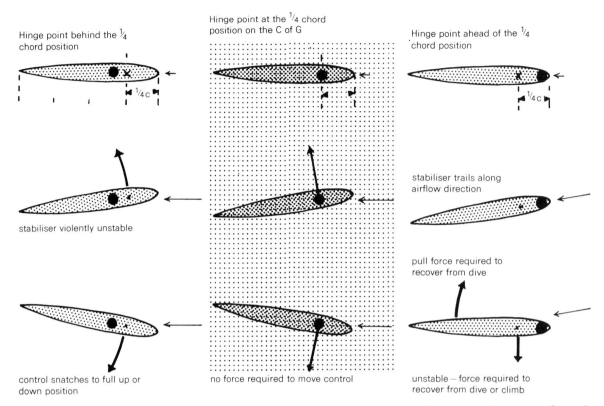

Hinge point behind the ¼ chord position

Hinge point at the ¼ chord position on the C of G

Hinge point ahead of the ¼ chord position

stabiliser violently unstable

stabiliser trails along airflow direction

control snatches to full up or down position

no force required to move control

pull force required to recover from dive

unstable – force required to recover from dive or climb

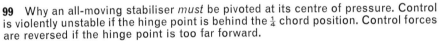

99 Why an all-moving stabiliser *must* be pivoted at its centre of pressure. Control is violently unstable if the hinge point is behind the ¼ chord position. Control forces are reversed if the hinge point is too far forward.

The main disadvantage of springs is that they do not provide any extra increase in control force during manoeuvres at higher speeds. It is just as easy to move the stick sharply at 130 knots as it is at 40 knots and, therefore, it is not difficult to overstress the machine.

Anti-balance tabs, however, do become more powerful with speed, so that the control becomes heavier. With this arrangement, like the conventional tailplane and elevator, the pilot can judge by the feel of the stick forces how fast he is going and also how much load he is putting on the aircraft in a particular manoeuvre.

When the all-moving tailplane with spring trimmer was introduced on the K6E after many years of being considered unsafe, there was concern that pilots might inadvertently overstress their machines. However, because pilots are careful not to overcontrol at speed and because aerobatics are not normally carried out in these machines, there has been a good safety record.

Compared with the tailplane and elevator the all-moving tailplane has improved efficiency when it is under load. In a dive, when the net load is

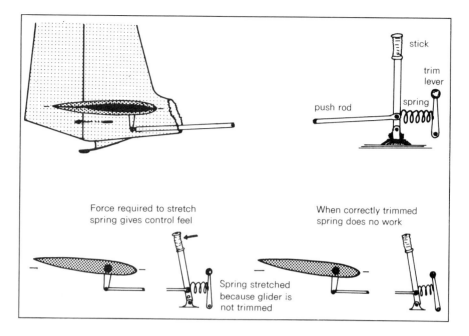

100 Spring trimming on an all-moving stabiliser. Without the spring the all-moving stabiliser requires no stick forces for manoeuvring. The spring produces some feel and enables the aircraft to be trimmed.

downwards, the aerofoil is at a less negative angle as a result of the movement forward on the stick. It also has an unbroken and unkinked surface giving a cleaner and more efficient aerofoil. Notice that in order to trim out the forward pressure on the stick created by an anti-balance tab (if one is fitted) the section has to be retrimmed to the perfect symmetrical section with the tab in line with the rest of the aerofoil. This is because the symmetrical section requires no load at any normal angle, and therefore centralising the tab puts the machine in trim.

For maximum efficiency, therefore, the glider with an all-moving tailplane and anti-balance tabs should be retrimmed immediately it is apparent that a stick force is being applied, whereas with a tailplane and elevator this may result in having the tab at a large angle and so creating higher drag.

Glider design is in an interesting state at the moment because there are so many variations in the design of the empennage (tailplane and fin and rudder). Each type has its own advantages and disadvantages and it is far too early to say which will prove most practical and efficient. At present the choice is largely a matter of fashion (Fig. 101).

The tailplane has proved to be one of the most vulnerable parts of a glider, particularly if the pilot chooses his field badly and lands in tall crops. Although one piece of straw can be broken easily, the force of literally

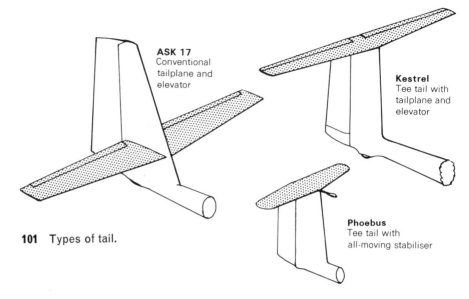

ASK 17
Conventional tailplane and elevator

Kestrel
Tee tail with tailplane and elevator

Phoebus
Tee tail with all-moving stabiliser

101 Types of tail.

hundreds of straws per second striking the tailplane leading edge at 30 or 40 m.p.h. can cause a surprising amount of damage. The tailplane is often broken in pieces and the fuselage may be severed just ahead of the tail! This kind of damage, although occurring only in long crops, has influenced most designers in their choice of position for the tailplane.

Many modern machines have it mounted at the top of the fin, well clear of any crop (the Tee tail). Others have it half way up, and a few have combined tailplanes and rudders in a Vee tail. It is worth discussing the pros and cons of each type to dispel some fallacious ideas about them.

The Tee tail In this case the tailplane is mounted on top of the fin (Kestrel, Nimbus, Standard Cirrus, LS1, Pilatus B4 and many others). The main advantage is, as already mentioned, that it is well clear of crops.

It is also well clear of the fin and rudder, so that they are not blanketed by the tail during the spin or recovery, and acts as an end plate for them, probably making them a little more effective. Another advantage is that at all normal speeds it is well above the downwash from the wing and out of any disturbance caused by the fuselage. This reduces the drag slightly by helping the airflow over the tailplane to remain smooth and laminar. The tailplane will also be slightly more effective, because with a normally positioned tailplane the downwash acts as a slight de-stabilising influence. This may make very little difference with an all-moving tailplane, but will result in a loss with a tailplane and elevator, which will have to be compensated for by being held at a less efficient angle. There is also a drag reduction because the junction between the fin and tailplane is cleaner than with a tailplane mounted either on the fuselage or half-way up the fin. The joint involves only two, instead of four, corners where the flow will be disturbed.

162

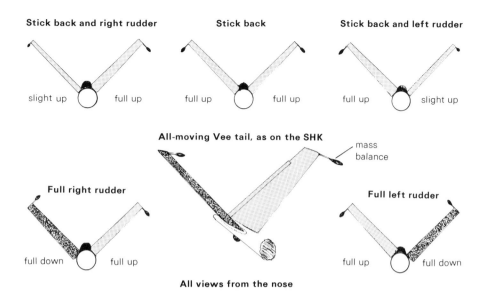

Stick back and right rudder

slight up   full up

Stick back

full up   full up

Stick back and left rudder

full up   slight up

All-moving Vee tail, as on the SHK

mass balance

Full right rudder

full down   full up

Full left rudder

full up   full down

All views from the nose

102   Vee tails. Elevator and rudder movements are combined. If the total area is comparable to the usual stabiliser and fin and rudder, stability and control are quite normal.

Structurally, the Tee tail is not quite so advantageous. The fuselage has to be stronger and torsionally stiffer to resist the effects of any bad swing or ground loop. Otherwise the weight of the tailplane mounted at the top of the fin will result in damage to the fin, or even a broken fuselage, if a swing occurs. Also, of course, the fin itself has to be much stronger and this adds to the weight.

Summing up, the Tee tail is a good solution to any risk of crop damage, but tends to be rather heavy and more prone to serious damage in a ground loop. It is more efficient than the normal tail, particularly if an all-moving tailplane is fitted.

The Vee tail   At first sight the Vee tail appears to have much to commend it as it reduces the number of surfaces and the number of junctions involved. It would, therefore, be reasonable to expect a much lower amount of drag.

With the Vee tail fore and aft movements of the stick and movements of the rudder are combined to give the movements of the control surfaces shown in Fig. 102. The Vee tail can be either all-moving, or have fixed portions with separate control surfaces.

With Vee tails it is usually impossible to get the full rudder movement combined with a full movement of the elevator, but this is of no real importance. The movements possible are still more than adequate.

The risk of crop damage is small because the roots of the tailplanes are protected by the fuselage and the tips are up out of reach of the crops.

If the area of the surfaces is large enough to give the equivalent stabilising effects and control of a normal tail, the handling can be very similar to that of an aircraft with a normal tail. However, in the past the designer very often made them smaller in an effort to reduce the weight and drag. This resulted in poor stability and directional control, just as it would with a conventional tail.

There are a number of factors which have to be considered from the aerodynamic and structural point of view when comparing the Vee tail with other layouts, and as a result it is not at all clear which is preferable.

The tails may be set at various angles between 60° and 90°. If we consider the effects of fore and aft movements on the stick, and of the tail producing stabilising loads up or down, it will be seen that only a small proportion of the 'lift' produced by each surface is actually doing any useful work. It would appear, therefore, that the drag induced by producing a given up or down force is bound to be much greater than when the surface is a plain, horizontal one. However, this is not the whole story because the size of the surfaces, and in particular their length or span, is far greater, and this will make them more efficient than a shorter tailplane of lower aspect ratio.

With rudder movements, the forces are again acting in the wrong direction, so that larger forces are needed for control and a very large twisting force occurs with full rudder. The rear fuselage must, therefore, be much stronger and heavier to allow for this.

There has been some doubt about the spinning and spin recovery characteristics of gliders fitted with Vee tails in the past, but this is thought to have been the result of the designers using much too small an area, combined with a rather short fuselage. Extensive tests carried out in wind tunnels and on powered machines just after the war showed that, on test, the Vee tail had better anti-spin characteristics as well as lower drag than a normal tail.

Most of the gliders with Vee tails that I have flown have a small, but noticeable, difference in handling which takes a few flights to get used to. This is due to the slight pitch changes and torque effects which occur whenever the rudder is applied.

In fact, the BG135 prototype is the only aircraft I have flown in which it is difficult, if not impossible, to feel the effect of the Vee tail.

Horn balances and balance tabs

Large powered aircraft often have problems with the controls being too heavy for the pilot to operate comfortably. In this case, since power-assisted controls are expensive, some form of inset hinge or horn balance may be used on the control surfaces. Alternatively, geared servo tabs may be fitted to help reduce the loads. Sometimes a horn balance is incorporated in the top of the rudder, as in Fig. 103, and this has two effects. Besides reducing the effort required by the pilot to move the rudder, the tendency to overbalance and lock over during sideslips is reduced by a horn balance. (This phenomenon is explained on page 188.)

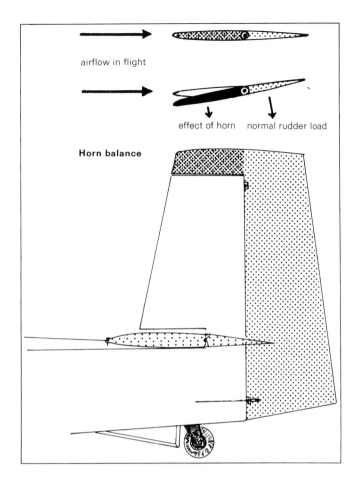

airflow in flight

effect of horn   normal rudder load

Horn balance

103 Horn balance. The horn produces a force which helps the pilot to apply the rudder. Horn balances are sometimes used on the ailerons and elevators of large aircraft in order to make the controls lighter for the pilot.

It is seldom, if ever, necessary to make the elevator control on gliders much lighter. Any geared tab will usually be arranged to increase the loads and so increase the stick free stability. A great advantage of using a geared, anti-balance tab of this kind is the freedom it allows the designer to modify the feel of the control during the flight tests. By the simple expedient of changing the gearing of the tab in order to increase or decrease the loads on the control column, the whole 'feel' of the glider may be changed and in this way it is often possible to experiment during the test flying to get the controls nicely harmonised.

Mass balancing   Particularly in the case of the elevator the feel of the control is affected by manoeuvres unless the control surface is at least partially mass balanced. (Fig. 104.)

If no mass balance is fitted, the weight of the elevator will make it drop down onto the stops while the machine is stationary on the ground. In flight, the air loads will make it trail along the direction of the airflow with a very slight droop caused by the weight. When the aircraft is pulled into a loop, or a tight turn, the increase in loading increases the effective weight of the elevator. This means that the pilot has to apply even more force on the stick to keep it back. Lack of mass balance increases the force required for manoeuvring or, in other words, it increases the stick force per 'g'.

It also affects the feel of the control if the aircraft flies through bumpy air. If the aircraft sinks rapidly, for example, the fixed portion of the tailplane moves immediately with the aircraft while the inertia of the elevator results in it being left slightly behind. The upward movement of the elevator makes the tail produce an increased down load, helping it to move further. When the tailplane has stopped the inertia of the elevator means it will continue to move, so that the surface overshoots.

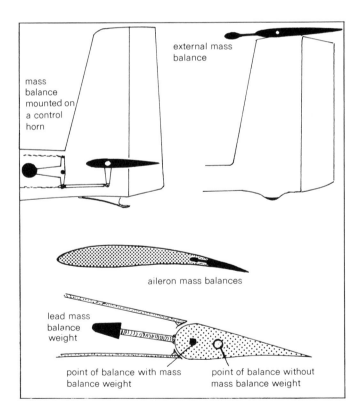

external mass balance

mass balance mounted on a control horn

aileron mass balances

lead mass balance weight

point of balance with mass balance weight

point of balance without mass balance weight

104   Mass balancing improves the feel and reduces the risk of flutter.

This is the same combination of factors that occurs during the flutter of a control surface, but, in this case, all that may be noticed is a slight 'kick' through the stick in rough air and a distinct tendency for it to jump out of the pilot's hands during a bouncy landing. This effect on landing is particularly noticeable on the Falke and on the Auster Terrier.

If the construction of the elevator is very light and most of the weight is close to the hinge point, mass balancing may be unnecessary. Obviously the designer does not want to carry any unnecessary ballast in the tail of a glider and if it is possible to achieve acceptable handling without special mass balancing he will do so.

However, if the tailplane is an all-moving one, a high degree of mass balance will be needed. With anti-balance tabs, the amount of mass balance is generally reduced gradually during test flying until it is the minimum which eliminates any tendency for the stick to oscillate badly in bumpy air. The damping effect of the tab helps to get rid of this problem but without enough mass balance the gearing of the tabs has to be so high that the stick forces are objectionally large.

When the tail is not fitted with tabs and relies entirely on the feel produced by the spring trimming device, the elevator must be balanced at its hinge

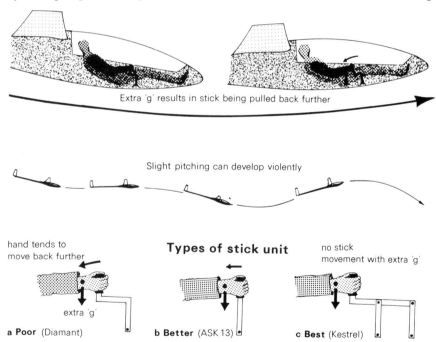

Extra 'g' results in stick being pulled back further

Slight pitching can develop violently

Types of stick unit

hand tends to move back further

extra 'g'

a Poor (Diamant)

b Better (ASK 13)

no stick movement with extra 'g'

c Best (Kestrel)

105 Pilot induced oscillations (P.I.O.s). If the elevator control is very light P.I.O.s may occur at high speeds. This kind of oscillation can increase and become catastrophic! With some types of stick unit inadvertent movements tend to accentuate any pitching. The cure is to reduce speed, prevent the stick moving, or take the hand off the stick.

point. This completely eliminates the effect of inertia on the tailplane itself. However, an effect similar to a lack of mass balance of the control surface will occur if the design of the control column puts the weight of the pilot's arm behind the pivot point. Fig. 105 shows that with the arrangement **a** any sudden bump will move the stick forward or back because of the inertia in the pilot's arm. The stick movement will in turn result in a further pitching of the aircraft and another inadvertent movement of the stick. At high speed this may set up a pilot induced oscillation (P.I.O.) which is difficult to stop and is also a very unpleasant and potentially dangerous state of affairs. **b** and **c** show arrangements which avoid this problem. **c** is used on the Kestrel and prevents up and down movements due to bumps being translated into fore and aft movements of the stick.

The amount of weight required to balance the control surface will depend on the position of its own centre of gravity in relation to the hinge point. Obviously the designer will use all his cunning to keep the rear part of the stabiliser as light as possible. The mass balance may be concealed in the fuselage on a small arm, or take the form of a streamlined bob weight mounted out in front of the surface so that less weight is needed.

When comparing the various forms of tail the weight of mass balancing must not be ignored and, because of the need for this extra weight, an all-moving tail may frequently turn out to be heavier than a normal tailplane and elevator.

Practical aspects of fore and aft stability, trimming and control

When a glider is sharply disturbed from steady flight at the trimmed speed, it will generally behave in one of two ways when it is left to its own devices. It will either oscillate gently nose up and down several times until it settles down again at the original speed and attitude, or it will oscillate gently initially, with the oscillations becoming larger and larger until a stall occurs. The latter behaviour may be quite acceptable, provided that the oscillations are slow enough to present no control problem. This kind of oscillation is called a phugoid. Exactly what a particular type of glider will do depends on its degree of stability. This is affected, of course, by the position of its C of G (i.e. cockpit load at the time).

The important point, however, is to understand how this tendency to phugoid affects the glider in normal flight. If the glider pitches nose high for a few moments it will *always* drop into a diving attitude a few seconds later, unless the pilot stops it doing so by making a counter movement on the stick. In fact, it will oscillate up and down until the pilot stops it, or until the oscillation dies out by itself. A student pilot will often not recognise what is happening, and by slightly mistiming his corrections, he will keep the phugoid going, instead of stopping it. In hazy conditions, when it is difficult to spot the changes in attitude quickly, the pilot will realise that the nose is high by the loss of speed (usually detected by the lack of noise). However, by this time the glider is almost over the peak of the phugoid so that his correction as he eases forward to prevent a stall is too late and merely helps

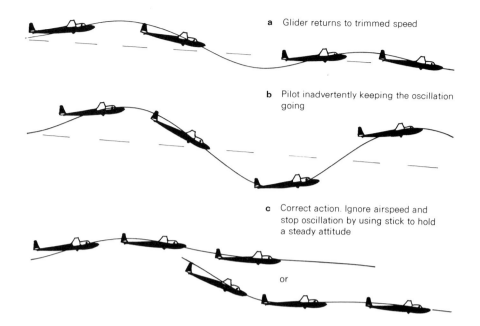

a Glider returns to trimmed speed

b Pilot inadvertently keeping the oscillation going

c Correct action. Ignore airspeed and stop oscillation by using stick to hold a steady attitude

or

106 Gentle phugoid oscillations and how to stop them. The built-in stability always tends to correct any disturbance and care is required not to accentuate the pitching movements instead of stopping them. **a** Following any disturbance the glider will settle down at its trimmed speed after several oscillations. **b** If the pilot suddenly becomes aware of low speed and eases forward to correct it, the dive is accentuated. By the time speed is excessive the stability has started to raise the nose and the pilot's correction comes too late, so that the oscillations are perpetuated. **c** Correct action.

the nose down further. A moment or two later, he realises that the glider has excess speed and applies a correction by easing back on the stick. But by then the stability has already pulled the nose up, so that again he is too late and just perpetuates the motion (Fig. 106).

This is a very common mistake during thermal soaring. The answer is to check the oscillation by holding a steady attitude *against the horizon*, if it can be seen, or to break the cycle by stopping the movement up or down, even if, for a few moments, the glider is flying too slowly.

It is a help (and a comfort) for the beginner to understand that whenever the nose is too high it will drop automatically to a 'too low' position. If the nose is too low, or the speed is higher than the trimmed speed, then the next thing will be a nose up movement – all caused by the stability of the aircraft.

Friction in the elevator circuit Both the stability and the handling of any aircraft are adversely affected by any stickiness or excessive friction anywhere in the elevator control circuit. In particular, it will make it very difficult to trim the aircraft so that it will fly 'hands off'.

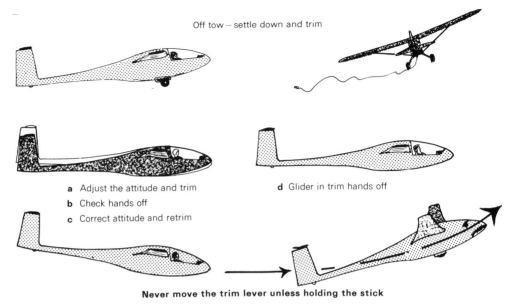

Off tow — settle down and trim

a Adjust the attitude and trim
b Check hands off
c Correct attitude and retrim

d Glider in trim hands off

Never move the trim lever unless holding the stick

107 How to trim the glider. **a** Adjust the attitude to obtain the desired speed and then adjust the trim for no apparent load on the stick. **b** Check the trimming by relaxing on the stick to see if the glider remains in the same attitude. **c** If the glider is not correctly trimmed use the stick to hold it at the correct attitude and speed and readjust the trimmer.

If a trimming tab is fitted and the elevator is, in effect, momentarily jammed by excess friction, any attempt to retrim will move the tab which will act as if it were a movement of the elevator. For example, if the trimmer lever is moved back to make the aircraft a little more tail heavy, the tab will move down (a trim tab always moves in the opposite direction to the control surface). However, if the elevator is held stationary the result of the movement of the tab will be a nose down change, instead of the expected nose up one. This can be extremely confusing. Even a very small amount of stickiness spoils the feel of the control and makes trimming difficult – the cure is often only a matter of a few drops of light oil in the hinges and bearings of the control system.

Trimming   When the elevator control circuit has very little friction the aircraft will always return to within plus or minus 1 or 2 knots of the same speed, after it has been slightly disturbed nose up or nose down. The correct procedure when trimming in flight is to adjust the attitude until the aircraft is flying at the required speed. Once the aircraft has settled down at that speed the trimmer should be adjusted until there is no detectable pressure one way or the other on the stick. The test is then to relax all the pressure on the stick and watch what happens. If the nose moves up or down the aircraft was not trimmed exactly. It is at this point that most beginners go wrong. The correct procedure is to use the stick to reposition the nose in its original position and *then* make a small correction on the trimmer. Do not try to adjust the trimmer to bring the nose back into position but use the main control (Fig. 107).

The other common mistake is to attempt to trim the aircraft while it is still in the wrong attitude and flying at the wrong speed. Although a very approximate trim position can be set in order to reduce the stick pressures, the final adjustments can only be made accurately when the machine is flying *at the desired speed*. Beginners often try to rush the process of trimming and, for example, when attempting to trim for 45 knots they will trim out for 'hands off' flight at 50 knots and then wonder why a backward pressure is needed at the lower speed. This shows a complete lack of understanding of trimming and longitudinal stability. If the machine is stable (and it is very unusual to encounter one which is not) it will always return to the attitude and speed for which it has been trimmed. There will be a different attitude and speed for each position of the trimmer, and when it is trimmed for one speed it is bound to be out of trim for all others.

It should also be apparent that if a glider is trimmed for 45 knots in straight flight it will be out of trim and will require a backward pressure during any turn. The trim position will vary according to the angle of bank and speed required (Fig. 108). This is important because for prolonged circling in thermals, and particularly when flying in cloud or poor visibility, it will be noticeably easier to keep an accurate turn if the glider is retrimmed to a 'hands off' situation. However, in spite of being in a turn the phugoid motion, alternatively nose up and nose down, will still occur. Once any pitching begins it will have to be stopped by a movement on the stick.

A common cause of the nose dropping is a gust making the bank increase during a turn. Unless the appropriate extra backward movement is applied immediately the bank increases the nose will start to drop. As the speed increases the stabilising effect of the tailplane will raise the nose to above the normal attitude. A few seconds later when the speed has become very low, because of the stability, a further nose down pitching movement will occur. This phugoid may start very gently and then develop unless the pilot prevents it.

When the stability is less marked and the stick forces are very light, it will be much more difficult to trim accurately. Even small amounts of friction will make the aircraft return to a much wider range of speeds after it has been slightly disturbed.

If you are assessing the handling of a particular glider do not forget that your findings will depend very largely on your own weight. If you are very light you will be flying the glider near the aft position for the C of G and it will be far less stable than with a heavy pilot. A very stable machine will be much easier to trim and fly accurately. Moving the C of G forward makes the machine more stable by increasing the tail moment arm and also changes the trim, making it more nose heavy, so that it trims out at a higher speed. In an extreme case it may result in a lack of control because the stability makes

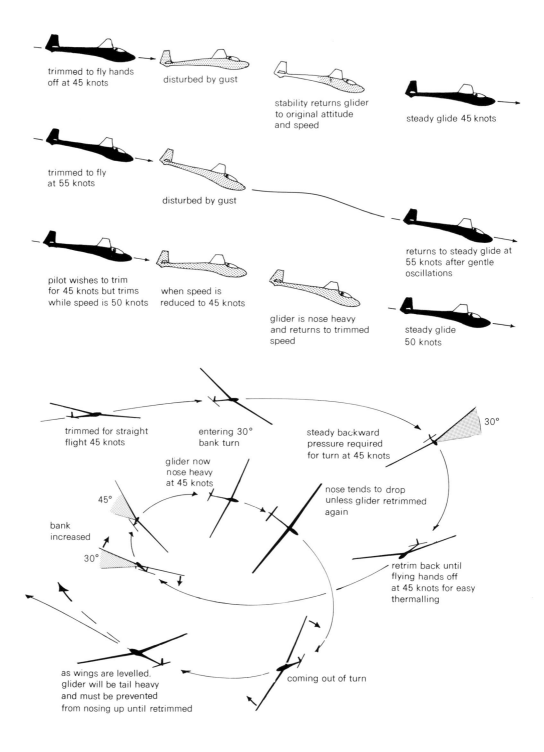

trimmed to fly hands
off at 45 knots

disturbed by gust

stability returns glider
to original attitude
and speed

steady glide 45 knots

trimmed to fly
at 55 knots

disturbed by gust

returns to steady glide at
55 knots after gentle
oscillations

pilot wishes to trim
for 45 knots but trims
while speed is 50 knots

when speed is
reduced to 45 knots

glider is nose heavy
and returns to trimmed
speed

steady glide
50 knots

trimmed for straight
flight 45 knots

entering 30°
bank turn

steady backward
pressure required
for turn at 45 knots

30°

glider now
nose heavy
at 45 knots

nose tends to drop
unless glider retrimmed
again

45°

bank
increased

30°

retrim back until
flying hands off
at 45 knots for easy
thermalling

as wings are levelled,
glider will be tail heavy
and must be prevented
from nosing up until retrimmed

coming out of turn

the control less effective. At low speeds the elevator may not be sufficient to round out for a landing, or to achieve a complete stall in level flight.

When the C of G is near the aft limit the aircraft will be slightly more tail heavy, very much lighter on the controls, and far easier to stall and keep in a spin.

During test flying a glider is flown with ballast in the tail to bring the C of G back to the position it would be with lighter pilots. The designer bases his initial stress calculations on the loads created when the C of G is within certain forward and backward limits. The test pilot must then fly the machine to find out whether the stability and handling are satisfactory at these limits and revise them if necessary. Finally, he must check the spinning characteristics because these also deteriorate as the C of G moves aft. The safe aft limit is sometimes determined by the spinning and sometimes by the stability and control.

Pilot induced oscillations

Whereas on early designs of glider the angle of glide deteriorated very rapidly with an increase in speed, modern machines often have gliding angles of over 20:1 at 90 knots or more. On a really good soaring day the between-thermal cruising speeds through sinking air may be close to the VNE, and at these speeds the pilot will get a very bumpy ride. With the very light controls and flexible wings of modern gliders it is possible to start pitching oscillations which are difficult to damp out. In fact the pilot may quite unwittingly induce them. Pilot induced oscillations are usually only likely when the stick forces are very low and the elevator is powerful, so that small movements on the stick cause quite large pitching movements.

There are many factors involved in P.I.O.s but probably the most important one on gliders is the effect of inertia on the mass of the pilot's hand and arm on the stick already mentioned (see Fig. 105). Any up or down movement is translated into moving the stick forward or backward and this results in a further pitching movement. This effect is similar to a lack of mass balance, and if the timing of a series of disturbances happens to be at the correct frequency it is difficult to prevent a violent oscillation developing. This has been the cause of serious damage on several gliders and the complete destruction of at least one, and the matter cannot be taken lightly. P.I.O.s can be set up at low speeds but are less serious, since the loads on the structure will be far lower.

The cure for P.I.O.s is to hold the stick firmly in one position to stop the oscillation, rather than try to apply corrections, which, if mistimed, only

108 (opposite) Trimming in turns and straight flight. Note that the glider must be flying steadily at the *desired* speed before accurate trimming is possible. If the glider is retrimmed to circle steadily hands off it will then only be accurately trimmed for that particular angle of bank and speed. When returning to straight flight it will require trimming again or it will be very tail heavy and tend to lose speed.

make matters worse. It is also essential to slow down by gently easing up into a climb or by opening the airbrakes, if it is possible to do this smoothly at speed.

An alternative theoretical method is for the pilot to take his hand off the control so that the normal stability damps out the oscillation. However, this is often impractical, particularly if the P.I.O. occurs on aerotow or at low altitude.

8 Lateral stability and control

Lateral stability

Strictly speaking, 'lateral stability' should refer to stability in the rolling plane. It might be expected to provide both resistance to the aircraft being tipped into a banked position and an automatic recovery to level flight.

However, there is little or no automatic tendency to recover until the aircraft starts to slip sideways towards the lower wing, when the effect of the dihedral angle (or sweepback) gives the lower wing extra lift and corrects the bank.

It will be seen how the combination of lateral and directional stability controls the characteristics of the aircraft in turns and sideslips. This combination is known as 'spiral stability' and determines whether the aircraft will tend to bring itself back to level straight flight, or whether it will continue to turn, with the bank getting steeper and steeper and the nose dropping.

Lateral damping

Even without dihedral angle any tendency to roll will be heavily damped. When a wing starts to move downwards the direction of the relative airflow changes slightly. The airflow meets the wing at a larger angle and gives it extra lift, which tends to stop the movement. The upward moving wing then has a slightly reduced angle and less lift, and this also helps to stop the motion (Fig. 30 on page 58). With a large wing span this damping is so marked that it is difficult to achieve a high rate of roll. The ailerons have to overcome this damping as the bank is applied or taken off.

Because of this the bigger gliders are normally much more sluggish in roll, and the designer must provide larger ailerons to give the glider the necessary manoeuvrability to centre quickly into thermals in rough air. It is a simple matter to achieve a high rate of roll on a glider of only 10 metres span but a very different matter with one of 20–25 metres. This is reflected in the design requirements for gliders (*The British Requirements, B.C.A.R. Section E*, is available from H.M. Stationery Office, Holborn, London) which lay down that at a speed of 1.4 Vs (1.4 times the stalling speed) the maximum time to move the glider from a 45° banked turn in one direction to a 45° banked turn in the other, must be less than 1 second for each 10 feet of wing span. For a glider with an 18 metre, or 59 foot span, this means 5.9 seconds are allowed to reverse the turn. Gliders such as the Skylark 3 and 4 just meet this requirement, However, more recent machines such as the Kestrel, Nimbus and ASW 17 meet it easily. (ASW 17 of 20 metres span – 65 feet – takes just over 5 seconds.)

The damping is also affected by the distribution of the wing area. A parallel chord wing will be much more highly damped than a tapered wing of similar span and area. Reducing the area at the wingtip improves the lateral control by reducing the damping and so increases the effectiveness of the ailerons.

Rolling movements are also affected by the inertia of the wing. A heavy wing, particularly if the mass of the wing is well out towards the wingtips, will reduce the effectiveness of quick movements of the aileron. It will also make it more difficult to stop a rolling movement once it has started. This will be particularly noticeable with large span gliders carrying water ballast in the wings for the wing weight may be increased by half as much again, so that the inertia is also considerably above the normal. The glider may, therefore, be noticeably slower to react to the controls whenever the bank is being changed.

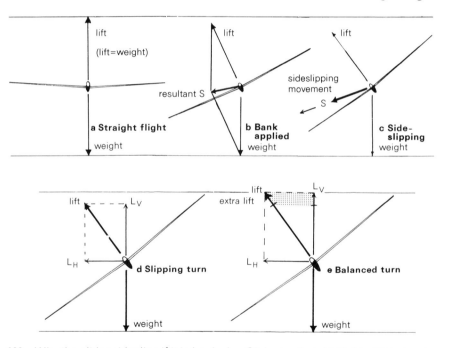

109 Why the glider sideslips if it is banked. **a** Glider in straight flight – lift balancing the weight. **b** Glider banked – the resultant lift and weight gives sideways and downward movement. **c** Steeper bank showing sideslipping movement. **d** Glider banked showing lift force split into vertical and horizontal components. Note that the vertical component LV is not sufficient to balance the weight. LH is the turning force. **e** A balanced turn. Extra lift supplied by a slightly larger angle of attack or more speed enables the vertical component to balance the weight.

176

This lateral damping is important because it makes all normal aircraft neutrally stable as far as disturbances causing small banking movements are concerned. Once the machine has become banked, the balance of the lift and weight is upset, as in Fig. 109, and it can be seen that the resultant S pulls the machine to the side and downwards in a sideslip.

Dihedral angle It is only as the aircraft sideslips towards the lower wing that dihedral or sweepback start to work to bring the wings level again. Fig. 110 shows how with dihedral the airflow meets the lower wing at a slightly larger angle, and with sweepback it meets the lower wing at a more efficient angle, so that extra lift is developed to bring it level. The effect of dihedral and sweepback occurs at any time when an aircraft is flying sideways through the air. For example, if rudder is applied to the right, the nose yaws to the right and the airflow starts to meet the whole aircraft at an angle. The left wing will meet the airflow at a larger angle of attack, or, in the case of the swept wing almost at right angles to the line of the leading edge, so that the lift on that wing is

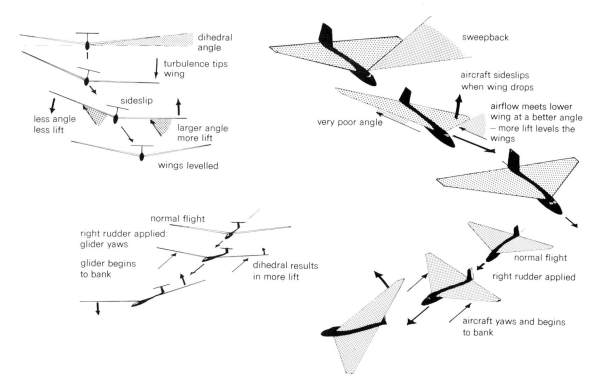

110 The action of dihedral and sweepback. When the aircraft banks and sideslips towards the lower wing, dihedral angle and sweepback result in it developing more lift so that the wings are levelled automatically. If rudder is applied, dihedral and sweepback result in the aircraft banking. This effect is sometimes referred to as the further, or secondary, effect of the rudder. It is not an efficient or safe way of applying bank for a turn.

increased. The result of applying rudder to the right will, therefore, be first of all a swing or yaw to the right, followed by a gradual banking movement in the same direction.

If we consider dihedral it will be seen that there is an inevitable loss caused by the lift from the wings working at a slight angle to the vertical. The dihedral angle is, therefore, kept to the minimum required to provide a small amount of lateral stability.

Model aircraft designed for free flight without radio control have to be much more stable than piloted full-sized gliders, since they have to be able to right themselves immediately if they are disturbed by a gust. Designers of models will often resort to using several changes in dihedral along the wing in order to put the greatest dihedral angle close to the wingtip where it will have a larger leverage and a more powerful righting effect. However, unlike the full-scale glider, the stability of a model is all-important even at the expense of performance. A few early glider designs used gull wings, with a large dihedral angle at the wing root and then very little angle at all for the rest of the wing. This was not particularly efficient and was done mainly for aesthetic reasons, but it did give the wingtips a little more clearance above the ground, while keeping a good fuselage to wing joint.

Sweepback It has already been explained how sweepback acts in a sideslip to bring the wings level. However, the extreme angles of sweepback used on high-speed aircraft are not there for reasons of stability. Large angles of sweepback improve the high-speed characteristics by delaying the formation of shock waves and the resulting large increase in drag but they also create too much lateral stability, which is a disadvantage. One antidote is to use anhedral (anti-dihedral) with the sweepback to cancel out some of the unwanted stability. This is done on many very high-speed machines including the Harrier (Fig. 111).

For low-speed machines such as gliders sweepback has yet another disadvantage. It encourages an outward flow of the boundary layer of air close to the wing surface and so helps the airflow to break away at the tips, making them stall much earlier. This results in an undesirable tendency to drop one or other wing abruptly at the stall and it is generally necessary to resort to using washout at the wingtips to prevent it. The net result is that the lateral stability gained by sweepback on gliders has to be paid for by the loss of efficiency created by reducing the wing incidence at the tips. At fast cruising speeds the wingtip is dragging through the air at a negative angle, producing only a down load and extra drag. In fact, sweepback is usually a disadvantage and is avoided on gliders and normal light aircraft. However, it does have a special use on fully aerobatic machines. While dihedral becomes anhedral in inverted flight sweepback remains sweepback, no matter which way up the aircraft is flying. Machines designed specifically for aerobatics, such as the Zlin Trenor, Stampe, Pitts Special and Yak 18, use sweepback in preference to dihedral because it gives the same amount of stability either way up.

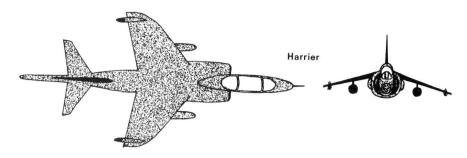

111 Sweepback with anhedral to reduce excess lateral stability.

Harrier

Sweep forward has the same characteristics as anhedral but reduces the tendency to tip stall. Washout is not normally needed on a glider using sweep forward, although extra dihedral will be required to give the same degree of lateral stability.

Both sweepback and sweep forward result in a greater tendency for the wings to twist when they bend upwards under load. For this reason, swept wings are always a little heavier than the equivalent straight wing.

On gliders, sweepback and sweep forward are generally only used as a means of moving the area of the wings back or forward, without moving the point at which they are mounted on the fuselage. For example, on many tandem two-seaters (ASK13, Bocian, Blanik) the wings are swept forward in order to keep the wing root behind the instructor's seat while avoiding having the C of G too far forward. This has the convenient result that the rear pilot is sitting very close to the C of G so that the glider may be flown solo without ballast and without a large change in the C of G position. However, sweep forward reduces the lateral stability so that compensating extra dihedral is necessary. This in turn has its advantages and disadvantages, which the designer must consider. The extra dihedral angle raises the wingtips and improves the ground clearance – and no instructor will grumble about that on a two-seater trainer.

Lateral control Conventional gliders and powered aircraft all use ailerons as the basic method of lateral control, but this was not always the case. Earlier machines, such as the Bleriot, had wing warping, or even wings which were pivoted at the fuselage so that one side could be moved to a larger angle of incidence than the other.

Simple free-flight model aircraft usually rely on the effects of the large dihedral angle, and turn by applying rudder only. The resulting skidding movement puts the outer wing at a larger angle to the airflow, giving it more lift. However, this is a very inefficient method of applying bank because the whole aircraft skids sideways through the air creating more drag.

This happens on all aircraft and is sometimes known as the 'further effect of the rudder'. From the pilot's point of view it is an after-effect of using the rudder to yaw the aircraft, which is seldom deliberately done in flying. It is most noticeable during a crosswind landing and in a poor turn. When the rudder is applied to 'kick' the aircraft straight for touchdown, some opposite aileron is necessary to prevent the yaw resulting in a banking movement. It will be noticed that during turns, corrections for slip and skid with the rudder also require a correction on the ailerons to keep the bank constant.

This tendency to over-bank is a useful warning against using too much rudder in a turn. If more than a small opposite aileron deflection is needed to hold the bank steady this is a sign either that the speed is becoming danger-ously slow, or the pilot is applying far too much rudder. In either case the situation is nearing the danger point as the glider will certainly drop the inner wing and try to spin if it stalls.

The glider tends to become laterally unstable close to the stall and banks more and more steeply. Over-ruddering has the same result but causes a loss of speed and height as well because of the additional drag caused by the sideways movement of the fuselage through the air.

A few high-speed machines use lift spoilers in addition to ailerons, but regardless of what method is used the principle is the same. In order to bank the aircraft one wing must develop more lift than the other.

Fig. 112 shows the operation of the ailerons and how the loads they create at the wingtips tend to twist the wing. If much twisting does occur the result is far less effective control, or even a reversal of control.

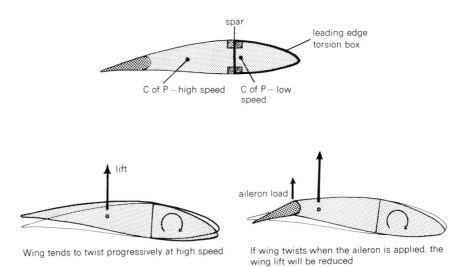

Wing tends to twist progressively at high speed

If wing twists when the aileron is applied, the wing lift will be reduced

112 Aileron reversal. At high speed the wing tends to twist to a small angle and the torsion box is vital to prevent it failing. The downgoing aileron increases this tendency and if the wing does twist, the reduced incidence results in *less* lift and therefore a reversal of the effect of the aileron.

Several of the aircraft in the film *Those Magnificent Men in Their Flying Machines* suffered from this kind of problem because they had originally been designed with very flexible wings for wing warping control, and had then been adapted to use ailerons. In spite of stiffening and extra wire bracing the wings warped when the ailerons were used, so that there was very little lateral control. This kind of problem would develop on most aircraft if they were flown in excess of their design speeds, but, with these particular aircraft, a state of no control was reached at about 50 or 60 knots. Fortunately, the rudder could be used to help matters, since all these aircraft had a reasonable amount of dihedral, and, if all else failed, the wing could usually be raised by applying rudder away from the dropped wing.

Although the cause of this problem was not really identified until the 1950s, most early glider designs in fact suffered from wings which were far too flexible. The aileron control on gliders such as the T21b began to get very sluggish on aerotow and at speeds of over 60 knots and this was mainly due to lack of torsional stiffness. Most gliders of this period resorted to very large, wide chord ailerons in an effort to get better control, but these also tended to flex and the large surface and wide chord gave high loads on the stick.

When the first of the laminar flow wings was introduced the much thicker ply skins necessary to keep an accurate contour and ripple-free surface also had the effect of increasing the stiffness. The ailerons immediately became far more effective and much smaller surfaces could be used. The penalty of extra weight was offset by the greatly improved gliding performance due to the lower wing drag.

Aileron drag Whenever extra lift is being developed it is bound to induce extra drag – in this world, you never get something for nothing!

When the ailerons are being used to apply or take off bank one wing is given more lift and the other less in order to start the banking movement. Since extra lift means extra drag, the lifting wing is dragged back, and, in addition to the banking movement, the aircraft tends to swing or yaw in the opposite direction. If this is allowed to happen the aircraft slips sideways through the air creating very high drag. The long wings and short fuselage of the glider accentuate this tendency so that the 'adverse yaw', as it is known, is very pronounced. Light aircraft with much shorter, stumpy wings are scarcely affected by it (see Fig. 21 on page 46).

There are several ways of reducing the aileron drag and adverse yaw, the most important of which is the use of differential gearing of the ailerons. Fig. 113 shows how it works. The downward moving aileron always moves through a much smaller angle than the upward moving one and this reduces the extra lift, but also keeps the drag low. This is due to the fact that ailerons and flaps like these increase the lift for the first 8°–10° with only a small increase in drag. Beyond that angle the drag rise is much more rapid, until above about 25° the increase is very nearly all drag. The use of differential ailerons does not significantly reduce the rate of roll. However, it does lessen

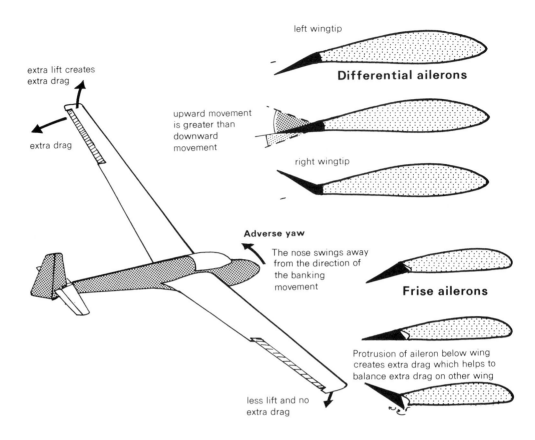

113 Methods of reducing the adverse yaw caused by aileron drag. Differential ailerons are used on all modern gliders and some use Frise ailerons as well.

the adverse yaw which, if allowed to occur, reduces the rate of roll for a few seconds, and also results in high drag from the fuselage battering its way sideways through the air. All modern gliders use differential ailerons and the upward moving one usually moves about twice the angle of the other.

Spoilers have been used on a few experimental gliders to assist in increasing the rate of roll without increasing the aileron drag. They are not very effective and have very little 'feel', but do produce some extra drag on the down-going wingtip. For example, on the Sigma experimental glider the very tiny ailerons were supplemented by spoilers when the stick was moved across the last few inches to apply full aileron. Spoilers of this kind are also used on some airliners and have a particular advantage over ailerons which is that they do not tend to twist the wing.

Generally speaking, the glider pilot will like the handling of a glider if it has light controls, a reasonably high rate of roll, and only a small amount of adverse yaw. Some designers use Frise ailerons in order to even out the drag of the wings while the aileron is being applied. In this case the upward moving aileron is arranged to project a little below the lower surface of the wing. This increases the drag on that wing and at the same time acts as a small horn balance which helps the pilot to move the control, making the ailerons much lighter. This system is usually used on powered aircraft and can be seen on the Auster, Super Cub and Beagle Pup, and on the Cobra and Olympia 463 gliders, and Falke motor gliders.

Many of the glider designs using full span flaps for extra cruising performance move their flaps and ailerons in conjunction with each other. For example, the Kestrel, Nimbus and ASW 17 all raise and droop their ailerons in conjunction with the flaps in order to keep a similar wing section over the whole span and to avoid the large drag losses which would occur if the flaps and ailerons were at different angles in normal flight. Additionally, on some designs, because the ailerons and flaps move up or down together the aileron in effect runs the whole length of the wing. This is undoubtedly an improvement as far as performance is concerned, but it does mean that when the flaps are down for low speed circling the aileron drag is once again rather high. The downgoing aileron is moving to quite a large angle, creating considerable extra drag with not much increase in lift and this results in slightly less lateral control than when the ailerons and flaps are in the neutral position. This effect is sufficiently marked to make it worth starting the take off run with no flap deflection so that the ailerons are powerful. As soon as speed and good control are gained the flaps can be lowered.

It requires fine engineering and structural design to make the flaps and ailerons work freely, in spite of the bending of the wing which may be as much as 4–5 feet under load.

A few older glider designs resorted to geared tabs on the ailerons to reduce the pilot effort needed to make a full stick deflection. This is very common on medium-sized powered machines but should not be necessary on gliders or light aircraft.

Aileron flutter
The feel of the ailerons is sometimes spoilt by a snatching of the control, or a tendency for them to oscillate in bumpy air. The pilot likes, and expects, to feel a progressive increase in pressure on the stick when moving it further and further over to move the ailerons. If, during a full deflection, the loads suddenly cease to increase, it will give the pilot the impression that the control is snatching or moving itself for the last part of the movement. This may be due to poor rigging if the aircraft is fitted with Frise ailerons or, on prototype machines, if the Frise shape is incorrect. In these cases the balancing effect of the Frise suddenly occurs after the aileron has moved a certain amount. Another possible cause is lack of mass balance on the ailerons. Complete mass balancing of the controls is not mandatory and on many machines little or no mass balancing is used. If the aileron itself is rather heavy, and so has its mass well behind the hinge point, snatching and oscillations will happen in bumpy air. The test pilot checks for this by flying

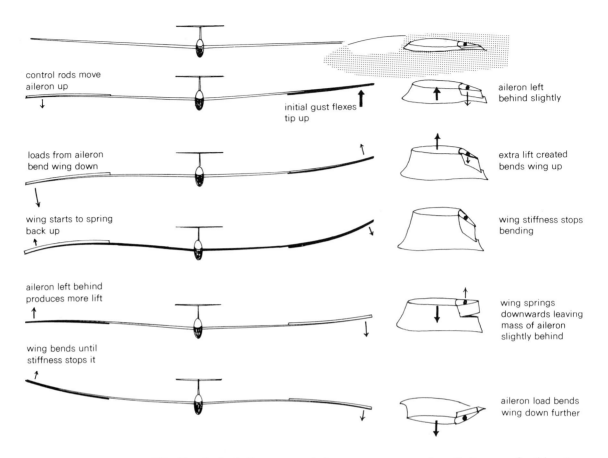

control rods move
aileron up

initial gust flexes
tip up

aileron left
behind slightly

loads from aileron
bend wing down

extra lift created
bends wing up

wing starts to spring
back up

wing stiffness stops
bending

aileron left behind
produces more lift

wing springs
downwards leaving
mass of aileron
slightly behind

wing bends until
stiffness stops it

aileron load bends
wing down further

114 How lack of aileron mass balance can cause serious flutter on a flexible wing. The oscillations tend to build up until structural failure can occur.

at gradually increasing speeds and giving the stick a sharp sideways tap. Normally the stick will just return to the central position without oscillating, or it may overshoot and then come back. If the aileron has insufficient mass balance it will oscillate to and fro several times and in bumpy air this will feel very twitchy and unpleasant, although it might not be dangerous. However, if the wings are rather weak or flexible this kind of oscillation may start a serious flutter.

Fig. 114 explains why this flutter occurs. It may seem rather academic to include an explanation of flutter in this book, but it is likely to become a more common phenomenon with glass fibre machines. Even a few extra coats of paint on the control surfaces will upset their balance point and make them liable to this kind of flutter, particularly if there is any excessive play in the control circuit. Any snatching or twitchiness of the controls should be taken seriously and investigated immediately.

The risk of flutter increases rapidly at higher speeds when the air loads become greater and tend to flex the structure more. With design diving speeds of less than 130 knots it is sufficient for the designer to show that the structure is reasonably stiff and that there is no tendency for flutter up to that speed during the test flights. If it is intended to fly the aircraft above this speed it is desirable for all control surfaces to be fully mass balanced. Many experienced pilots do not seem to understand that all structures will flutter if the speed is increased far enough. In fact, the critical speed may be only a few knots above the 'never exceed speed' and this is based on a glider in perfect condition as it left the factory. There have already been an alarming number of catastrophic failures with gliders being flown at excessive speeds in turbulent conditions and it is vital to realise that even the V_{NE} refers only to smooth air conditions and is not intended to be a speed for normal operations.

Flutter is not confined to the ailerons, and the production models of several types of glider have had to be modified because of flutter problems which did not become apparent during the manufacturers' test flying. Because of the relatively flexible fuselages there have been several cases of rudder flutter at high speed. This can be cured by mass balancing the rudder surface in the same way as the elevator and ailerons, or by putting a friction damper in the control circuit. There have been at least two miraculous escapes from the possibility of complete structural failure due to flutter. A case of rudder flutter resulted in such violent twisting of the fuselage that the canopy fell off when the canopy catches failed. The other was a case of an experimental machine which had flutter in the all-moving tailplane and anti-balance tabs. The damage included a complete failure of the torsion box on one wing and a broken stabiliser spar. However, in spite of the damage the glider was flown down to a safe landing by the somewhat worried test pilot. Flutter is dangerous!

9

Directional and spiral stability and control

Directional stability

It is important that the glider has a built-in tendency to align itself with the direction of the airflow in order to remain streamlined. This is known as directional or weathercock stability. The aircraft should behave like a weathercock, swinging itself into line with the airflow so that the fuselage presents the minimum frontal area all the time.

This is mainly a question of having a large enough fin and rudder. In Fig. 115, showing the side view of a modern machine, the fin and rudder are kept small in order to reduce the weight and drag, but they are still large enough to provide adequate stability and control.

Compared with modern powered aircraft gliders have far less directional stability and, as a result, they depend upon the pilot using the rudder to keep the aircraft pointing in the right direction. In fact, this is all the rudder does in normal flight. Without the rudder movements the glider would tend to swing off sideways from time to time and the movement of the fuselage through the air would create very high drag and ruin the gliding performance.

If the fin is made larger to improve the directional stability a larger rudder will probably be needed to provide control on the ground and prevent the tendency to swing when taking off or landing with a crosswind. It will, however, be heavy to operate and the whole tail will weigh more and will create more drag, as well as requiring a stiffer fuselage to support it. Obviously the size of fin and rudder is largely a matter for the designer and the glider pilot soon learns to adjust himself to minor differences between one machine and another.

The fin and rudder power must be adequate for good spin recovery, for preventing adverse yaw when full aileron is used to apply or take off bank and for good directional control during the take off and landing run.

When the rudder is applied for a sideslip the glider yaws to the side until a balance of forces occurs. The yawing of the rudder is balanced by the tendency for the directional stability to weathercock the fuselage back into line with the airflow. If the rudder power is strong and the stability weak, a large angle of yaw will result. When the directional stability is very strong

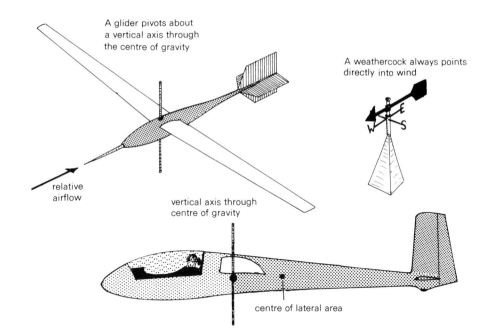

A glider pivots about a vertical axis through the centre of gravity

A weathercock always points directly into wind

relative airflow

vertical axis through centre of gravity

centre of lateral area

115 Directional or weathercock stability. The fin and rudder ensure that the centre of the lateral area is behind the C of G. An aircraft always tends to realign itself with the relative airflow like a dart or arrow.

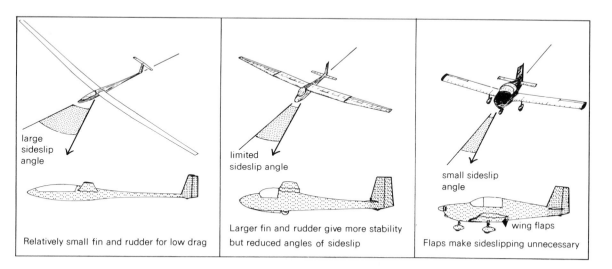

large sideslip angle

Relatively small fin and rudder for low drag

limited sideslip angle

Larger fin and rudder give more stability but reduced angles of sideslip

small sideslip angle

wing flaps

Flaps make sideslipping unnecessary

116 Directional stability and sideslipping. The angle of sideslip is limited by the power of the rudder and the directional stability. High-performance sailplanes use small tails for low weight and drag. Modern light aircraft are directionally very stable because of the large fin and rudder areas and higher flying speeds. Effective flaps steepen the approach and make sideslipping unnecessary.

and the rudder power rather weak, only very small angles of yaw can be obtained. Each type of aircraft will vary in its angle of yaw in a full sideslip (Fig. 116). Modern powered aircraft will hardly sideslip at all because of their strong directional stability. However, since most modern powered aircraft have effective flaps to make the approach steeper, sideslipping is seldom necessary as a means of losing height. Gliders and old powered aircraft, such as Tiger Moths, will sideslip relatively well. If the angle of sideslip is much greater than the maximum angle of the rudder deflection the airflow itself will hold the rudder over in a sideslip. This overbalance, or reversal of rudder loads during sideslipping, is a common, though undesirable, feature of many modern gliders. On machines with a wide-chord rudder or a very large rudder surface the pilot may need to use considerable force to recentre the rudder during recoveries from sideslips and from spins.

As with all lifting surfaces, the fin and rudder are far more effective if they are of reasonably high aspect ratio (tall with a small chord) and, of course, the length of fuselage boom from the C of G determines the leverage and therefore has a great influence on the directional stability and control.

Moving the C of G back or increasing the side area of the fuselage ahead of the C of G (for example by lengthening the cockpit to bring the pilot forward slightly) will, as with model aircraft, reduce the directional stability, unless the fin and rudder are enlarged. Additional dihedral on the wings when they flex upwards under an extra load may also reduce the effective directional stability, besides increasing the lateral stability.

Directional stability and control on the ground

The position of the main wheel in relation to the centre of gravity has a considerable influence on the control and stability of the aircraft while it is running on the ground. This is because the aircraft then pivots about the wheel instead of, as in flight, about the C of G. On most modern gliders and on tail wheel aircraft the weathercocking effect is extra powerful, because with the forward position of the wheel there is much more side area behind the wheel than behind the C of G. On the K8, K13 and other gliders fitted with a forward main skid, there is less side area behind the wheel and directional stability on the ground is less good.

In strong crosswinds an aircraft with the wheel ahead of the C of G will have a very much stronger tendency to swing itself into wind and the rudder will be less effective at stopping it. This is a very real problem with modern gliders.

If the friction between the ground and the tail wheel or skid is sufficient to prevent a swing, a normal straight take off or landing run will be possible. However, if the friction is low, the pilot will be unable to prevent a swing into wind while the glider is still at low speed and rudder control is not yet effective.

Extra caution is needed with gliders or powered aircraft operating from smooth, hard surfaces like tarmac runways. If they have a tail skid instead of a tail wheel there will be very little resistance to swinging and at low

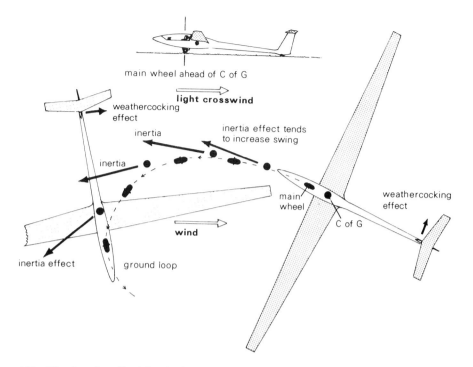

117 The inertia effect tends to accentuate any swing when the main wheel is ahead of the C of G as in modern gliders. In light winds the inertia effect becomes more powerful than the weathercocking effect.

speeds the pilot will be unable to stop a swing into wind. On grass or softer ground it may be a help to keep the tail down at low speeds. A backward movement on the stick will increase the friction and the resistance to the tail skid moving sideways over the ground.

In no wind conditions it might be expected that the longer moment arm of the rudder on an aircraft with the wheel ahead of the C of G would give better directional control. However, there is one vital factor which cancels out this apparent advantage. When the wheel is ahead of the C of G the inertia of the aircraft also accentuates any swing (Fig. 117). In windy weather this is unimportant because of the powerful weathercocking effect. In light winds, and particularly in light crosswinds, once the glider has started to swing badly the inertia will keep the swing going and a ground loop will be inevitable.

When the main wheel is behind the C of G the inertia tends to keep the aircraft straight and serious swings or ground loops will not occur, unless the wingtip touches the ground and causes the swing (Fig. 118).

This problem is accentuated by the higher landing and take off speeds of many modern gliders and by their rather ineffective aileron control at low

189

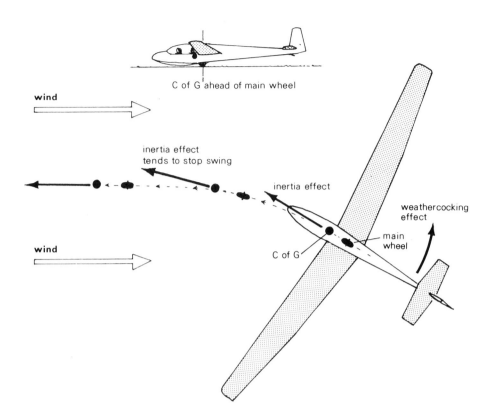

118 Weathercocking effect with main wheel behind the **C of G**. Inertia effect tends to reduce the swing on the ground run.

speed. This makes it much more likely for a wingtip to touch the ground or catch in long grass and start a swing. In these aircraft it is safest during take off to have the wingtip holder on the *downwind* wing so that, if he drags the wingtip at all, he is swinging the glider out of wind. Otherwise he may cause an uncontrollable swing and the take off may have to be abandoned.

The golden rule on take off is to allow extra room in case it proves impossible to keep straight. It is always wise on a crosswind take off to anticipate a possible swing by starting the run with full rudder to prevent the glider swinging into wind, and then reduce it as the speed increases and the controls become more effective.

Spiral stability (Fig. 119.)   The balance between directional and lateral stability controls what is known as 'spiral stability'.

The easiest way to understand the essentials about spiral stability is to describe two extreme situations, one when the lateral stability is very marked but the directional stability is weak, and the other when directional stability

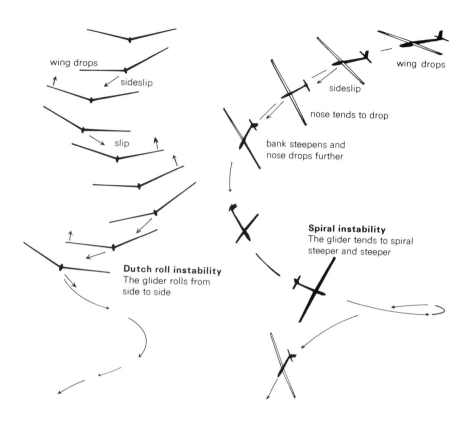

119 Spiral stability is the balance between directional and lateral stability. Too much dihedral or sweepback or lack of fin and rudder result in Dutch roll instability. Too much directional stability or insufficient dihedral give spiral instability with the aircraft tending to go into an ever-steepening diving turn. Most gliders are slightly spirally unstable and go into an ever-steepening turn when 'hands off'.

is strong and lateral stability is weak. Most aircraft are designed to be slightly spirally unstable. The desirable degree of spiral instability is somewhere between the two extremes and is largely a matter of opinion.

When an aircraft has a relatively large amount of dihedral (or sweepback) even a very small amount of yaw will result in a powerful banking movement. (This is so severe in many high-speed aircraft that, if the unexpected failure of an outboard engine causes a swing to one side, the resulting rolling movement may be difficult, or even impossible, to stop. Even a very large airliner may bank past the vertical before it can be stopped!)

Any slight yawing movement from one side to the other will produce a rolling movement which is known as 'Dutch roll'. If the directional stability is made much stronger by enlarging the fin and rudder there will be very little tendency for the aircraft to yaw out of line with the airflow. Alternatively, just reducing the dihedral angle (or sweepback) would have much the same effect by lessening the tendency to roll. (This problem of excess lateral stability is usually dealt with on high-speed aircraft by operating the rudder automatically to damp out the yaw before it has time to develop. The detector, which is far quicker and more sensitive than any pilot, senses the start of the yaw and applies just enough rudder to stop it. This is known as a yaw damper.)

When the directional stability is strong and the lateral stability is weak the aircraft becomes spirally unstable. If the aircraft is tipped into a banked position by a gust it will begin to sideslip towards the lower wing. This will result in an increase in lift being developed by the lower wing, because of the dihedral, and this would normally level the wings again. However, the directional stability is also working at the same time, and this will make the aircraft tend to swing into line with the relative airflow. If the left wing drops the glider will slip to the left and weathercock round further in the same direction. This effect will then continue to swing the nose round and down to the left. The yawing motion will result in more lift from the outer wing and the outcome will depend on whether it is stronger than the lift on the lower wing. If the lateral stability is strong the wings will tend to be levelled, but if the directional stability is strong, the aircraft will continue in an ever-steepening diving turn or spiral dive. (Fig. 112.)

A pilot will never usually attempt to measure spiral stability and the gliders that we normally fly feel quite pleasant to handle, although most of them are spirally unstable and will only right themselves from a gentle bank. Spiral stability also varies with speed and at very slow speeds most gliders are more unstable. During all turns at thermal flying speeds the bank will tend to increase and it is quite normal on gliders (but not on most other aircraft) for a control movement to be needed to prevent this overbanking. At lower speeds, as the glider gets close to the stall, this tendency becomes very marked and a larger and larger aileron movement is needed until control is finally lost and the bank will increase despite all the aileron movement being used to prevent it.

After these rather lengthy explanations of the stability and control of a glider and conventional light aircraft it is worth recapping with some short notes.

Summary of longitudinal stability

Longitudinal stability depends on the tail volume, i.e. tailplane times its distance to the C of G. Stability is increased as the C of G is moved forward, but fore and aft control is made heavier. The aircraft trims out to a higher speed and runs short of nose up control at low speeds.

Stability decreases as the C of G is moved back, the control becomes lighter and more powerful, and the aircraft trims out to a lower speed and tends to run short of nose down control so that recovery from stalls and spins becomes more difficult. When the aircraft is trimmed for a certain speed it will tend to return to that speed after any small disturbance. Larger disturbances may result in a phugoid, or nose up and down oscillation which may continue, get worse, or be damped out after a few cycles. If the machine is stable it will require either a bigger and bigger movement on the stick to increase or decrease speed progressively (stick fixed stability) or a greater stick force (stick free stability).

It may be satisfactory to have neutral stick fixed stability provided that the stick free stability is positive. In simple terms, provided that the pilot has to push harder to go faster, he will not mind whether he actually has to move the stick forward or if it stays in the same position.

When an aircraft is unstable, stick movements and pressures have to be applied to prevent the machine going into an ever-steepening dive or climb. This is not acceptable and is dangerous.

The C of G aft limit (the minimum allowable cockpit load in a glider) is often determined by the need to maintain fore and aft stability. However, on some types of glider it is limited by the spin recovery characteristics. The further back the position of the C of G the more difficult it is to make a recovery from a spin. The importance of observing the cockpit limitations, and in particular the minimum cockpit load, cannot be too strongly emphasised. If necessary, extra ballast must be carried to fulfil these requirements.

Summary of lateral stability

Lateral stability is normally provided by dihedral, which gives a righting action whenever the aircraft slips sideways through the air. Rolling tendencies are damped out and, at normal speeds, all gliders tend to resist them.

With gliders, the large wing span and relatively poor directional stability caused by the short fuselage create special problems with aileron drag. Differential and Frise ailerons are used to reduce the adverse yaw caused by aileron drag, but it cannot be eliminated. (More lift always means more drag.)

The rate of roll is largely governed by the wing span.

Summary of directional stability

Directional, or weathercock stability is provided by the fin and rudder. It is important that the whole aircraft should point directly at the relative airflow so that it is streamlined. Good weathercock stability reduces the amount of rudder movement required to keep the fuselage pointing in the right direction.

The power of the fin and rudder must be adequate to provide control at very low speed on the ground, to overcome the adverse yaw from the ailerons at normal flying speeds and to provide good spin recovery.

Summary of spiral stability

Gliders usually have slight spiral instability and any turn tends to steepen itself and develop into an ever-steepening spiral dive. The pilot prevents this with a small counter-move on the stick to stop the bank increasing. This instability becomes more marked at very low speeds and acts as a warning of imminent danger from stalling in a turn.

Applying rudder yaws the nose so that the airflow meets the aircraft at an angle. The dihedral angle results in extra lift on the outer wing so that the aircraft starts to bank in the direction in which the rudder was applied. In this way, the rudder tends to result in banking movements, although these are after effects. The very large increases in drag caused by using the rudder to apply bank make it a most undesirable thing to do.

The ideal glider A glider will be pleasant to fly when the controls are well harmonised – that is, when they require approximately the same force to move them. The control forces should increase progressively at higher speeds and the ailerons should give a high rate of roll with low aileron drag. The fore and aft stability should be sufficient to make the machine easy to trim to, and hold, a steady speed, yet the stick forces should be low enough to avoid the necessity for retrimming every few moments. There should be no twitchiness, or tendency for any of the controls to oscillate or snatch. At the same time the glider must be comfortable, have an adequate range of cockpit loads and a good performance at both low and high speeds. A well-sprung undercarriage, effective wheel and airbrakes and a low landing speed will make landings in fields safe and easy.

In addition to these flying characteristics the designer must also make the machine easy and light to handle on the ground if it is intended for club use, and it should also be quick and easy to rig and de-rig.

10 Flight limitations

Airworthiness requirements

In order to be a good soaring machine a sailplane must be both lightweight and aerodynamically efficient, but it is also essential that it is structurally sound and safe to fly. However, unlike a fully aerobatic powered aircraft, a sailplane will never be strong enough for the pilot to throw it about with careless abandon. The fact is that the machine will either be good for soaring or it will be good for aerobatics.

The design of any new glider, or any other type of aircraft, is controlled by the National Airworthiness Authority. Different countries may have slightly different requirements but since they all aim to ensure a safe but efficient machine, the differences are very minor.

Every glider has (or should have) a flight limitation placard in the cockpit stating the loading limitations (maximum and minimum cockpit loads) and the permitted speeds and manoeuvres. The main limits, such as the maximum launching speeds, rough airspeed and never exceed speed are given on the placard but it would not be practical to show all the limitations (Fig. 120).

The strength requirements for a glider for normal soaring must cater for all the usual flight loads likely during launching and general flying, plus the effects of flying into turbulence and up- and down-gusts. In good soaring conditions the pilot will sometimes want to be able to cruise at high speeds and to pull up steeply and circle tightly as he comes into a strong thermal. These pull-ups may mean an increase in the loading to about three times that of normal flight (3g) so that the minimum design strength of such machines has to be at least 5g, to allow for the effects of rough air with a reasonable amount of margin of safety.

The maximum load for which a glider is designed is known as the proof load, and theoretically it should be possible to apply this without any damage occurring. Beyond this load some damage is to be expected and, in the case of a metal machine, permanent deformation may occur which weakens the structure. In order to allow for differences in the material used and for gradual deterioration during service, the design ultimate loads are normally

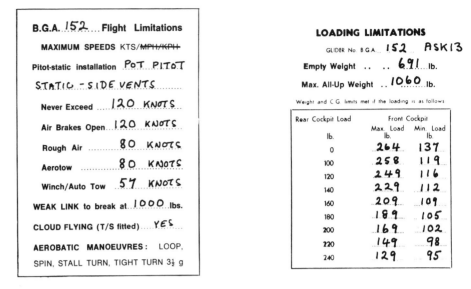

LOADING LIMITATIONS

GLIDER No. B.G.A. *152 ASK13*

Empty Weight .. .. *691* lb.

Max. All-Up Weight .. *1060* lb.

Weight and C.G. limits met if the loading is as follows

Rear Cockpit Load lb.	Front Cockpit Max. Load lb.	Min. Load lb.
0	264	137
100	258	119
120	249	116
140	229	112
160	209	109
180	189	105
200	169	102
220	149	98
240	129	95

120 Typical flight limitation and cockpit loading placard for a two-seater glider. The maximum and minimum load in the front cockpit depends on the rear cockpit load.

50% more than the proof loads. Experience shows that this is a reasonable allowance.

Although a sailplane is not intended to be flown upside down there will be occasions in rough air when the effects of flying into a severe downdraught will result in negative 'g'. Most gliders are only designed for negative loads of about half the positive ones.

Unless the assumption is made that the pilot will be reasonably sensible about the handling of the controls, the glider would have to be excessively strong and heavy. Most gliders are not strong enough to allow the pilot to use a full deflection of *any* of the controls at speeds of more than about two and a quarter or two and a half times the normal stalling speed. This represents a very serious limitation on the use of both the ailerons and rudder, since they may be light enough to be applied fully at much higher speeds. Since the loads increase in proportion to the square of the speed it requires only a small excess of speed to produce loads which are far above those for which the glider has been designed. Similarly, the reserve of strength is rapidly used up by flying at speeds in excess of the 'design diving speed' (VD) quite apart from the risks of flutter.

Flight envelope In order to simplify the designer's task the minimum strength is defined in terms of the airspeeds and load factors in a graphical form known as the 'flight envelope'. (Fig. 121.) This indicates the maximum loads and speeds which the pilot should never exceed and for which the designer must stress the glider. The effect of gusts is superimposed on this graph and this means that some extra strength is provided to reduce the risk of damage in turbulent conditions.

Pilots tend to assume that there are large margins between the design loads and speeds and those shown on the placard. It is as well to be realistic about them. As far as the placard 'never exceed speed' (V_{NE}) is concerned this is 0.9 of the design diving speed (V_D). This does allow a small margin for accidentally exceeding the V_{NE} and for minor instrument errors but 10–15 knots is not much of a margin in a modern sailplane which gains speed so rapidly in a dive. During the test flying it is usual to go to 0.95 V_D to ensure that there are no problems at the lower placard speed. Above this speed you are flying in conditions which have not been fully explored and by 1.25 V_D the loads in the highly stressed areas such as the tailplane and rear fuselage will be reaching the ultimate design loads and failure will be imminent. In addition to the excessive loads this is the speed at which flutter is likely to cause failure. However, without full mass balancing of all the controls, speeds of over 130 knots may result in flutter, and at V_{NE} it is possible for present-day designs to be very close to their flutter speed without any obvious sign of trouble. A little extra play caused by wear in the control system may be enough to tip the balance at these speeds and any damage or excess wear on control surface drives and hinges cannot therefore be tolerated where the normal operating speeds are close to V_{NE}, as in high-performance machines.

Loads on the wing structure

The main loads on the wing structure are the result of changes in the amount of lift developed. For example, when the aircraft is recovering from a dive or is being pulled round a tight turn the force required to make the change of direction is provided by the lift from the wings. When the pilot moves the stick back in order to recover from a dive, the result is to pull the wing to a larger angle of attack so that it develops more lift. The extra lift provides the force to make the aircraft change its flight path and, of course, produces the extra bending loads on the wing. (See Fig. 18 on page 43.)

At any given speed the load on the wings will depend on how large an angle of attack is reached. At lower speeds a wing will stall before the loads become excessive and this means that, however strong an up-gust or however sharply the pilot pulls back on the stick, the wing will always stall before the load becomes critical. At higher speeds, the pilot could easily overstress the glider by pulling back sharply. Most modern machines are designed to take positive loads of up to 5g or 6g and, since the stalling speed varies with the square root of the load factor, at speeds below about two and a quarter or two and a half times the normal stalling speed the wing will always reach the stalling angle before the loads reach the design limit. At higher speeds it is a very different matter and the pilot is expected to use discretion in handling the controls since it is only too easy to reach the design loads, particularly in gusty conditions.

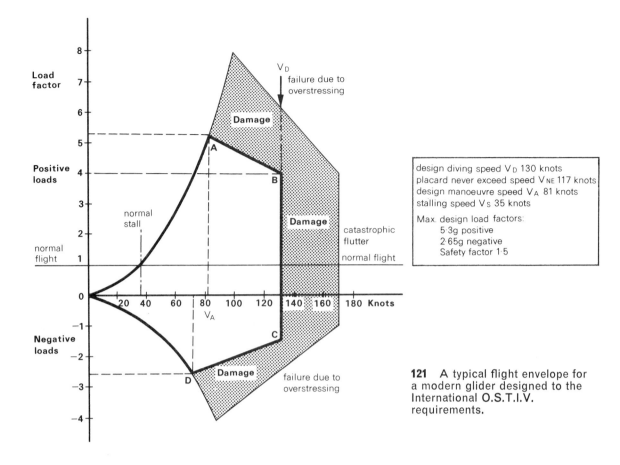

design diving speed V_D 130 knots
placard never exceed speed V_{NE} 117 knots
design manoeuvre speed V_A 81 knots
stalling speed V_S 35 knots

Max. design load factors:
5·3g positive
2·65g negative
Safety factor 1·5

121 A typical flight envelope for a modern glider designed to the International O.S.T.I.V. requirements.

Special care is needed during cloud flying and aerobatics since it is easy to build up excessive speed in a steep dive. This places the pilot in a critical situation, since it will be easy to pull too hard in an attempt to prevent the speed rising beyond the placard speed while failure to pull back soon enough will inevitably mean overspeeding and risk of flutter.

Experience has shown that, while most pilots are aware of the maximum 'g' loadings for which their gliders are stressed, few of them understand some of the other limitations to which the glider has been designed. This is a dangerous state of affairs since some of the design limits can be exceeded easily and there is a tendency to believe that because no damage or failure occurred it is safe to repeat the manoeuvres on other occasions.

Tail loads Because of the unstable movement of the centre of pressure of the aerofoil (explained in Chapter 7) there is a severe twisting force on the wing at high speeds. This results in a very large down load on the stabiliser. An even greater down load occurs if the glider is pulled up into a climb or a turn at high speed since the tailplane has to develop the extra force to produce the pitching acceleration. (See Fig. 98 on page 158.)

Unless flutter occurs, serious structural failure is almost always preceded by the tailplane or rear fuselage failing due to these high down loads. If a wing does fail it can almost always be traced either to exceeding the placard speed or to existing damage to the spar or torsion box which has gone undetected or has not been considered significant.

It is not uncommon to hear pilots in competitions or on record attempts boasting of flying between thermals at the placard speed (V_{NE}). In smooth air this would be reasonably safe, but in turbulent air such as the rotor flow of a wave system or in strong thermals, there is a very real risk of damage. It is important to realise what a narrow margin of strength remains if the placard speeds are exceeded or if the air is very turbulent. Any structural failure at high speed is likely to be catastrophic, with the pilot subjected to such high negative 'g' that he is unlikely to be conscious enough to escape and use his parachute.

In competition flying the start line is a critical point, since it can save several minutes flying time to cross the line just below 1000 metres and as near V_{NE} as possible. The speed is then turned into extra height and distance. This means starting with an extra 400 or 500 feet about a mile away from the line and diving down to gain speed and to cross just below the maximum allowable height. The exact height loss to gain this speed is found by trial beforehand but may be upset by lift or sink during the actual dive. Lift is particularly dangerous, since diving off the extra height in a modern machine can only result in exceeding the placard speed. If there is a risk of crossing the line too high for a 'good start', the pilot may, in the heat of the moment, accidentally overspeed, and there was a case of a glider disintegrating over the start line in World Championships because of this. Fortunately the pilot was thrown clear and parachuted to safety.

In the same way the pilot may be tempted to fly too fast for safety on final glide, but in this case he will be far too low to use a parachute. There is little to be gained by flying a few knots faster at this point since the time saved has already been wasted in climbing unnecessarily high. However, where the competition rules specify a maximum height for crossing the finishing line, extra height can be a real embarrassment.

Launching loads Aerotow launching causes little or no additional load compared with normal free flight and in *smooth air* it is not necessary to be concerned or to release if the placarded towing speed is exceeded. However, in turbulent conditions the speed must be kept within the limit or the loads during gusts may easily be more than those for which the aircraft was designed.

In the same way during winch and car launching, provided the air is smooth and normal piloting technique is used the structure is protected provided there is a weak link in the cable, since it will break long before the machine becomes overloaded. Once again, the loads can easily exceed the design limits in gusty conditions if the launching speed is too high. The weak link will not necessarily break before the loads become excessive and cause damage. In addition to the effects of gusts, the loads on the launch can be increased by sudden surges in the cable.

Obviously, if the speed is approaching the maximum indicated by the placard the angle of climb should be reduced. Even then the structure could still be overstressed in severe turbulence and the only safe thing to do if the speed increases too much is to release and have words with the winch or car driver before the next launch!

The winch launch speed is usually well below the manoeuvring speed (V_A) because the bending moments on the wing are much higher than for the equivalent pull-out or turn. In a 2g turn or pull-up the wing lift of twice the normal is offset by the effect of twice the wing weight acting downwards and relieving the bending moments. This has a similar effect to putting fuel in the wingtip tanks of some powered aircraft. The weight of the fuel opposes the bending of the wing caused by the extra lift so that a significant saving of weight is possible in the wing structure compared with carrying the same fuel in the fuselage.

On a winch launch, however, the glider is subject to only 1g, while the wings have to balance both the weight of the glider and the weight and pull of the cable (Fig. 87 on page 141). The bending moments on the wing are, therefore, much greater than might be expected and the maximum launching speed is limited by this.

Aerobatic limitations

It is obvious that many pilots are not aware of some of the special problems of performing aerobatics in gliders. In their ignorance they not only risk their own safety but that of the next pilot to fly the aircraft. In many countries aerobatics are totally forbidden unless the pilot is specially qualified and is flying one of the few, fully aerobatic machines, such as the German Salto or the Swiss Pilatus. This seems an unnecessary restriction provided that pilots really understand what they are doing and are shown how to perform the permitted manoeuvres smoothly before they attempt them solo.

Gliders are not normally designed for aerobatics, but the structural requirements for soaring result in a machine which is also strong enough for some aerobatic manoeuvres. The majority of designs are cleared as 'Semi-aerobatic' and this allows only the manoeuvres prescribed on the placard to be performed – normally loops, stall turns, steep turns of up to $3\frac{1}{2}$g and spinning.

The speed below which it is impossible to exceed the permissible load factor is known, as explained, as the manoeuvring speed (V_A). This is normally the limiting speed for full deflection of *all* the controls and, above that speed, the amount of movement allowable is progressively reduced until at the design diving speed it is only one-third of the range of movement. This has implications which are particularly important for the glider pilot who enjoys aerobatics since, on some types of glider, it may be quite easy to apply full aileron and keep it on while the speed is building up far beyond V_A. This results in much greater loads than the designer has allowed for and might cause structural failure.

Spinning does not involve very large loads because the high drag of the stalled wings restricts the speed and therefore the loads. Care is needed when spinning high-performance machines because they may become unstalled and build up speed and high 'g' in a spiral dive. It is also quite easy to reach very high speeds after the spin has been stopped and the glider is being brought back to level flight again.

Weight limitations　The weight limitations (Fig. 120) are important because of the slightly different structure weight and weight of equipment of each machine. After major repairs or re-covering gliders must be re-weighed and the permissible cockpit loads recalculated. The minimum load is particularly critical because the centre of gravity moves back rapidly as the pilot weight is reduced. The limits are determined either by the stability or the spin recovery characteristics, both of which deteriorate with an aft C of G. Being overweight is less of a hazard. The glider becomes more stable, more difficult to stall and is usually unspinnable. Since the designer's strength calculations are all based on the placard maximum all-up weight, the load factor which can safely be applied is reduced when this is exceeded and it is most unwise to do aerobatics. Excessive pilot weight will also increase the tail loads at high speeds and heavy pilots should limit the flying speed to well below the V_{NE} as a safety measure. In addition to the increase in flight loads, the landing shocks will also be greater and therefore more likely to cause damage.

Loops　It is only when the glider is flying at over 70 knots or so (V_A) that there is any possibility of overstressing it during a pull-up in smooth air. Below this speed the wing would stall before the loads became too great. A speed of 85 knots is usually ample for a loop in any type of glider and after diving to reach this speed a smooth, gentle, progressive backward movement on the stick is needed to start the loop. Unlike a powered machine the loop has to be tightened more and more until the glider has gone over the top. The backward movement must be gentle at first or the 'g' loading may become excessive. Then, as the glider is pulling up into the vertical climb, the stick is moved further and further back. By this time the speed is falling very rapidly and there is no longer any risk of overstressing. At the top of the loop the stick is usually right back on the stop and the speed may be well below the normal stalling speed. With gravity acting towards the centre of the loop the stalling speed is reduced to zero and the glider will inevitably drop over into a dive, even though it may feel very unpleasant for a few seconds. As the glider drops into the dive the backward movement must be relaxed a little or a high-speed stall may occur. The warning buffet is usually obvious, but if the backward movement were held on the glider would drop one wing and

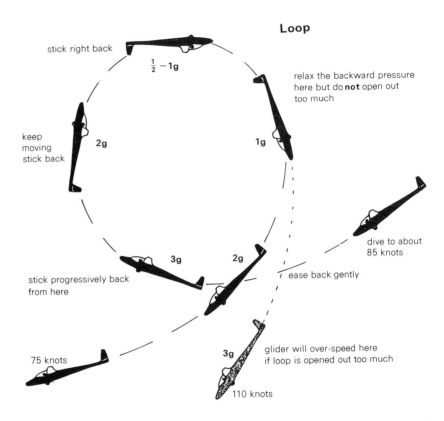

Loop

stick right back

$\frac{1}{2} - 1g$

relax the backward pressure here but do **not** open out too much

keep moving stick back

2g

1g

3g

2g

dive to about 85 knots

stick progressively back from here

ease back gently

75 knots

3g

glider will over-speed here if loop is opened out too much

110 knots

122 Looping. Dive to about 85 knots ($2\frac{1}{2}$–$2\frac{3}{4}$ times stalling speed). Ease back gently, increasing the backward movement progressively until stick is *right* back as the glider reaches the top. Relax the backward pressure slightly during the dive out.

flick as the elevator became effective again and the wing was pulled up to the stalling angle. Care must be taken not to open out the loop too much as, once the speed has increased beyond a certain point in a modern glider it will become excessive during the final stages of the manoeuvre. (Fig. 122.) Although this acceleration could be checked by opening the airbrakes this is not always a satisfactory solution. The airbrakes do tend to snatch themselves open violently at high speeds and unless the pilot is strong enough to prevent this it can result in damage to the wing structure around the airbrake boxes. Opening the airbrakes will result in an increase in the bending moment on the wing and most design requirements allow for this by reducing the stressing case when airbrakes or flaps are in use. In a typical instance this reduction means that the wing strength is reduced from 5g to $3\frac{1}{2}$g by opening the airbrakes or lowering the flaps. The lift is reduced over the wing in the area of the airbrakes so that the rest of the wing has to produce compensating extra lift and this effect can be seen clearly on large span gliders with rather flexible wings as the pilot opens the airbrakes on the approach. For example, the wingtips on the Nimbus can be seen to bend up about 2 feet as the airbrakes are opened and this gives a useful extra clearance between the wingtips and the ground during the landing. (Fig. 123.) Opening the airbrakes during a pull-out at high speed causes a frightening deflection. (The best advice here is not to look at the wingtips!)

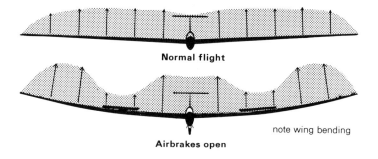

Normal flight

Airbrakes open

note wing bending

123 The redistribution of the lift when the airbrakes are open (exaggerated for clarity).

As explained, it is important during the final stages of a loop not to open out the loop so much that excessive speed is reached in the pull-out. When the snatching of the airbrakes is not serious excess speed can be avoided by opening them, but extra care is then needed because of the weakened wing structure. With powerful airbrakes there is no problem once they have been opened, unless the pull-out has to be made with a minimum loss of height. By limiting the speed it is far easier to limit the 'g' and the radius of the pull-out will also be greatly reduced if the speed is restricted.

If the type of glider is not cleared for looping manoeuvres you can be sure that there is a good reason for it. Many modern high-performance machines cannot be looped safely although they are structurally strong enough because the elevator power is often inadequate to make a reasonably tight loop, so that it is almost impossible to prevent the machine overspeeding during the recovery from the dive. (This will be more critical for heavy pilots.)

An average loop will give a maximum acceleration of $3-3\frac{1}{2}$g which is getting quite close to the design limits. This makes it sensible for an accelerometer to be fitted in gliders used for first attempts at aerobatics and for a manoeuvre to be demonstrated by a competent instructor before a pilot attempts it solo. Good loops can be performed by watching the needle of the accelerometer and pulling back to try to maintain $3-3\frac{1}{2}$g during the first half of the loop and again during the recovery. A moderately sharp gust can result in the glider being overstressed during looping and therefore aerobatics should only be performed in reasonably smooth air.

Many modern machines have all-moving stabilisers and rely on a spring device to provide some feel to the elevator control. Without any real control loads at high speed it is remarkably easy to pull excessive 'g' and overstress such machines and aerobatics are best avoided unless an accelerometer is fitted.

Stall turns, chandelles and tailslides

Whereas the stall turn is a perfectly safe and acceptable manoeuvre in a light aircraft it is far from safe in most gliders. For many years it has been discouraged in England and the chandelle (sometimes known as a wingover, or lazy eight) is recommended instead. Without the propeller slipstream to give the rudder some effectiveness at low speeds a glider is reluctant to yaw and there is a likelihood of it being left in a near-vertical climb with no means of preventing a tailslide. This is not only unpleasant but also dangerous as the reversed airflow tends to flap the control surfaces violently across against their stops and this may break them off at the hinges.

On several occasions this has actually happened but by the grace of God the glider landed safely with the rudder flapping on its cables! The large wing span and high inertia in yaw make it very difficult to initiate any yawing at low speeds with the rudder.

If at any time the glider is in a very steep nose up attitude and there seems to be a risk of it tailsliding, brace all the controls firmly in a fully deflected

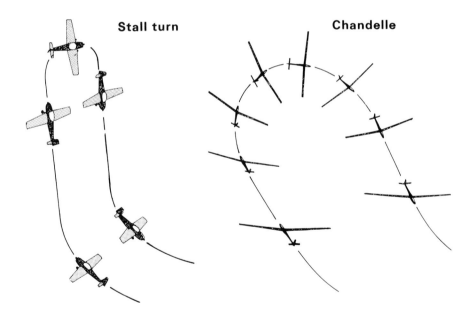

124 The stall turn and chandelle or wingover. The stall turn is not recommended for gliders since at low speeds the rudder control becomes inadequate to make the turn and a tailslide may occur. The chandelle is a combination of a steep turn and a loop.

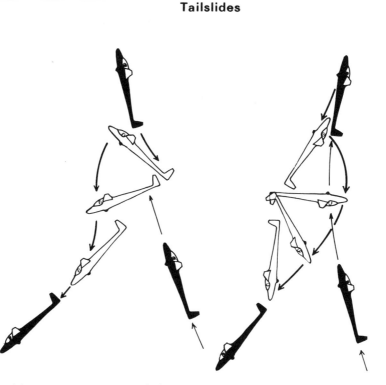

125 Tailslides can be dangerous. If a tailslide seems imminent, brace the stick and rudder firmly to prevent the controls being damaged.

position to prevent them snatching across and damaging themselves. The aircraft will usually slide backwards for a few feet as the nose drops violently and after a couple of seconds recovery can be made from the dive to level flight. A tailslide from an attitude beyond the vertical may result in a flip over backwards as in Fig. 125.

Applying full rudder as the glider is pulled up into the steep climb does not result in a satisfactory manoeuvre since it causes a violent skidding, which is usually followed by a rather undignified flop into the dive. Obviously the amount of rudder being applied must in any case be limited at high speed or the fin may be overstressed.

The manoeuvre we know as a chandelle is a safe alternative which is enjoyable to do and just as spectacular to watch as a true stall turn. It is really a looping manoeuvre and no harm occurs even if the glider gets very slow and more or less falls over the top. The easiest way to learn to do it is to start a series of steep turns changing over from left to right. During the changeover the nose is allowed to drop as the wings are brought level and then pulled up again as the bank is applied. It is important to remember to stop the bank when it reaches about 45° and then pull back on the stick to loop the machine over the top and back into a dive. As this is done the ailerons and rudder are used quite normally to bring the wings level, so that the recovery from the dive is made in the opposite direction to the entry.

Always apply the bank in plenty of time or the aircraft will lose too much speed before the turn is started.

It is usually easiest to start from a gentle turn in the opposite direction, rather than from a straight flight. Remember to stop the rolling movement or the aircraft will perform part of a barrel roll and will go past the vertical, so that the recovery will be much more than 180° from the direction of entry. The important point is to *pull* back on the stick and *loop* the glider over the top. If the speed seems rather slow do *not* ease forward as this will leave the glider pointing skywards with the risk of a tailslide. Pulling back will help the glider over the top and it will soon regain speed as it dives away.

Throughout a chandelle the glider should be flown smoothly and accurately and the rudder is used merely to prevent slip and skid as the bank is being changed.

Rolling manoeuvres (Fig. 126.) It might be thought that since a glider is not subjected to any inverted loads during a barrel roll that they should be safe to do. However, the rate of roll on gliders is so poor that full aileron will be required throughout, and as the speed is bound to increase very rapidly during the last half of the roll the glider will invariably exceed the maximum speed for full aileron, or will sideslip out of the manoeuvre. In both cases the design limits will be exceeded by fairly large margins. This happens even in a near-perfect barrel roll and with any inaccuracy the situation is made worse by the much higher speeds.

Combinations of loops and rolls to form figure of eight or clover leaf manoeuvres also need extreme accuracy because the full aileron is applied while the speed is low and is held on until the desired direction is achieved, often without regard to the speed. The poor rate of roll on gliders makes it difficult to roll even through 90° without overspeeding.

Inverted flight It would appear from looking at the flight envelope that almost all gliders are strong enough for inverted flight. However, few are in fact safe for it, and none are safe unless the pilot has already learned to do the same manoeuvres accurately in a powered machine. While the speed at the top of a loop is seldom above 30 knots, a recovery by looping out from inverted flight is likely to start at 60 knots, or more, particularly on the first attempts. This will result in the V_{NE} being exceeded unless the airbrakes are opened fully in plenty of time. The only reasonably safe procedure is to slow down by pushing forward until the glider is almost stalled before pulling through to level flight, but this is not always possible (Fig. 127).

Once the aircraft is upside down the effective forward movement on the stick is far too small to get the nose back up and reduce the speed if it begins to build up. This is particularly true with rather high cockpit loads (heavy pilots). The difference between wing and tail incidence of 3° or 4° is designed for normal flight and therefore results in a drastic shortage of forward movement when the machine is inverted.

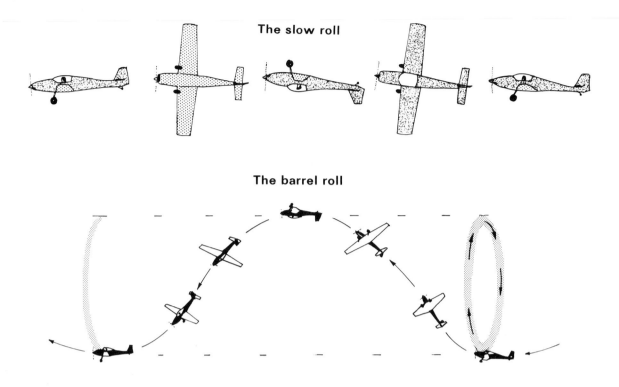

The slow roll

The barrel roll

126 Rolling. The slow roll requires skilful use of all three controls. The barrel roll is like a horizontal corkscrew and positive 'g' is maintained throughout. The poor rate of roll makes rolling impractical and dangerous in most gliders.

If the forward movement on the stick is not sufficient to keep the nose up the speed will increase to 70 or 80 knots within a few seconds and there is a grave risk of structural failure if an attempt is made to pull through and loop back into normal flight. It is no better to attempt the second half of the roll, as the speed will again exceed the limitations and it will in any case usually prove impossible to keep rolling because of the high forces involved. The only possible solution is to open full airbrake quickly and loop out carefully.

A very high degree of aerobatic competence is needed both to make safe slow rolls and for inverted flight in a glider, due to the poor rate of roll and the excessive aileron drag. Any instructor who has taught rolling manoeuvres in machines such as the Tiger Moths knows that, in spite of careful briefing, pupils never complete their first attempt at a slow roll. As the inverted position is reached the machine invariably stops rolling and tends to fall out into an inverted dive. They seldom remember to close the throttle and, without help, the situation would soon be completely out of their control. Modern light aircraft have much higher rates of roll and require less skill

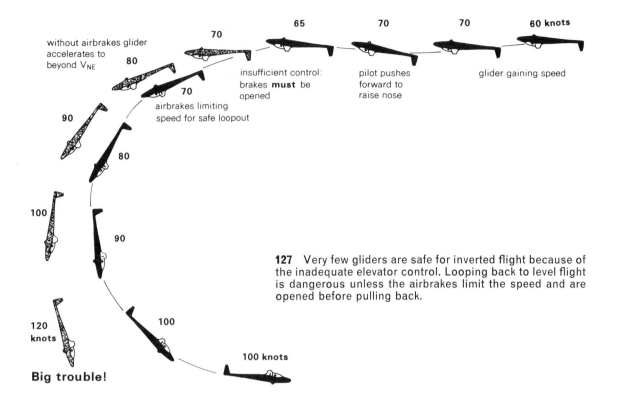

without airbrakes glider accelerates to beyond V_{NE}

airbrakes limiting speed for safe loopout

insufficient control: brakes **must** be opened

pilot pushes forward to raise nose

glider gaining speed

Big trouble!

127 Very few gliders are safe for inverted flight because of the inadequate elevator control. Looping back to level flight is dangerous unless the airbrakes limit the speed and are opened before pulling back.

to manoeuvre so that the only useful experience to be gained in them is familiarisation with flying upside down and the sensations involved.

It is unlikely that any pupils without previous rolling experience would complete more than half a roll without falling out into a dive, and there is no reason to believe that they would then remember to open the airbrakes quickly. The feeling of being upside down and being unable to keep the roll going is very unnerving and the resulting risks are quite unacceptable.

Tests involving *skilled* glider aerobatic pilots flying gliders fitted with strain gauges in the fin and rear fuselage showed that the loads involved in the final half of the roll frequently exceeded the design strength. The result is that very few types of glider are cleared for rolling manoeuvres.

Flick manoeuvres   Flick manoeuvres are only approved for certain aircraft and a few especially strong, fully acrobatic gliders. During a flick roll the aircraft is stalled violently at about one and a half times the normal stalling speed by using some rudder and aileron to induce one wing to drop. As well as the very asymmetrical loads on the wing itself during the violent rolling movement which then occurs, there are unusually high inertia forces acting on the tail, particularly if the tailplane is mounted on top of the fin. An error in the entry speed of only a few knots will result in a very much higher 'g' loading and this is usually the reason that the manoeuvre is prohibited in most light aircraft.

Common sense about aerobatics

If you really want to enjoy aerobatics it is cheaper, safer and far more satisfying to go to a power flying club and have half an hour in a really aerobatic machine instead of risking your neck trying advanced aerobatics in a glider.

To summarise these notes on flight limitations, you have no need to fear structural failures when flying gliders on normal soaring and cross-country flights if you:

1 Respect the placard speeds for launching and flying in rough air
2 Keep well below the V_{NE} at all times
3 Handle the controls smoothly at speeds above about 75 knots

If you enjoy aerobatics:

1 Resist the temptation to do them unless the air is reasonably smooth
2 Handle the controls smoothly and do not exceed $3\frac{1}{2}$g at any time
3 Do not attempt unapproved manoeuvres
4 Take care not to use large rudder or aileron movements above about 75 knots
5 Keep one hand on the airbrake lever and open the airbrakes if the glider seems likely to reach an excessive speed
6 Give yourself plenty of height and always wear a parachute
7 Inspect your glider carefully before any aerobatics

If you are a light-weight pilot (less than 150 lb) check the placard limitations and carry ballast when necessary to ensure you are well inside the C of G limits.

If you are heavy, check with an instructor that the type of glider you are flying is not seriously affected by being nose heavy. Limit your flying speeds to well below the normal V_{NE} and do not do aerobatics. Use extra speed on every approach in order to have sufficient elevator control for landing.

11 Glider structures

The glider pilot, unlike the average power pilot, is often in the position where *he* must decide whether his machine is safe to fly after some damage or deterioration has been noticed. He does not need to be a stress man or a designer but he should have a good idea how his aircraft is built and which areas are of critical importance.

The wing Without going into too much detail, the wing loads in flight can be summarised as up and down bending loads, drag loads, and twisting loads – when the glider is flying at high speeds and the ailerons are deflected.

In a simple structure the bending and shear loads are taken by the main wing spar and the drag and twisting, or torsional, loads are resisted by the leading edge D or torsion box. (Fig. 128.)

The spar If a single spar is used it consists of a large-sectioned boom at the top and bottom with one or two thin webs to prevent the booms from buckling and also to take the shear loads. When the wing is under load in normal flight the top boom is in compression and the bottom boom is in tension – most materials will buckle under compression long before a similar load causes a failure under tension. Near the wingtip the bending loads due to the lift will be small so that the spar size and depth can also be small. These loads are cumulative and reach their maximum at the fuselage.

The torsion box The wing is prevented from twisting in flight by the formation of a box section which has stiff skins of glass fibre, metal sheet or plywood. The whole wing can be skinned over in this way to contribute some stiffness or just the area from the main spar forward to the leading edge can be boxed in to form a D box.

At normal speeds the lift force acts at a point about one-third of the chord back from the leading edge, which is close to the deepest part of most wing sections and near the main spar. The loads just tend to bend the wing and not to twist it.

At high speeds the lift acts much further back and this causes both bending and twisting of the wing. As with the bending effect, the twisting loads are small near the wingtip and increase towards the fuselage. If the twisting was not stopped the wing would twist further and further, reducing the angle of

128 (opposite) Wing structures. Examples of various methods of construction using wood, metal and glass fibre. The main spar resists the bending loads created by the lift.

210

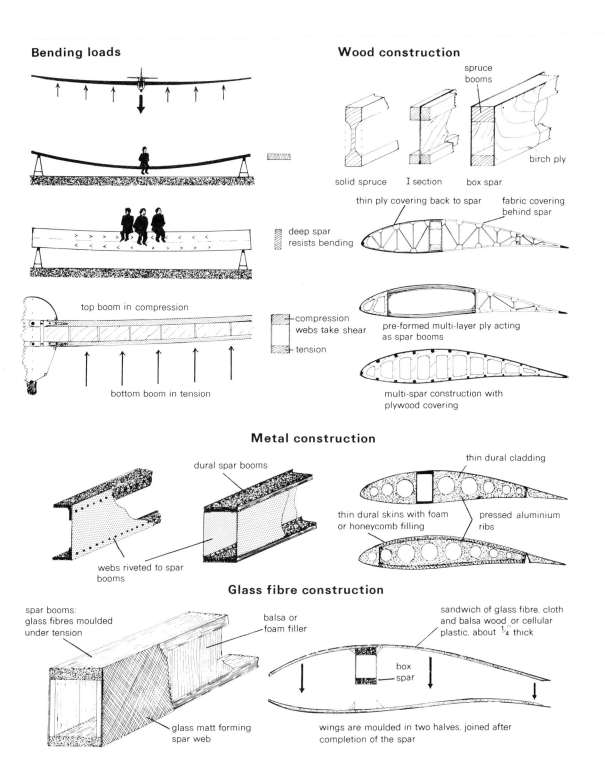

Bending loads

Wood construction

spruce booms

birch ply

solid spruce   I section   box spar

thin ply covering back to spar   fabric covering behind spar

deep spar resists bending

compression
webs take shear

tension

pre-formed multi-layer ply acting as spar booms

top boom in compression

bottom boom in tension

multi-spar construction with plywood covering

Metal construction

dural spar booms

thin dural cladding

thin dural skins with foam or honeycomb filling   pressed aluminium ribs

webs riveted to spar booms

Glass fibre construction

spar booms:
glass fibres moulded under tension

balsa or foam filler

sandwich of glass fibre, cloth and balsa wood or cellular plastic, about $\frac{1}{4}$" thick

box spar

glass matt forming spar web

wings are moulded in two halves, joined after completion of the spar

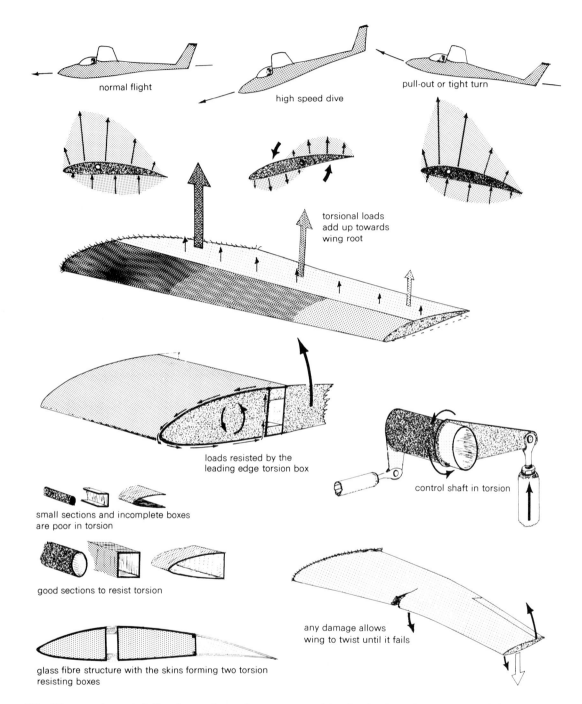

normal flight

high speed dive

pull-out or tight turn

torsional loads add up towards wing root

loads resisted by the leading edge torsion box

control shaft in torsion

small sections and incomplete boxes are poor in torsion

good sections to resist torsion

glass fibre structure with the skins forming two torsion resisting boxes

any damage allows wing to twist until it fails

129 The very large twisting forces in a wing are caused by the backward movement of the centre of pressure at high speed. These torsional loads are resisted by the leading edge torsion box and any damage to the torsion box is serious unless it is very close to the wingtip.

attack to a negative angle, until it failed downwards. The torsion box is therefore *vital* to the structure. Whereas the spar is concealed and protected the torsion box can easily be damaged by careless ground handling or bad trailer fittings and damage of any kind in the area out to about three-quarters of the span is very serious and must be properly repaired before further flight.

At the wing root the torsion loads are fed into the fuselage by spigots or pegs, or in some cases by a secondary spar. Any damage to these fittings, or to the root rib or secondary spar, is again very serious since it would allow the wing to twist at high speeds – such damage often occurs during a ground loop when the drag loads bend the wing backwards slightly.

Flying through severe turbulence, or a heavy landing, may cause damage to the wing surfaces, particularly around the airbrake boxes and at the corner of the aileron cut outs. These are points where the degree of stiffness changes abruptly so that when there is a sudden load the flexing occurs in a concentrated area.

Damage at the wingtips themselves is structurally unimportant, although it should not be left unattended to for long, as damp may penetrate the glider and cause further deterioration.

With a wooden glider minor damage to the wing ribs and trailing edge may be caused by careless handling. The trailing edge is relatively unimportant and in First World War aircraft it was often just a cord or wire stretched along for the wing fabric to be wrapped round. A badly warped trailing edge looks unsightly but may be quite safe for flying. However, a common reason for the trailing edge to fail is that a secondary spar has failed and in this case, or if in doubt, do not fly the aircraft.

The main rigging pins on most gliders are made stronger and larger than is necessary to take the loads in order to reduce the bearing loads and the wear. The root end spar fittings take very large loads indeed and should always be examined carefully after a heavy landing or excessive flight loads. The attachment point to the spars should also be checked for any signs of movement or damage and a crack in the paint along the fitting may be an indication that something is wrong.

The fuselage The largest flight loads on the fuselage probably occur during a pull-up from a dive at high speed. At this moment there is a very large down load on the tailplane plus inertia loads from the mass of the tail and rear fuselage, which all tend to bend the rear fuselage downwards while at the same time the nose of the fuselage is also being bent down by the inertia on the nose and pilot (Fig. 98 on page 158).

The biggest bending moment comes just behind the wing and this could cause the fuselage to buckle at that point. (In fact this happened to me during a demonstration of a prototype glider some years ago. Fortunately, it was only a partial failure and I was able to land safely and it was subsequently discovered that someone had done their sums incorrectly so that later machines were all strengthened.)

Again, most fuselage damage is caused by heavy landings and bad ground handling. Always try to trace the likely path of the loads after a heavy landing. For example, although the main skid may be undamaged check the fuselage structure immediately above the skid shock absorbers, check under the pilot's seat, around the wheel box and, if the wheel is a retractable one, lift the aircraft and check the retraction is still free and easy and that the structure and wheel brake mechanism are not bent.

Look for any signs of rippling in the skin or fabric which could indicate that a part inside has either failed or been distorted.

The tail wheel or tail skid and the structure immediately above it are particularly prone to damage which can be serious since the rear of the fuselage, which may be subjected to very high loads in flight, can be weakened.

Heavy landing shocks can also easily cause damage to elevator hinges and to the attachment parts of any mass balance weights for the elevator or rudder.

Always examine the fuselage skins very carefully for damage after a ground loop. Particularly on glass fibre machines even serious damage may be almost invisible and any signs of crazing of the jell-coat or minute hair-line cracks are almost certainly an indication of trouble. With a Tee tail the inertia of the heavy tailplane high above the fuselage will cause damage if the aircraft is swinging and the swing is then suddenly stopped by the tail wheel or skid hitting a rut in the ground.

With a metal structure damage can usually be spotted by a wrinkled skin or obviously pulled rivets and with a wooden structure by a crack mark along the paintwork, but with glass fibre a crack leaving only a fraction of the original strength may be almost unnoticeable and would not in any case look serious to the uninitiated.

Tail surfaces The stabiliser is subject to very large loads, especially when the glider is flying at high speed. For example, on some machines the ultimate design load is as great as the total weight of the whole glider with pilot! Imagine lifting the whole glider by the tailplane and it will be obvious why even minor damage is serious and must be repaired before the glider flies again.

The fin is also vital and should be inspected carefully – particularly near the base where it joins onto the fuselage. Damage may easily occur in this area if the glider swings badly on rough ground.

Rigging A large number of accidents and near-miss incidents are due to the pilot failing to rig his machine correctly.

It is often possible to cause expensive damage by carelessness, by trying to rig with too few people or by rigging in the incorrect sequence. For example, never fit the tail until last and always remove it first when de-rigging. The tailplane and the rear fuselage can be seriously damaged if

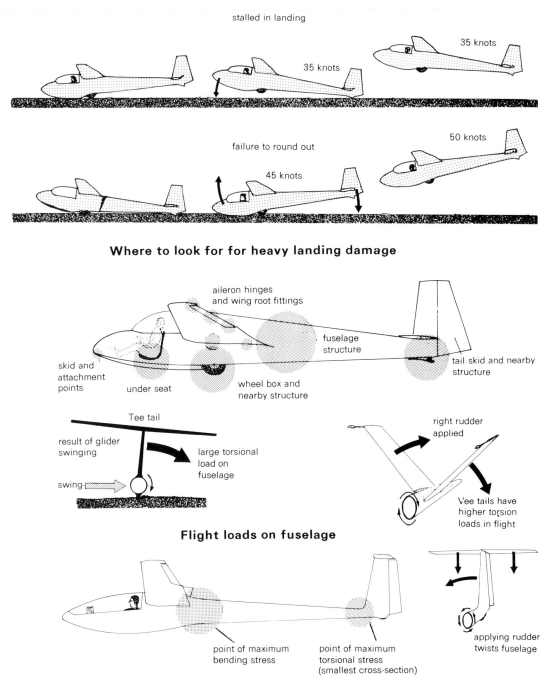

stalled in landing

35 knots

35 knots

failure to round out

45 knots

50 knots

Where to look for for heavy landing damage

aileron hinges
and wing root fittings

fuselage
structure

skid and
attachment
points

under seat

wheel box and
nearby structure

tail skid and nearby
structure

Tee tail

result of glider
swinging

swing

large torsional
load on
fuselage

right rudder
applied

Vee tails have
higher torsion
loads in flight

Flight loads on fuselage

point of maximum
bending stress

point of maximum
torsional stress
(smallest cross-section)

applying rudder
twists fuselage

130 Where to look for possible damage. The most severe landing damage usually occurs when the glider flies into the ground at high speed through failing to round out. Serious swings and ground loops often damage the rear fuselage and tailplane fittings as well as the wingtips and wing root fittings. Minute hairline cracks may signify serious damage with glass fibre machines.

the fuselage falls over, whereas little or no damage would have occurred if the tailplane had been removed.

Rigging trestles to support the wings during assembly reduce the risk of damage – and the number of slipped discs!

It is often possible to put on the tailplane or the wing so that the automatic coupling for the controls does not connect properly. If you are rigging a strange machine for the first time see if this is possible, and, if it is, you can be sure that somebody will manage to do it sooner or later. On some machines a control connecting pin can be put in either way which will cause a control jam, restricting the movement in one position. After connecting up the controls, recheck them and move them fully. Where the connections cannot be easily seen and checked by trying to separate the two fittings, recheck by getting someone else to hold the cockpit control while you make sure that the surface is not free.

A number of serious launching accidents happen because the geometric lock on the airbrakes is either worn or badly adjusted. Unless the airbrakes on both wings lock together the loads from one brake being sucked open may unlock and open the other and if the geometric lock is very light it may become almost non-existent when the wings are flexing upwards during a launch. A badly adjusted airbrake lock is a serious defect and usually only takes a few minutes to put right. If the airbrakes open on a winch launch and the cable happens to break, a crash is almost inevitable.

Check all trim tabs for the correct movement and tabs, control surfaces and flaps for any play in the control circuit. There is very real risk of flutter if either the trim tabs or the flaps and control surfaces have any appreciable slop. For instance, I experienced elevator buzz at only 90 knots on one modern machine and this was traced to slight wear in the elevator drive. The trailing edge could be moved about a tenth of an inch up and down while the stick was held stationary.

Daily inspections Keep a D.I. (Daily Inspection) book or notebook in the aircraft and keep a record of any minor snags or damage and any work done each day. If the glider has just been assembled always make a point of rechecking the rigging before signing the book. Whenever possible, ask someone else to check the rigging – it only takes a moment but it provides a sensible double check.

A daily inspection is not intended to be a full certificate of airworthiness (C of A) inspection but any sign of damage or of overstressing and any maladjustment of the controls must be carefully investigated.

1 Check the D.I. book for any minor defects previously reported and make sure that the machine is not unserviceable i.e. that the C of A has not expired.

2 Check all the controls for full and free movement in the correct sense.

3 Move around the aircraft systematically checking for: hangar or ground handling damage, heavy landing damage, excessive wear or maladjustment on all the controls, tyre pressures and correct rigging.

4 Recheck all the controls; check the flaps, airbrakes, trimmers, releases, harness, instruments. Look for loose objects which might cause a control jam, check the canopy lock and hinges and the perspex for cracks.

5 Sign the D.I. book noting any minor defects.

Then install the sealed barograph, switch it on and leave it recording until you de-rig or put the glider into the hangar. Every year thousands of Silver and Gold 'C' heights and distances are missed because a barograph was not carried or it had been turned off during the day. With the normal drum type of instrument it can be left on all day and there is no harm in having a second trace running over some insignificant earlier flight.

12 Converting from gliders to powered aircraft

Many glider pilots decide to learn to fly powered machines either to help with the launching of their club gliders, or to fly motor gliders. Of course, their gliding experience is a great help and learning to fly a powered machine is largely a matter of mastering the various minor differences in technique and of getting used to the engine handling.

I make no apology for including a chapter on converting to powered machines because it will be useful and of interest both to glider pilots and instructors. In some countries to fly a motor glider or self-launching sailplane requires the equivalent of a full Pilot's Licence but the average glider pilot will find absolutely no difficulty in flying a motor glider, since the very low power produces a minimum of engine effects. Once the engine has been stopped, it is just another glider to fly and to soar.

Where to learn If you are already a competent glider pilot you will probably consider obtaining a Private Pilot's Licence at some time or another. For a pilot with a Silver 'C', this is an easy step and it only takes an hour or two of dual practice to reach solo standard.

Since many people may not be aware that they are colour blind, or have other problems which bar them from holding a licence, the first step is to take the medical examination to apply for a Student's Pilot's Licence.

There are several things to bear in mind when you are choosing where to go for training. The nearest flying club will probably work out better and cheaper since you will be able to fly more frequently. It is not worth travelling an extra 50 miles to save a small amount on the hourly flying rate and you will soon get tired of the journey if you arrive to find that you cannot fly that day.

It is a great advantage to have an instructor who has flown gliders and,

218

therefore, can understand your particular needs. I have known many instances of very competent glider pilots, and even gliding instructors, who have been given several hours of dual instruction on the effects and further effects of the controls, just as though they were beginners! This is an absolute waste of money and shows either a complete lack of understanding on the part of the instructor, or else a deliberate policy on the part of the flying club to 'milk' the student for as much money as possible.

The best thing is to ask your C.F.I. (Chief Flying Instructor) and any gliding friends who have recently obtained a P.P.L. about the local flying clubs, which should help you to avoid any rather inefficient ones.

Obviously the needs of each glider pilot will vary enormously, but an English Silver 'C' pilot should be capable of reaching the licence standard in about 10–15 hours dual and 3–4 hours solo. This assumes either that he gets good ground instruction or that he reads up and learns all the relevant information on his own. Any course shorter than this may mean neglecting exercises such as navigation and precautionary landings, of which the average glider pilot has only a limited experience. Appendix A outlines the kind of syllabus of flying which might suit the Silver 'C' glider pilot.

If you are only obtaining the licence to be able to tow gliders, extra training in navigation and radio aids will not be essential. However, if you intend to go air touring, or even to retrieve gliders from cross-country flights, the standard required for the licence is really inadequate and you would be wise to have extra training. It is very embarrassing to be lost in an aircraft and can also lead to heavy fines if you happen to infringe any controlled airspace, whatever your excuse.

Unfortunately, most flying clubs are equipped with modern aircraft fitted with nose wheel undercarriage while most gliding clubs use tail wheel machines for glider towing. Coming from gliders you should find no real difficulty in adapting to either type but once you are used to nose wheels it becomes much harder to convert back to tail-wheelers.

A higher degree of skill is required to take off and land with a tail wheel machine since it tends to swing and bounce if given the chance to do so, while a nose machine does not do this and is therefore much easier to master. While converting from a tail wheel to a nose wheel machine is only a matter of one, or at the most two familiarisation flights, it may take several hours of dual instruction for a pilot trained on a nose wheel to become safe for solo on a tail dragger. In fact, I have known pilots who learnt on a modern nose wheel aircraft, bought Austers or similar machines and have given them up and sold them because they could not master the take offs and landings.

My own advice, supported by most other experienced power instructors who *have no vested interests*, is to learn on a tail wheel type if you have the choice. It may not be such a nice looking, modern machine, but once you have learnt to fly on one you will find everything else easy in comparison.

However, if you intend to do a lot of air touring you will need experience with radio and radio aids and it is easiest to get this during your basic training.

In this case, learn on a fully-equipped modern machine.

The cost of power flying will vary from club to club. The most inexpensive are usually the flying groups operating just one aircraft. The instruction is carried out by members and the cost is kept low by doing some of the maintenance work on a self-help basis. Before joining a club like this make sure that there are not too many keen members under training or you will find it difficult to get enough flying. You must also accept the fact that if your aircraft becomes unserviceable there may be no flying for you, or anyone else, for several weeks. At a larger club these difficulties seldom arise.

The cost of flying is usually calculated by the time from 'chock to chock' – that is, from the time you start to taxi out to the time that you stop the engine after the flight. At a very busy airport, where you have to taxi for miles and then queue up to wait for your turn to take off, an hour of circuits and landings may mean less than 40 minutes of actual flying. Calculated on this basis the flying can be very expensive and it can save money to go somewhere less congested.

Once you have decided where you are going to go, visit the club and buy a copy of the text book the instructor recommends to cover the P.P.L. syllabus. At the same time try to get copies of all the cockpit checks and circuit procedures so that you can start to learn them by heart. You can save yourself time and money this way and your instructor will be very relieved not to have to spend time going through them with you each time. Power flying involves a slightly more systematic approach than gliding and you will not be allowed to go solo, however well you can fly the aircraft, until you have learnt all your checks and can carry them out accurately.

As soon as you have started circuits and landings find the time to sit in the cockpit and practise going through the cockpit checks and the procedures for the complete circuit until you are word perfect. You will find the actual flying fairly easy but you must also get the procedures right or you will fail your General Flying Test (G.F.T.).

The use of the rudder

While the rudder on a glider is used almost exclusively to overcome the effects of the aileron drag, the rudder on a light aircraft is used mainly to overcome the yawing effects caused by altering the power. These effects of power are really the only completely new thing you have to master if you already fly gliders. With an American engine, for example, full power causes a distinctive yaw to the left and during the climb some right rudder has to be applied all the time. (British engines often rotate in the opposite direction.) It is usual for the machine to be built or trimmed so that in level flight at normal cruising power no rudder is needed. This means that at full power some right rudder must be applied and in the glide some left rudder will be needed. For the experienced glider pilot it is probably easiest to glance at the slip indicator and check whether it is showing accurate flight. If the wings are kept level with the ailerons and the ball (or slip needle) is out to the left, more left rudder is required to bring it back to the centre. This kind of

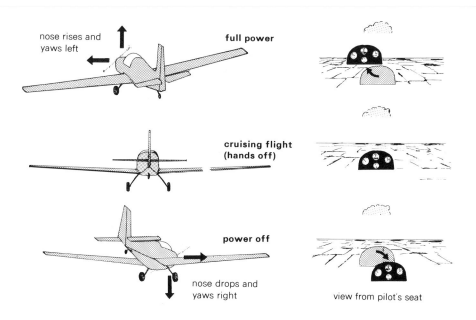

131 The effects of changing power cause pitching and yawing movements. The worst case is during an overshoot when the aircraft is trimmed back for the glide. Applying full power results in a marked nose up pitching movement and swing to the left which must be controlled until the aircraft is retrimmed.

yawing is almost entirely caused by the slipstream effect described later.

Very little rudder will be needed going into or coming out of turns, except when flying at low speeds, and because of this a glider pilot will always initially tend to over-rudder. No rudder is required on most modern light aircraft during a turn, except for any needed to overcome the yaw due to any variations in the power, as already mentioned. In normal flight, turns are made by applying the bank and easing back on the stick.

Trimming Powered aircraft are generally much more stable fore and aft than gliders and this makes them heavy to fly, unless the trimmer is used. In addition, any change of power or speed upsets the trim so that it has to be readjusted. More power results in a *nose up* pitching movement and reducing power in a *nose down* one. (Fig. 131.) After any change of power or attitude you will be expected to retrim quickly and accurately and the correct sequence to follow when going into climb is Power, Attitude, Trim. First the throttle is adjusted to give the power required, then the attitude is adjusted until the correct speed is reached and, lastly, the trimmer is adjusted until there is no load on the stick.

Never move the trimmer unless you are holding the stick. The elevator trimmer on some powered machines is so powerful that if it is moved quickly when the aircraft is flying at high speed a very large force would be put through the elevator and structural damage could result. (Remember, most light aircraft are not stressed for such high load factors as gliders!)

On the first flight you should try and memorise the approximate positions of the nose for climbing, straight and level flight and gliding so that, when you are changing from one to another, you can put the nose into the correct attitude quickly. A few minutes of concentrated practice in going from one position to another and then retrimming will be invaluable before you start on a circuit.

Going from straight and level flight at cruising power into a glide the procedure is as follows. Throttle back the engine smoothly and apply carburettor heat; prevent the nose from dropping and keep straight with the rudder (using left rudder with American engines) as the speed falls to the correct gliding speed; readjust the attitude to hold the correct speed and trim back. (During any prolonged glides the engine must be cleared and warmed from time to time by opening the throttle fully for a few moments.)

The procedure for going into the climb is similar. First apply the required amount of power, usually full throttle (moving the carburettor heat to cold); prevent the nose from rising above the climbing attitude and keep straight with the rudder (right rudder with American engines); readjust the attitude to obtain the exact airspeed required and retrim forward until the aircraft will fly 'hands off'.

With other engines the yawing effect will be in the opposite direction if the propeller turns anti-clockwise as viewed from the cockpit.

Most of the problems in keeping straight during the final approach and landing can be traced to failing to counteract the yaw caused by reducing the power. A quick glance at the slip indicator will show whether the correct amount of rudder is being used and accurate trimming for the approach will help you to keep a steady speed and attitude and make the landings easier.

Control during take off and landing

On a machine with a nose wheel there is little or no tendency to swing at any time on the ground, even in a strong crosswind. No finesse is needed to produce a reasonable landing but the nose wheel will not stand a very heavy thump, and this can happen if the hold off is *far* too high. In this case the aircraft will pitch forward hard and it will also, of course, be damaged if it is flown into the ground without any round out.

On touchdown the aircraft normally tends to pitch forward gently onto the nose wheel and this reduces the lift from the wing by reducing the angle of attack, so that no bouncing can occur. Nose wheel machines are therefore, non-bouncing and non-swinging.

Tail wheel machines are unstable directionally and tend to bounce, unless they are landed either 'three point' or very tail high (known as a wheel landing and only used in special circumstances such as strong crosswinds). For the same reason they will tend to swing on take off unless the pilot keeps them straight with the rudder.

There are several interesting reasons for swinging on take off, not the least of which is the pilot over-controlling with the rudder. I will explain these in detail although *their total effect is not very great* and can *always* be overcome by the prompt use of the rudder. The actual take off is simply a matter of keeping the aircraft straight as it gains speed and of easing back gently on the stick to lift the machine off the ground. With a tail dragger, the tail is raised into the flying position as soon as there is sufficient speed for good control. As it reaches flying speed a gentle backward movement on the stick will lift it off the ground. With a nose wheel type, the aircraft is already sitting in the flying attitude and therefore it is only a matter of easing back on the stick just before flying speed is reached. (Fig. 132.)

Propeller slipstream effect

The slipstream from the propellers which comes back over the aircraft in a spiralling motion and strikes the fin and rudder on only one side (Fig. 133) is the most important cause of the yawing movement and swing on take off. Obviously at full power the slipstream is most powerful and has most effect but the speed of the aircraft is also significant. At low speed the spiral is tightly packed, as in Fig. 133, and the sideways force on the fin and rudder is large, while the effect of the fin and the power of the rudder at low speeds is poor, so that the swinging tendency is difficult to stop. At higher speeds the spiralling slipstream is much more spread out, making it less strong, and the

Remember — open throttle smoothly to full throttle and keep straight

a

Line up: straighten tail wheel · Stick back: open throttle: keep straight · Lift tail: keep straight · Ease back gently

b

Line up: straighten nose wheel · Open throttle: keep straight · Stick gently back to lift nose wheel · Ease back gently

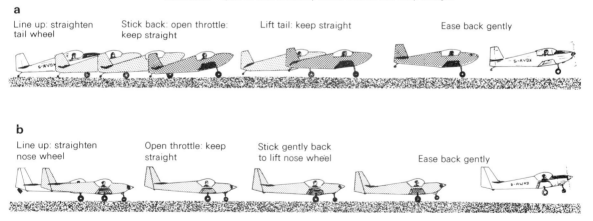

132 The take off. **a** Tailwheel type. Line up for take off and move forward a little to straighten up the tail wheel. Holding the stick back to keep the tail down for better steering, open the throttle smoothly to *full* throttle, keeping straight with the rudder. Then ease forward on the stick to lift the tail into the flying attitude and keep straight. Ease back slowly to lift the aircraft off the ground as it reaches flying speed. **b** Nose wheel aircraft. Line up for the take off and move forward a little to straighten up the nose wheel. Holding the stick slightly back (right back on very soft or rough ground) open the throttle smoothly to *full* throttle keeping straight with the rudder. As the aircraft gains speed, ease back gently to take the weight off the nose wheel and as it reaches flying speed it will leave the ground.

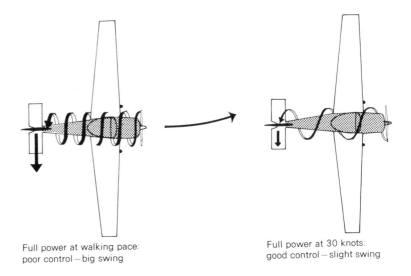

Full power at walking pace:
poor control – big swing

Full power at 30 knots:
good control – slight swing

133 Slipstream effect – the major cause of swinging on take off. Full power at low speed results in a big swinging tendency. Full power at 20–30 knots gives little swing and rudder control is already good. Do *not* open the throttle too quickly.

fin and rudder have much more power so that the swinging can be controlled. Apart from causing swinging on take off the slipstream improves the airflow over both the rudder and elevators and makes them a little heavier and more effective under power than when gliding at low speeds. However, this factor is not significant except to explain the noticeably better response on the elevator and rudder during a powered approach at low speeds compared with a glide.

Fairly obviously, the swinging effect caused by the propeller slipstream can be minimised by opening the throttle smoothly, so that full throttle is not reached until the aircraft has gained enough speed for good directional control. Avoid opening the throttle suddenly, as this may cause the engine to falter and will certainly make it more difficult to keep the aircraft straight.

The designer can help to reduce this effect by mounting the engine at an angle, as on a model aircraft. If the thrust line is offset it will cancel out most of the slipstream effect in cruising flight and during the climb.

Offset thrust effect Whereas propeller slipstream affects all single-engined propeller-driven aircraft, offset thrust only occurs on tail wheel machines. Fig. 134 explains this.

While the aircraft is moving along the ground in a tail down position the thrust of the propeller is slightly offset. During each rotation the downward moving blade moves forward much further than the upward going one and this results in it producing more thrust. The thrust is in the same direction as that of the propeller slipstream and again is greatest at full power and while the aircraft is moving slowly. As soon as the tail is raised, both upward and downward moving blades move the same distance per turn and there is no further offset blade effect. Since the nose wheel machines sit in a more or less horizontal attitude for take off they are not affected.

Gyroscopic effect When a heavy propeller is turning very rapidly it has the properties of a gyroscope and precesses when it is tilted (Fig. 135). This happens with a tail wheel machine when the tail is raised during the take off run. The result of lifting the tail quickly is to produce a force which tends to swing the aircraft and this is again in the same direction as the slipstream and offset thrust effects. Gyroscopic effect can be minimised by raising the tail slowly after the aircraft has gained a fair speed and by doing this any swing can be controlled easily with the rudder. Gyroscopic effect does not affect the take off on a nose wheel machine because the pitching movements are very small and the effect as the nose is lifted is only slight and creates a swing in opposition to the other factors.

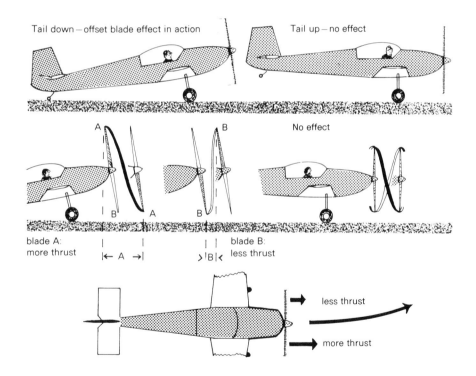

134 Offset blade effect – a minor but interesting reason for swinging on take off. While the tail is down, the downgoing blade A moves much further forward, creating extra thrust.

225

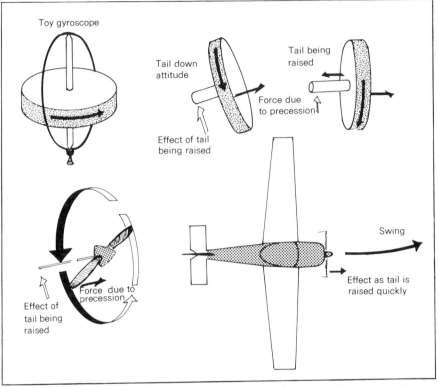

135 Gyroscopic effect. This can be minimised by lifting the tail gradually during take off. The propeller acts as a gyro and precesses when tilted. This is a very small effect except with very powerful engines and heavy propellers.

Torque

Torque is the least important of all these factors, although it is often mistakenly blamed for them all. Torque is the tendency for the aircraft to roll over in the opposite direction to the rotation of the propeller and it is a surprisingly small force except on very high-powered propeller aircraft (Fig. 136). The later versions of the Spitfire, for example, had very powerful engines and a very narrow track undercarriage, with the result that there was a distinct tendency for the aircraft to roll over onto a wingtip if the throttle was opened too quickly. However, this in itself did not cause any great swing. On the Typhoon and Tempest fighters, which had even more power and a very wide undercarriage, the effect of torque was much more serious. With a wide undercarriage any rolling increases the load on the wheel on one side, thus

136 Torque – a non-effect on most light aircraft. Torque is the reaction to the rotation of the propeller and tends to roll the aircraft in the opposite direction. It causes a slight extra load on one main wheel and the resulting friction could start a slight swing.

increasing the friction. This was accentuated by the extra leverage of the wheel about the C of G compared with the narrow spacing on the Spitfire. The result could be a much more violent swing if the throttle was opened too quickly.

The effect of torque is very small on modern light aircraft and can be ignored.

Summary of the causes of swinging on take off

All these engine effects act in the same direction and swing the aircraft in the opposite direction to the rotation of the propeller. The tendency to swing can be minimised by opening the throttle smoothly and slowly so that the aircraft has a chance to gain some speed before the engine reaches full power. This gives the pilot more control. The tail should be raised slowly to the flying position to reduce any gyroscopic effect and, if the tail wheel is coupled to the rudder for positive steering, it is best to keep it firmly on the ground at the start of the take off run. This will make it far easier to stop any slight swing until sufficient speed has been gained to give adequate rudder control.

On most nose wheel aircraft none of these factors has much influence on the take off and any swinging is almost certainly started by the pilot over-controlling on the rudder. On these machines the nose wheel should be lifted *just* clear of the ground as soon as possible in order to reduce the loads, particularly on rough ground. However, any attempt to drag the aircraft off the ground before it has reached flying speed may delay the take off and in an extreme case may prevent the aircraft ever reaching the flying speed.

It is common for pilots to over-control with the rudder during take off. Always select a point ahead on the airfield boundary, or beyond, and aim towards it so that the start of any swing can be detected. The power of the rudder depends upon the airspeed at the time and increases rapidly during take off. Any correction made to stop a swing has to be taken off almost immediately or it will start a worse swing in the other direction. With a tail wheel machine it takes quite a number of take offs and landings to become competent at keeping straight and, since these aircraft are violently unstable directionally on the ground, you must never relax on any take off or landing.

The landing

The landing itself should present few problems to a well-trained glider pilot. The essential difference is the need to level out 3–4 feet higher than in a glider. If the approach has been made using some power the throttle is closed completely during the round out. However, one hand should always be kept on the throttle ready for instant use in the event of a bad landing. (In fact, one hand should be kept on the throttle throughout the take off and climb in order to make sure that it does not creep back with the vibration.) With a nose wheel machine, a steady backward movement on the stick during the hold off will guarantee a satisfactory landing. (It is not normally possible to touch the tail on the ground. See Fig. 137.) Tail draggers require a fully held off landing or they will bounce. Compared with a glider the final backward movement of the stick has to be much larger and quicker as the power of the

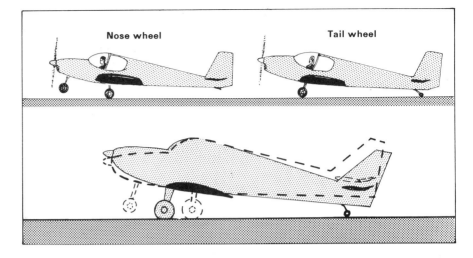

137 A comparison between nose wheel and tail wheel undercarriages. The designer sets the wing on the fuselage at a slightly larger angle of incidence on the nose wheel machines to prevent the tail touching the ground during a fully held off landing. A fully held off landing with a tail wheel machine results in the main wheels and tail wheel touching down together.

elevator declines rapidly at low speeds. Do not try to get too close to the ground or the machine will inevitably touch down prematurely with the wheels and bounce off again. Try to touch down tail first. This is practically impossible with most tail wheel machines but by trying there is at least a better chance of coming down on three points. (A three point landing is one with the two main wheels and tail wheel touching down together which is the ideal landing for a tail dragger.)

If the hold off is made a little too high, or the aircraft bounces or balloons, a small amount of power should be applied to prevent a heavy landing. This will check the rate of descent in the same way as reducing the airbrakes does on a glider. If the ballooning is bad or the aircraft bounces into a nose high position, always open the throttle smoothly to *full* power and go round again for another circuit. At first, most glider pilots forget that this is possible and it is a good idea during training to practise one or two overshoots deliberately. If the touchdown is going to be more than half-way up the field and there is the slightest risk that there will be difficulty in stopping in the space left, go round again. Remember to prevent the nose rising with full power.

There should be very little tendency during a landing to swing more in one direction than the other and if this does happen the most likely reason is a crosswind. As with gliders, very light winds are the worst because the speed increases the inertia effects and once even a slight swing begins – unless the pilot corrects it immediately – there is a risk of swinging right round in a ground loop. This cannot happen with a nose wheel machine since the inertia effects cancel out any swing.

On machines with a non-steerable tail wheel any tendency to swing at low speeds after landing must be stopped with rudder *and* a touch of wheel brake if necessary.

Straight and level flight
It is important to realise that for any given amount of power there can be two speeds for level flight. One is the cruising speed with the aircraft flying cleanly in the normal, rather nose down attitude, and the other is a speed just above the stall with the nose much higher (Fig. 138). In this case, the aircraft is mushing through the air with so much induced drag that the power is only just sufficient to maintain height. This makes it important always to gain plenty of speed before reducing the power for the cruise – for example after climbing to height.

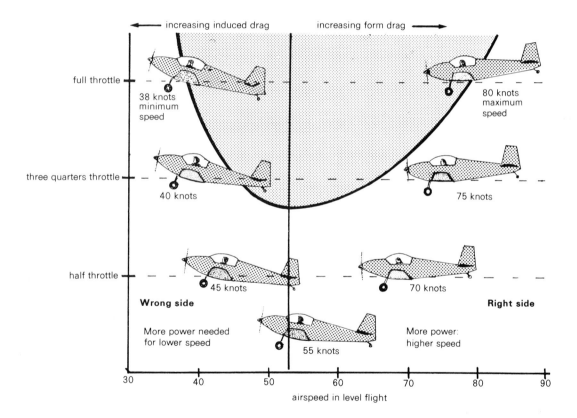

138 The effect of the drag curve – there are usually two speeds for level flight for a given power setting. Always level out and gain speed before reducing the power or you will be left at low speed flying on the wrong side of the drag curve.

There are two distinct methods of settling down to fly straight and level. On the circuit, for example, the exact cruising speed is usually unimportant but it is desirable to maintain a constant height, normally either 800 or 1000 feet above ground level. At other times it may be much more important to fly an exact speed.

To level out at a set height after climbing the first action is to lower the nose gradually to increase the speed while holding the height constant until the normal cruising speed is reached. The power is then reduced with the throttle to set the cruising r.p.m. and the aircraft is trimmed. It is then easy to check the altimeter and vertical speed indicator (known as the V.S.I. and which is just a poor variometer to the glider pilot) and stop any gain or loss of height by lowering or raising the nose slightly and retrimming as necessary. Using this method the effect of any lift or sink is cancelled out by diving or pulling up the nose slightly and height is maintained at the expense of variations in the airspeed. The majority of pilots use this method most of the time and memorise the r.p.m. required for the normal speed for flying round the circuit.

For really accurate navigation it is usual to calculate the courses and estimated time of the flight for a definite airspeed. In this case the first thing to do after climbing to the required height is to adjust the attitude with the elevator to give the desired speed and set the r.p.m. you think should give you level flight at that speed. After retrimming, a glance at the V.S.I. or altimeter will show if the height is remaining constant. If the height is increasing, the power must be reduced slightly, maintaining the correct speed with the elevator. After one or two small adjustments of the throttle both a constant height and the chosen speed can be obtained.

This method emphasises an important principle. The elevator and attitude control the airspeed and the throttle, or power, controls the rate of climb or descent. This is the basis of a powered approach. Of course when the power is altered a small change of attitude (and trim) will always be required to maintain the same speed. For example, when the power is increased to reduce or stop the rate of descent, the nose will have to be raised a little in order to prevent a slight gain in airspeed.

Circuit flying The pilot will be expected to fly a neat, accurate rectangular circuit with the downwind leg at exactly the correct height. This is not as easy as it sounds, particularly in thermic conditions. (Fig. 139.)

It is essential to learn to settle down at the correct speeds and height quickly. Any delay in levelling out and retrimming after climbing to circuit height, for example, will result in a very wide circuit with the airfield almost out of sight. You will also find that unless you know your downwind checks off by heart you will have difficulty completing them in time for a turn onto the base leg in a normal position.

Although many instructors encourage powered approaches, glider pilots usually find it easier to start with glide approaches which keep the approach

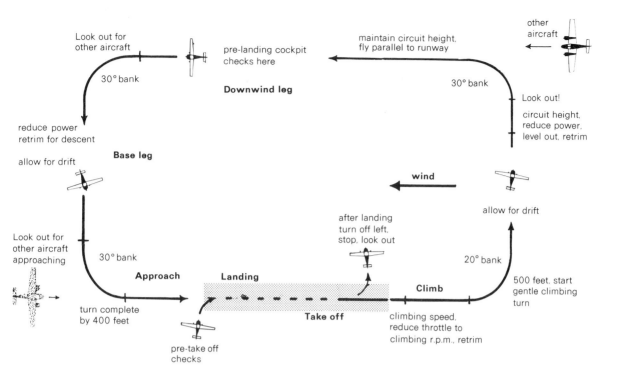

Look out for other aircraft

30° bank

pre-landing cockpit checks here

Downwind leg

maintain circuit height, fly parallel to runway

other aircraft

30° bank

Look out!

circuit height, reduce power, level out, retrim

reduce power retrim for descent

Base leg

allow for drift

wind

allow for drift

after landing turn off left, stop, look out

Look out for other aircraft approaching

30° bank

Approach

Landing

Climb

20° bank

500 feet, start gentle climbing turn

turn complete by 400 feet

pre-take off checks

Take off

climbing speed, reduce throttle to climbing r.p.m., retrim

139 A typical power circuit. Your flying instructor will give you details of the actual checks to be carried out. Circuits are usually standardised at 800–1000 feet above airfield level.

shorter and avoid the last-minute changes in trim and the yawing tendency when the throttle is closed during the round out. Unfortunately, at most airfields there are a number of pilots who habitually make huge 'Transport Command' circuits forcing following aircraft to make equally large, or even larger circuits to avoid cutting them off on the approach. Fig. 139 shows a typical circuit for a light aircraft. The initial climbing turn and the final turn onto the approach are made at 500 feet and the instructor will expect the circuit height to be held to within about 50 feet while the downwind checks are being completed. This will take a little practice!

Forced landings Genuine engine trouble on a modern aircraft is now extremely rare but practising what to do in such an eventuality is still an essential part of converting to powered machines. An experienced glider pilot will have little difficulty and may even be able to give the instructor a few tips about field selection. The main difference is the much higher rate of descent and faster speeds involved. If the aircraft is fitted with flaps, the final approach can be steepened with them in much the same way as with airbrakes, except that they cannot normally be safely raised again to extend the glide if they have been lowered too soon.

Always select the largest available field which has a reasonable surface and good approaches, for the penalty for a missed approach is much more severe than in a glider. The most common fault, as with glider field landings, is to keep too close to the field. Remember that the much higher gliding speed than in a glider results in a much larger radius of turn, so that plenty of room must be left for this.

Far more actual forced landings and broken aircraft happen during training than from real engine trouble. Most of them are due to incorrect engine handling, so that the engine fails to pick up when the throttle is opened at low altitude. This can be caused by carburettor icing, or just by allowing the engine to get too cold, or the plugs to become oiled up. One of the most important lessons to be learnt from practising forced landings is what to check for, and how to put right or avoid the causes of a partial failure. Without training, most glider pilots would just select a field and land, when a quick check might reveal only the need to change fuel tanks or adjust the mixture control to restore full power again.

Carburettor icing is a very real menace and can occur at almost any time when there is moisture in the air, whether the day is hot or cold. The ice builds up very quickly when the engine is running at low power or idling and the first symptom is often its cutting out altogether, or refusing to pick up when the throttle is opened. Since the carburettor air heat is supplied from the exhaust system there will be insufficient heat to melt off any ice unless the engine is kept reasonably warm. During descent, most engines need to be warmed up by opening them to full throttle for a few moments every 500 feet or so. The carburettor heat should be used whenever the engine is throttled back for a prolonged glide or whenever the conditions are very moist. The hot air reduces the engine power slightly and therefore it is only used when really necessary.

Sometimes an engine will ice up and stop while taxying out for take off on a cold, damp morning unless the engine is warmed up well and the hot air is used. In cruising flight, the symptoms of icing are rough running and a gradual loss of power. It is a wise habit to apply hot air every 15 minutes or so as a precaution and if icing is happening the hot air will result in an increase in r.p.m. after a few moments as the ice melts. The control should then be returned to cold unless the problem is severe. In very cold weather it is possible that hot air may only result in bringing the air temperature in the carburettor *up* to the freezing range. In this case leaving the hot air in the 'on' position might cause icing instead of curing it. (Most modern aircraft have very efficient systems so that the hot air always brings the temperature well above the freezing range.)

The most likely, and the most critical, time for mechanical failure is just after take off, because the engine is at full power with the aircraft climbing at a low speed. Below 500–600 feet a landing *has* to be made more or less straight ahead since the loss of height in a turn, particularly while attempting to regain speed, makes it almost suicidal to attempt to turn back to the airfield. Remember that even landing in a wood or other obstruction is far safer than risking a stall and spin while trying to turn.

Precautionary landings (forced landings with power)

Unfortunately it is easy to fly into bad weather, or run short of daylight, or fuel, so that a landing in a field becomes necessary. The vital thing is to act decisively and carry out the landing before the situation becomes desperate.

If the time and weather permit, the procedure is to pick a suitable field and make at least one low run over it to make sure that it has a good surface and is large enough for a safe landing and, later, a safe take off. Whenever possible it is best to make a complete preliminary approach down to a few feet before actually attempting the landing. The second approach will usually be better organised and more accurate than the first one.

The recommended technique is to make a powered approach with full flap and a rather lower speed than normal. In this way, with practice, a very accurate approach and touchdown can be made. The rate of descent is controlled with the throttle while the speed is maintained by co-ordinated movements on the elevator. At the lower approach speed the aircraft will sink onto the ground immediately the throttle is closed, giving a very precise touchdown.

Apart from crosswind landings, these precision landings are probably the most exacting flying a pilot will normally ever do, and this makes them interesting and fun to practise. The aircraft is often being brought in at, or even slightly below, the normal power off stalling speed and this requires a high degree of skill and judgement (see Appendix B on level flight at very low speed). Sooner or later the value of having practised precautionary landings will be obvious, especially if the weather closes in unexpectedly and a quick landing has to be made into a field. If it is necessary to fly low down, the main thing to remember is to use extra power for any turn and *full* power for any steep turn. In poor visibility lowering a small amount of flap gives a better view and more manoeuvrability but the most important thing is to keep plenty of power and speed.

Stalling and spinning

The main thing to remember is that the loss of height in a stall is many times greater in a light aircraft than in an average glider. No deliberate spinning is advisable below 4000–5000 feet, so that the recovery can always be completed by about 3000 feet.

The loss of height in a stall can be reduced considerably by applying full power as the stick is moved forward and this is always the correct procedure unless the aircraft has flicked into a steep nose down attitude. It is easy to stall most light aircraft in a turn because of the more powerful elevator and this may result in quite a violent flick one way or the other. The short wing span tends to make any wing drop or spin much more rapid than on a glider and this is a little nerve-racking at first. The standard spin recovery, as on gliders, should stop any spin within a turn or two. However, the spin will not stop on many types of machine until the stick has been moved well forward and it is therefore vital to make it a progressive movement *until* the spin stops.

As a precaution against stalling in steep turns more power is *always* applied in turns of more than 45° of bank to help maintain speed. This is particularly important at low altitude.

Bad weather   Glider pilots seldom have much experience of flying in drizzle or heavy rain and the dangers are difficult to appreciate. The cloud base can drop from 1500 feet to ground level in only a few minutes and it is unrealistic to expect to be able to turn back into any clearer weather. The pilot is usually trapped and has to make a landing. Never risk climbing up through the cloud in the hope of finding a gap elsewhere. If the cloud gets down to 500–600 feet above the ground, remember the serious risks in staying in the air at all. This is the time to carry out a precautionary landing. Be decisive and do not delay! Select a good field and make a landing while there is plenty of height and time to make a proper job of it.

A very large number of accidents occur while making precautionary landings because the decision has been left too late. Lack of experience in bad weather makes glider pilots particularly vulnerable to this kind of hazard and also to getting lost. The flying may be easy, but never forget that 'All aircraft bite fools'.

Motor gliders   The shape and form of motor gliders may well change several times in the next decade as new and better forms of power plant become available. At present they tend to be rather low-powered, so that their rate of climb and take off performance is limited. A few elementary precautions should be taken.

Engine handling   Because of the low climbing speed of the present motor gliders the cooling of the engine is usually marginal and prolonged climbs at low speed in hot weather may result in excessively high cylinder head and oil temperatures. The engines are often not fitted with a cylinder head temperature gauge (C.H.T.) so that the pilot is unaware of the damage he may be doing by climbing steeply at low speed. The oil temperature gauge gives very little indication of this severe overheating and high oil temperature is more often a warning of oil shortage. High oil temperature can only be reduced by reducing the power setting and by increasing the flying speed, and in very hot weather it may be necessary to fly in a series of saw-tooth climbs, levelling out every thousand feet or so. Low oil pressure is a warning of impending trouble and the engine should be shut down immediately if the oil pressure falls below the minimum allowed.

Good engine handling may significantly increase the working life of the engine. For example, immediately after starting, an engine should be run slowly until the oil pressure has risen and then at 1000–1200 r.p.m. for a period of several minutes in cold weather. At idling speeds there is often a tendency for the sparking plugs to foul up and with aero engines it is safest not to leave them ticking over at low revs for more than a few moments. If the engine has been running for 4–5 minutes it will generally be warm enough for a safe take off.

Many motor glider engines have single ignition and the only checks that are possible are of the oil temperature and pressure gauges. Always make sure that the engine responds without spluttering to a quick opening of the throttle and confirm that the engine r.p.m. is normal at full throttle. It is essential to check the r.p.m. on *every* take off and if it is below normal, or the engine is not running smoothly, the take off should be abandoned immediately. With such a small reserve of power the misfiring of even one cylinder may prevent a safe take off and climb and the pilot must never just hope that it will get better, especially if it would be dangerous if the performance got worse.

Take off Motor gliders and other low-speed, low-powered aircraft are particularly susceptible to the effects of a change in the slope or surface of the ground. Even a slight uphill gradient will almost double the take off run. The low climbing speed also makes them especially vulnerable to the effects of wind gradients and turbulence and even a relatively small downdraught may prevent them climbing normally.

Avoid taking off towards high obstructions or hills whenever possible and always try to build up some extra speed before climbing in an area where turbulence is likely. A faster speed, although reducing the rate of climb, will reduce the loss of height in a bad area and will also ensure that you have ample speed for a safe turn, if one becomes necessary.

Whenever possible, allow the engine to cool off slowly before stopping it. Rapid cooling, like rapid heating, sets up high stresses in the cylinder heads and may cause distortion and extra wear.

Restarting in the air Allow plenty of height and time for setting up and restarting the engine on a motor glider in the air unless you are within easy gliding range of a field you are willing and prepared to land in. You must not expect immediate starting and full power at a moment's notice and, with non-electric starters, it is wisest to select a landing area before attempting a restart and to give up if it does not work by about 600 or 700 feet. Otherwise there is a very real danger of the circuit planning being left dangerously late because of frantically trying to restart. If you have landed safely in a field do not forget that the most dangerous accident is on a failed take off when the decision to abandon it is left far too late. Always survey the field and if the distance is at all short mark the last point at which you know you could stop before running into the hedge. Then, if the aircraft is still on the ground at that point, shut the throttle immediately and stop. However inconvenient a road retrieve may be it is always cheaper, safer and quicker than running into a hedge at near flying speed.

Many engines can be restarted by diving to high speed so that the propeller windmills round until the engine starts. Do not forget that if priming or choke are required for a normal cold start they will also be needed for a dive restart. Extra speed will also help to reduce the load on the starter. But do not expect the engine to start to windmill while the aircraft is only going at 50 or 60 knots, even though it normally continues to windmill at that speed after the ignition has been switched off. It always takes a much higher speed to *start* windmilling and if the compression is good it may be almost impossible to restart by diving. Dive restarting is not a last-minute measure to be tried when all else fails. It usually takes a dive of at least 600 feet, and could leave you in an embarrassing position for a field landing if it were left to the last moment!

Experience shows that many accidents are caused by the engines failing to start when the soaring conditions have failed and a landing seems likely. Even with a motor glider, it is essential to select a suitable field for landing so that the landing can be made safely if the engine fails to start.

With the self-launching sailplanes fitted with engines which retract into the fuselage just behind the wing, the rate of descent with the engine up for starting is very much higher than normal. This means that if the engine fails to start, there is unlikely to be time to align the propellor and retract the engine before landing. It is therefore vital to practise landings with the engine up and to realise that every actual field landing will be made that way. Obviously if the engine does start, a landing in a field would not be necessary.

Similarly, if the engine fails shortly after take off, with the extra drag of the engine and propellor it would be dangerous to attempt to turn back to land on the take off area. Like a normal powered aircraft, the choice is limited to landing ahead with a slight turn to avoid solid obstructions.

A partial engine failure giving rough running and a loss of power is particularly dangerous. It is instinctive for a pilot to try to keep flying and this results in a loss of speed. With the high drag of the engine and propellor, it becomes difficult to regain the speed, and any turn will then be semi-stalled and may result in a spin.

A comprehensive chapter for power pilots converting onto gliders is included in my previous book, *Beginning Gliding*.

Appendix A   Suggested syllabus for training a Silver 'C' glider pilot to P.P.L. standard

1   Introduction to pre-flight external checks, the cockpit layout and engine starting procedures.

   Instruction and practice at taxying, take off, climbing. Changing from climbing to straight and level cruising (at circuit flying power settings) from straight and level into the glide and back into the climb to learn to correct yawing and changes in trim with changes of power. The correct method of trimming. Stalling, emphasising use of power during recovery. Turns, emphasising small amount of rudder required and need for extra power for steep turns.

   The procedure for rejoining the circuit. Two circuits and landings with the instructor talking and explaining the routine. Taxying and shut-down procedure. (Flight time about 45 minutes.)

   Post-flight discussion. The student should be given, or should make, written notes of all the 'vital actions' checks and details of the normal circuit procedure and should go home and *learn* them.

2   Taxying, take off, changing from climb to straight and level flight and gliding and vice versa. Stalls and spins. Forced landing procedure. Circuits and landings. (Flight time 45 minutes to 1 hour.)

   Post-flight discussion to cover forced landings, engine failure after take off, and action in event of fire.

3   Circuits and landings. Overshoot procedure. Practice at engine failure after take off. (Flight time 30 minutes, or as required.)
   Solo circuits, if flying satisfactory. (20 minutes solo.)

4   Revision spinning, stalling off turns. Forced landing procedure. Two circuits and landings. (Flight time 1 hour.)
   Solo stalls and spins. Circuits and landings. (Flight time 45 minutes.)

5 Precautionary landings, or forced landings with power. (Flight time 45 minutes.)
Solo circuits, powered approaches. (Flight time 45 minutes.)

6 Navigation cross-country. Setting course, turning onto headings and using the directional indicator and compass. Flying accurate courses at pre-determined speeds. Practising precautionary landings and at least one crosswind landing. (Flight time 1 hour 45 minutes.)

7 Solo cross-country. (Flight time 1 hour 30 minutes.)

8 Navigation Flight Test. (Flight time 1 hour 30 minutes.)

9 Revision and dummy General Flying Test (G.F.T.). (Flight time 1 hour plus.)
Solo practice, precautionary landings and any weak points. (Flight time 1 hour.)

10 G.F.T., or further dual and solo as required. (Flight time 1 hour 20 minutes.)

Dual	7 hours 50 minutes
Solo	4 hours 20 minutes
Total	12 hours 10 minutes

Note: In addition to the flying listed above, the student is required to do 4 hours of instrument appreciation and 2 hours of slow flying and stall awareness.

This is not intended to be a comprehensive syllabus but is merely a guide, or working basis, for an instructor taking glider pilots for the first time. As with all other students, the standard of flying skill between different pilots will vary and some will require far more dual instruction than is suggested here. The exact requirements for a P.P.L. will, of course, vary for each country.

Appendix B Vectors and force diagrams simply explained

A triangle or parallelogram of forces is a simple, practical method of finding the direction and magnitude of the forces on a body in motion, or to solve problems of movement such as the effects of the wind on an aircraft flying from place to place.

Equilibrium
A body is said to be in a state of equilibrium if it is at rest or in a state of uniform motion. When something is in a state of equilibrium the forces acting on it are exactly balanced. This is the situation with a powered aircraft whenever it is in a steady, straight climb at a constant speed, in straight and level flight at a constant speed, or in any steady straight descent at a constant speed. Unless the forces concerned were exactly balanced the aircraft would be accelerating in one direction or another.

Fig. 140 shows two examples of equilibrium and the balance of forces concerned. In each case the forces are represented by a vector. A vector is just a line representing the size of the force or velocity and giving its direction and point of application. When drawing a diagram representing several forces or velocities any convenient scale or unit may be used, providing that the same scale and units are used for all the forces or velocities involved.

In the first example, a man is pushing against a wall with a force of 30 lb, applied at right angles to the wall. There is no movement and therefore the forces must be in equilibrium and balanced. The push force is exactly balanced by the equal and opposite reaction produced by the wall. Choosing a suitable scale of 1 unit of length representing 10 lb of force, we can make a scale drawing, or vector diagram, to show what is happening.

The second example shows a car in motion. While the car is gaining speed, the power from the engine produces a force T which is greater than the friction and the air resistance of the car at that speed, so that the car continues to accelerate. However, as the car gains speed, so the resistance increases, until eventually the two opposing forces are exactly balanced, in this example at 30 m.p.h. Any increase in the propelling force would accelerate the car and any decrease would result in a loss of speed until once again the forces were in balance. To be more precise, the weight force acting vertically downwards and the opposing reaction from the road should also have been included.

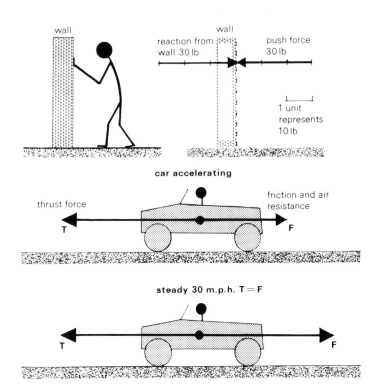

140 Forces in equilibrium. When thrust equals friction the car maintains a steady speed.

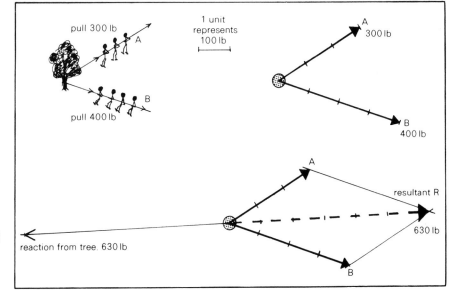

141 Finding the resultant of two given forces. The resultant R is found by completing the parallelogram of forces and measuring the diagonal.

Resultants and components of forces

A force may either be balanced by an equal and opposite force or by the result of several forces acting together. In flying we are often concerned with the result of two forces acting together and the method of finding the resultant of any two forces is shown in Fig. 141. Again, a scale drawing is made to show the size and direction of each force. A parallelogram is completed and the resultant of the two forces is the single force represented by the length and direction of the diagonal of the parallelogram. This is always the case, regardless of the direction and size of the forces concerned.

It is sometimes necessary to find two forces to balance the effect of a given single force, or to split up a single force into two component forces acting in specific directions. In Figs. 142a and b the given force of 40 lb is represented by the vector OF. Vector OR has been drawn equal and opposite to OF and therefore balances it exactly. There is an infinite number of components of OR, since each will be different for every different angle chosen for each component – a and b are just two examples of component forces of OR.

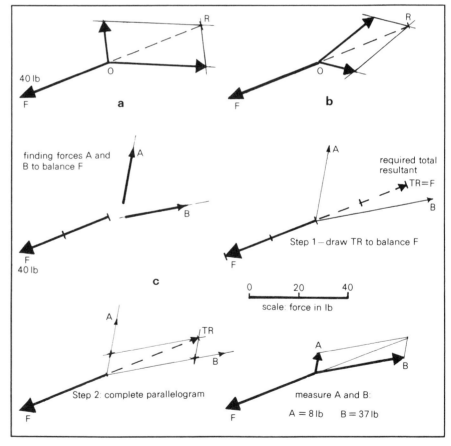

142 **a** and **b** show two examples of the infinite number of different components which would have the combined effect of **R**. **c** Explains the method of finding the actual forces involved.

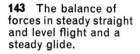

143 The balance of forces in steady straight and level flight and a steady glide.

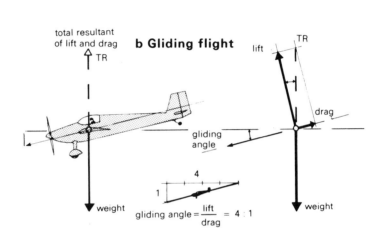

a Straight and level flight

lift

thrust

weight

lift

thrust   drag

weight

total resultant of lift and drag
TR

b Gliding flight

lift   TR

drag

gliding angle

weight   weight

$$\text{gliding angle} = \frac{\text{lift}}{\text{drag}} = 4 : 1$$

4

1

The exact method of finding the size of the component forces is explained step by step in **c.**

Two forces having the same effect when combined as a single force are known as *components* of a force. The result of two given forces is known as the *resultant*.

Forces on an aircraft in flight

When a powered aircraft is in steady, straight and level flight at a constant speed it is in a state of equilibrium and the forces must therefore be exactly balanced. The lift equals the weight and the thrust equals the drag, as in Fig. 143a. In gliding flight there is no thrust and the weight must therefore be balanced by lift and drag since there are no other forces acting on the aircraft. Fig. 143b shows how the relative sizes of the lift and drag forces can be found by completing the parallelogram. By definition, lift always acts at right angles to the relative airflow, which in still air is the exact opposite to the flight path. Drag always acts along the flight path, tending to slow the aircraft down. It can be seen that the glide ratio (in this case 4:1) is proportional to the ratio between the lift and drag. Here there is 4 times as much lift as drag. Lower drag, or more lift for less drag, would result in a better gliding angle.

Similar kinds of force diagrams can be drawn for any flight situation where the aircraft is in a state of equilibrium. Fig. 144 shows a special case for straight and level flight in a powered machine at low speed and demonstrates how we can use vector diagrams to help to reason out what is happening in flight. The angles are exaggerated for clarity. At very low speed the aircraft is in a nose high attitude with the thrust inclined upwards. This 'up-thrust' is obviously helping to support some of the weight so that it might be expected that less lift than normal would be required from the wings themselves. In order to achieve a balance of the forces the resultant of the lift and thrust must be balanced exactly by the resultant of the weight and drag and the resultant of weight and drag is found by completing the parallelogram and drawing in the diagonal. The equal and opposite resultant of lift and thrust (R) can then be drawn so that the other parallelogram can be completed and this gives the relative sizes of the lift and thrust forces. The vector diagram shows clearly that less lift is required from the wings than in normal level flight since the thrust is contributing to the lifting force available to support the weight. This results in reduction in the possible minimum flying speed in this situation, i.e. a lowered stalling speed, provided that the engine continues to produce that amount of thrust and does not stop! This advantage is made use of for very short landings in powered aircraft.

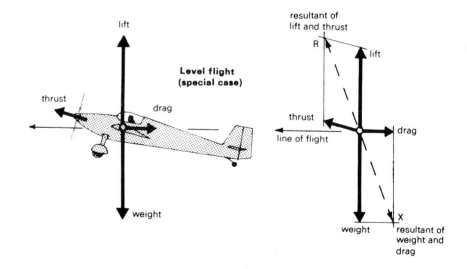

144 Straight and level flight at low speed with the thrust contributing to the lift. Less lift is required from the wings so that the stalling speed is reduced.

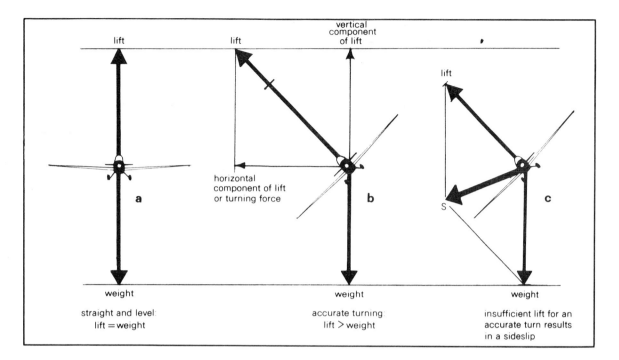

145 The balance of forces in a turn. Extra lift is always required for a turn.

Forces in a turn   Although, strictly speaking, a turn is not a state of equilibrium because of the constant change in direction, there is a balance of forces and vector diagrams can therefore be used to show the forces involved. In straight and level flight the lift is equal to the weight as in Fig. 145a. For an accurate turn, sufficient lift is required to turn and support the weight. **b** shows the extra lift required and the total lift force split into horizontal and vertical components. The vertical component balances the weight and the horizontal component does the work of pulling the aircraft round the turn. **c** shows what happens if the bank is applied and no extra lift is produced. The resultant of the lift and weight forces is S, a force pulling the machine downwards towards the lower wing in a sideslip.

Triangles of velocity   Problems of navigation can be solved by drawing vector triangles and parallelograms in a similar way to those already described. In these cases the vectors represent velocities, i.e. speeds and direction of movement instead of the size and direction of forces.

Consider a motor glider flying from the Lasham Gliding Centre to the Midland Gliding site at the Long Mynd in Shropshire on a windy day. (Fig. 146.) Rather than map-read his way from village to village, the pilot will want to calculate a course to steer to fly direct, allowing for the effect of the rather strong wind which happens to be blowing almost at right angles to his track. First he gathers all the facts he can. He draws a line joining the two gliding sites on his map and measures its direction and distance. This line is known as the track and his measurement of its angle from a vertical grid line or line of longitude shows it to be 320°, and the distance to be 102 nautical miles (n.m.). According to the Met. man the wind at 2000 feet should be south-west and about 20 knots. This is known as the wind velocity, and is written as W/V 225°/20 knots. In this case the pilot is in no particular hurry and decides to cruise at a speed of 60 knots. (The distances and speeds might just as easily have been kilometres or miles per hour provided that the same units are used throughout any calculation or triangle of velocities.)

He can now make his scale drawing, orientating it correctly as on the map so that the angles are correct in relation to true north and using any convenient scale to represent an hour's flying time. If there was no wind he would simply head along the direction of the track to reach his destination. Fig. 147a shows what would happen if he ignored the effect of the strong crosswind and steered straight for the Long Mynd. Obviously he must head much more to the left in order to allow for the drift. b shows the correct solution. In no wind, heading in this new direction the aircraft would reach B, 60 n.m. from Lasham after 1 hour of flying at 60 knots. From B a balloon

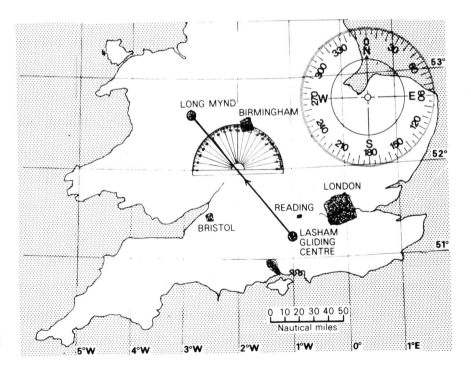

146 Measuring the track angle from Lasham to the Long Mynd. (Track 320° [true] distance 102. n.m.)

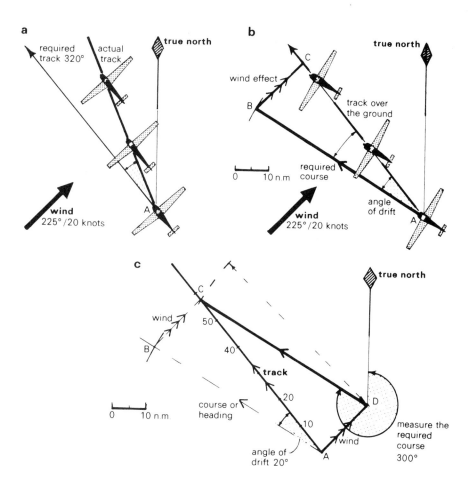

147 Using a triangle of velocities in order to calculate the course and ground speed in a crosswind. Required course is 300° (true) and the ground speed (AC) is 57 knots.

or a circling aircraft would drift 20 n.m. downwind to point C in an hour. The net result of flying for 1 hour in the new heading, together with the drifting effect of the wind for 1 hour is, therefore, to arrive at point C which is directly on track for the Long Mynd.

In practice it is easiest to draw the triangle of velocities by allowing for 1 hour of wind effect from the point of departure (AD in Fig. **147c**). From D and radius 60 n.m. (1 hour's flying at 60 knots) strike an arc to cut the track line at C. Then the course to steer for the Long Mynd from Lasham is the direction of DC, namely 300°. The length of AC is the distance travelled over the ground in the 1 hour flight, 57 n.m. in this case. This means that the whole flight of 102 n.m. should take 102/57 hours, or about 1 hour and 48 minutes. (57 n.m. in 1 hour is a ground speed of 57 knots.)

Note that for simplicity's sake no mention or allowance has been made for variation, which is the difference between the magnetic north and the true north as measured from the map.

The principle of the triangle of velocities and the use of the Dalton Computer, which is a simple and speedy way of drawing these vector triangles, has to be understood for the ground tests for a Private Pilot's Licence.

Appendix C   Conversion tables

Metres		Feet	Kilo-metres		Miles	Kilo-grammes		Pounds
0.305	1	3.281	1.609	1	0.621	0.454	1	2.205
0.610	2	6.562	3.219	2	1.243	0.907	2	4.409
0.914	3	9.843	4.828	3	1.864	1.361	3	6.614
1.219	4	13.123	6.438	4	2.485	1.814	4	8.818
1.524	5	16.404	8.047	5	3.107	2.268	5	11.023
1.829	6	19.685	9.656	6	3.728	2.722	6	13.228
2.134	7	22.966	11.265	7	4.350	3.175	7	15.432
2.438	8	26.247	12.875	8	4.971	3.629	8	17.687
2.743	9	29.528	14.848	9	5.592	4.082	9	19.842
3.048	10	32.808	16.093	10	6.214	4.536	10	22.046
6.906	20	65.617	32.187	20	12.427	9.072	20	44.092
7.620	25	82.021	40.234	25	15.534	11.340	25	55.116
15.240	50	164.042	80.467	50	31.069	22.680	50	110.231
30.480	100	328.084	160.924	100	62.137	45.359	100	220.462

SPEED CONVERSION SCALE

RATE OF CLIMB
CONVERSION SCALE

SPEED CONVERSION SCALE — columns: KNOTS, MPH, KM/H, FT/SEC

RATE OF CLIMB CONVERSION SCALE — columns: KNOTS, METRES PER SEC, FT MIN, FT/SEC, KM H, MPH

CONVERSION FACTORS

	To convert	into	Multiply by
Distances			
	Metres	Feet	3.281
	Feet	Metres	0.3048
	Centimetres	Inches	0.394
	Inches	Centimetres	2.540
	Kilometres	Miles	0.6214
	Miles	Kilometres	1.609
	Kilometres	Nautical Miles	0.5396
	Nautical Miles	Kilometres	1.853
	Miles	Nautical Miles	0.869
	Nautical Miles	Miles	1.151
Speeds			
	Kilometres per hour	Miles per hour	0.6214
	Miles per hour	Kilometres per hour	1.609
	Km h	Knots	0.5396
	Knots	Km h	1.853
	Metres per second	Feet per second	3.281
	Feet per second	Metres per second	0.3048
	M.p.h.	Knots	0.869
	Knots	M.p.h.	1.151
	Feet per minute	Metres per second	.00508
	Metres per second	Feet per minute	196.85
	Knots	Metres per second	0.515
	Metres per second	Knots	1.944
Areas			
	Square metres	Square feet	10.764
	Square feet	Square metres	0.093
	Square centimetres	Square inches	0.155
	Square inches	Square centimetres	6.451
Weights			
	Kilogrammes	Pounds	2.205
	Pounds	Kilogrammes	0.454
Wing loadings and tyre pressures			
	Kg per square metre	Lb per square foot	0.205
	Lb per square foot	Kg per square metre	4.882
	Lb per square inch	Kg per square centimetre	0.07
	Kg per square centimetre	Lb per square inch	14.3
Weight of Water			

1 Imperial gallon	= 4.546 litres	= 1.2 US gallons,	weighs 10 lb
1 litre	= 0.22 Imperial gallons	= 0.264 US gallons,	weighs 2.2 lb
1 US gallon	= 3.8 litres	= 0.83 Imperial gallons,	weighs 8.3 lb

Index